RICHE

OF TI

The Life of St.

reached its climax when he

...ed his father's wealth

renounc...
to become a beggar, and
follow a life of piety.

Theodore Maynard has
given this lively, humorous,
and deeply religious man the
sort of biography he might
have wanted—warm and sym-
pathetic yet factually accurate. He traces the development of the Franciscan Order
and recounts graphic...
fervent wors...
co...

Richest of the Poor

The Life of Saint Francis of Assisi

BY THEODORE MAYNARD

Biography: RICHEST OF THE POOR: THE LIFE OF SAINT FRANCIS OF ASSISI · DE SOTO AND THE CONQUISTADORES · THE ODYSSEY OF FRANCIS XAVIER · APOSTLE OF CHARITY: THE LIFE OF ST. VINCENT DE PAUL · QUEEN ELIZABETH · THE REED AND THE ROCK : PORTRAIT OF SIMON BRUTÉ · ORESTES BROWNSON: YANKEE, RADICAL, CATHOLIC · PILLARS OF THE CHURCH · TOO SMALL A WORLD: THE LIFE OF MOTHER CABRINI · MYSTIC IN MOTLEY: THE LIFE OF ST. PHILIP NERI · HUMANIST AS HERO: THE LIFE OF SIR THOMAS MORE · A FIRE WAS LIGHTED: THE LIFE OF ROSE HAWTHORNE LATHROP · *Through My Gift*

History: THE STORY OF AMERICAN CATHOLICISM

Poetry: POEMS · THE LAST KNIGHT · EXILE AND OTHER POEMS · MAN AND BEAST · NOT EVEN DEATH · COLLECTED POEMS

Criticism and Essays: CARVEN FROM THE LAUREL TREE OUR BEST POETS · PREFACE TO POETRY

Fiction: THE DIVINE ADVENTURE

Anthologies: A TANKARD OF ALE · THE BOOK OF MODERN CATHOLIC VERSE · THE BOOK OF MODERN CATHOLIC PROSE

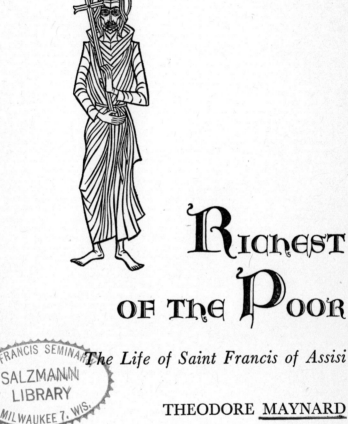

Richest

OF THE Poor

The Life of Saint Francis of Assisi

THEODORE MAYNARD

DOUBLEDAY & CO., INC., GARDEN CITY, N.Y. 1948

NOV 1948

IN MEMORIAM SARA MAYNARD

THIS RICHEST OF POOR MEN
—*First Life* by THOMAS OF CELANO.

CONTENTS

INTRODUCTION

It will be immediately evident that this is not a piece of original research. But neither is it (I hope) another example of the kind of popularization of St. Francis of which there have been too many. These almost invariably contain only the pretty features of the Franciscan story, either omitting all reference to the painful disagreements that occurred within the Order, even during the saint's lifetime, or presenting them in so oversimplified or one-sided a fashion as to leave a misleading impression.

In contrast with such works we have that of the learned and skeptical Paul Sabatier, whose book upon its appearance in 1892 was almost simultaneously—and deservedly—crowned by the French Academy and put upon the Index. This seems to advance the thesis that there was an irreconcilability between the Franciscan idea and the life of the Church. A false antithesis is created, with the idealism of St. Francis on the one hand, and, on the other, what is alleged to be the opportunism of the ecclesiastical authorities. The saint is used as a stick with which to beat the Pope. Yet it is only fair to remark that M. Sabatier in later writings, of which his essay "L'Originalité de Saint François" is a case in point, considerably modifies his earlier contentions. Probably the most important factor in bringing this about was the publication of Archbishop Robinson's *The Real St. Francis of Assisi.* It should further be said that in the *Vie* itself, though Sabatier rejects miracles, not on the usual ground of their being physically impossible but as a moral affront, he fully accepts the great miracle of the stigmata, admitting the incontestability of the evidence. His study stands as a starting point for virtually everything subsequently written on the subject.

I prescind from all the difficult problems of the textual criticism of the sources. A good concise discussion of this matter is in the *Short Introduction to Franciscan Literature,* published forty years ago by Archbishop Robinson. A more detailed work along somewhat similar lines is Mr. Moorman's *Sources for the Life of St. Francis of Assisi,* issued in 1940. Yet perhaps the best examination of these matters is to be found in Johannes Jörgensen's *St. Francis of Assisi* and Father Cuthbert's book of the same title, both of which appeared in 1912. They are closer to one another than either is to Sabatier. Several of his most cherished textual theories, though fruitful errors, are now recognized to be untenable.

The basis of this biography is Thomas of Celano's two *Lives* of St. Francis. But there are other contemporary or near-contemporary biographies that have been drawn upon almost as freely —St. Bonaventure's *Legenda Major,* the *Legend of the Three Companions,* the *Fioretti,* and the *Mirror of Perfection.* That the two last-named record, to a greater or less degree, only what is serviceable to the Spiritual party of the Franciscans need not trouble us unduly; the storms have blown themselves out, and it is not very difficult to recognize what should be taken with some reserve. Nor is it too hard to distinguish between the legendary and the strictly historical; and as even the critical Bollandist Père Delehaye has said, "Legend, like all poetry, can claim a higher degree of truth than history itself." As that is often true, I do not feel it necessary to exclude everything that is legendary or to enter into a discussion as to the precise degree of weight that should be given to each thing related of St. Francis. I shall, however, try, by some cautious phrase, to indicate what I believe to be more certain and what less.

The *Fioretti*, though it contains much that is fabulous and a little that is ridiculous, is more often sober history than has sometimes been supposed. Coming late in its Italian form—nearly two centuries after the death of Francis—it tends to embellish its stories, but there can be little doubt that the Latin original was compiled by men who had access to the notes left by the saint's friends, particularly Brother Leo, his most intimate friend of all. And it should be remembered that Leo survived Francis by forty-five years. The account given in the *Fioretti* of the crowning event of this life, the stigmata, is of all such accounts the most ample, circumstantial, and convincing.

With regard to the *Mirror of Perfection* I must remark that, while using its story of the voice speaking out of the sky to confirm the Rule, I think I should say here quite plainly, as I do also in the text, that I do not believe such an incident ever happened. My disbelief is not because of the obvious partisan purpose of that story (though that would be enough to arouse suspicion), and still less because I think that such a thing is physically impossible. My disbelief rests on psychological grounds. Yet though the *Mirror* has here and elsewhere several signs of having been retouched, the book contains a great deal of the highest value, and the larger part of its contents receive corroboration from other sources about which there can be no question. Even if some of it was probably written in 1318, other parts—and this is true also of the *Fioretti* and the *Legend of the Three Companions*—seem to have been before Thomas of Celano when he wrote his *Lives*. In short, the basis of a great deal in all these books may be assumed to be Leonine. Confusing as the chronological arrangement of the first lives sometimes is, they give what is by far the most complete and vivid picture of any person of that age, and their minor discrepancies make all the more striking their agreement as to what kind of man Francis of Assisi was.

Though St. Clare's life had less incident than that of her friend Francis, his story would be incomplete without hers. Here the principal authority is again Thomas of Celano, for though her life was written anonymously, it is usually attributed to him.

The best edition of any English translation of St. Francis's own works is that published by Archbishop Robinson in 1906. It uses the definitive Quaracchi text but is rather more than a translation of it, as the editor includes also the "Canticle of the Creatures" along with excellent introductory and other notes.

Good biographies from the Protestant point of view are those by Canon Knox Little (1904) and Mrs. Oliphant (1870). Francis has been regarded from many aspects—sociological, skeptical, medical, as well as religious. Without being, I trust, too invidious, I may say that I rate most highly the following: the Abbé Léon le Monnier's *Histoire de Saint François d'Assise* (1890), Father Hilarion Felder's *Die Ideale des heilige Franziskus* (1923), and the lives by Father Cuthbert and Jörgensen already mentioned. Though the definitive work remains to be written, it seems to me that the last two of these, if they could be boiled down and the mixture strained off, would come close to being definitive.

Writing as I do for the general reader, I have not felt it desirable to give page references. Even the general references to my sources that were in my first draft—"as Celano says," "according to the Three Companions," and the like—have been removed except when they appeared to be indispensable, as these might slow down the movement of the story. But I offer the assurance that I have gone to the best authorities and that I have not tampered with my material.

Although this is biography and not fiction, I admit that in some of the earlier chapters, where there occasionally seemed to be need of it, I have ventured upon a little reconstruction. The first introduction of Clare, seen as a child, is a case in point. But Francis must have known her then, as Assisi was a small place and she lived only round the corner. She was a cousin of the priest Sylvester from whom Francis did, in fact, buy stone for repairing St. Damian's. Without the kind of explanation I give, the record, as it stands, does not make much sense. I claim, therefore, that what I have done is not only permissible but necessary. As the precise chronological sequence of events cannot always be determined, I have had to use my judgment about this, though without any certainty that I am correct. Rich as the Franciscan material is, it is also meager at some points, and I cannot hope to have avoided all the pitfalls that beset everybody who ventures into this field.

I happen to share the faith of St. Francis, and it should be evident that I admire as well as love him. But I do not consider him always beyond criticism or that the later development of his idea, though it was in some respects painful to him, was along the wrong lines. Here, however, my criticism is really of those who, in the days of controversy within the Order, overemphasized some aspects of him in accordance with their own partisan feelings. I have done my best to portray him as he was, or at least as he appears to me.

For the generous loan of books I have to thank the superiors of the Holy Name College at Washington, St. Bonaventure College, Allegheny, New York, and St. Mary's Abbey, Newark, New Jersey. For the reading of my manuscript and many useful suggestions I have to thank the Rev. Michael McCloskey, O.F.M., of the Franciscan Institute, and my wife.

ROMANTIC SHOPKEEPER

Peter Bernardone, the rich cloth merchant of Assisi, was a man well satisfied with himself. He was making money fast, and the opportunities for making it were increasing every year. Though he was not greatly liked in the community—partly because he was rather grasping, but also because he was very vainglorious—he was not much troubled by that fact. Standing before his wife, arms akimbo and his stocky body tilted back from the waist, he asked her, "What do you expect, Pica? When a man is getting wealthy, he is sure to be envied. But I also have respect. Money gives one a place in the world."

Lady Pica looked at him with gentle scorn. "Place of a sort," she conceded. As he was proof against this in his complacency, she tried to shake him with a question, "But, Peter, is it *only* envy? Those twelve bolts of red cloth you sold at Foligno—three were good, but you knew that the others were shoddy."

He took this as a compliment and laughed. His laughter had an unpleasant note in it, suggesting something at once harsh and oily. "Hah, Pica, but that is trade! The buyer could have examined all the bolts. More fool he that he did not, and all the more clever a man your husband!"

He also considered himself clever in having married her. For though he came of a Lucchese family that had already made money in the cloth business, not every burgess obtained a bride of noble blood. Her claims to gentility were perhaps a trifle vague, but as they derived from distant Provence, they could not be disputed in Assisi. Peter always made a point of referring to her as "Lady Pica." Bernardone was a bit of a snob like many other prosperous merchants, and he was proud of this attestation of his wealth and position. Great as was the importance he attached to his moneybags, he had an uneasy sense that there were even more important things, though most of these also reposed upon money. In his way he, too, was a romantic shopkeeper.

His eldest son, the cause of the world's remembering Peter Bernardone at all, was born while he was away from home on a journey with his heavily baled pack horses to a distant fair. He was often away, sometimes for long periods, his journeys extending as far as the Provence where he had met his wife. These could almost be described as expeditions, with a long train of horses and mules escorted by a company of heavily armed men. When he got back, toward the end of 1182, he found, to his delight, that Pica had borne his child late in September. He was not so pleased that she had not waited for his return to name her baby John. To that same font of the cathedral of San Rufino, where all Assisian children were baptized, were soon taken other children also destined to become famous: the Scifi sisters Clare and Agnes, who achieved sainthood; and one very far from being a saint, the future Emperor Frederick II. It was the Bernardone baby, however, who was to attain so vast a celebrity that Assisi is the only city in the world of which it is impossible to think without thinking at once of its great Saint. He was Francis of Assisi.

Peter Bernardone was distinctly annoyed that his lady Pica had not postponed the baptism and that she had taken it upon herself to give the child a name without first having consulted him. "You know that the choosing of the name is the father's right," he told her.

She wailed, "But you were not here, Peter."

"What of that? You knew I would be back. You should have waited."

"I did not know when. The bambino might have died unchristened."

"No danger of that! You hurried this on so as to forestall me. I do not care what the priest called him. He is to be Francis. Remember, you are never to call him anything else."

This name, since so common, had perhaps never been used before. "The Little Frenchman"—when Peter softened and dropped his pomposity, Pica decided that Francis was after all very fitting. "I wanted it to be a compliment to you, Pica," her husband explained. "And look, cannot you see that he has a French look, so fine and delicate. It must be from you that he gets this. He is your son. We will teach him to talk French, which even I know a little. When he grows up I will take him with me when I have goods to sell at Carcassonne and Avignon and the fair at Grenoble."

Francis he became—Francis of Assisi. Peter Bernardone is more than a mere footnote in history because a time was to come, twenty-five years later, when he was to behave with such fantastic violence toward his son that the world has never forgotten it. In 1182 and during the years that followed he was watching a charming child —a prince from babyhood, everybody said—grow into a still more charming young man.

Though Francis was not as yet specially remarkable for anything except sweetness of temper and affability of manners, these he had to a quite exceptional degree. Those who knew him and were able to look back upon the young Francis saw, as all ages have seen, that here was the foundation of his sanctity, even though sanctity does not always crown such gifts, or repose upon them. At the time, even the many citizens of a more staid sort (and of these there were many), who had misgivings about the vivacious youth, thinking him a roisterer with his French songs and his free-handed parties, all heartily liked him. It was impossible not to like him. Nobody was able to understand how the closefisted and mirthless cloth merchant Bernardone had sired such a son. The only explanation anybody could think of was, "But of course there is Lady Pica." To which the invariable rejoinder was, "But Pica is so quiet and gentle and good." In the end it had to be admitted that if the jovial Francis could hardly be described as quiet, he was gentle and nobody knew anything bad of him.

On the other hand, nobody looked for anything to come from him. He would sober down and marry and be as commonplace as everybody else. Only in later years did Assisi recall (or invent) little incidents that had pointed from the start—had people only noticed their significance—to what he was to be.

One of these stories was that when his mother's hour had come, her labor was so difficult that it was feared the child could not be born at all. Just then a stranger came to the door and said that to bear her son she would have to go to the adjoining stable. There, like Mary, she gave birth to her son lying upon straw. As for that stranger, he is supposed to have held the child at the font in the cathedral, in confirmation of which there are pointed out on the stone flag below what appear to be the marks of the angelic feet.

For good measure, it is said that this mysterious sponsor, upon taking the child into his arms, announced: "There have been born today in this street two children, one of whom will be one of the best men in the world. The other will be the worst." That "worst" has been taken to apply to the man who succeeded Francis as the ruler of the Franciscan Order, Brother Elias. Yet, apart from the question as to whether Elias was as bad as all that, there is reason to believe that he was not born in Assisi at all, but nearby; and nobody knows the exact date of his birth. A legend of this sort clearly sprang from the hatred Elias came to arouse—that and the disposition of the later Franciscan mythology to draw parallels between the life of Christ and that of Francis. By hook or by crook, Francis had to be provided with a Judas.

The boy got some little education at the school connected with the church of St. George. This was very near the Bernardone house, and there he was taught Latin, this being still a living language, though the vernaculars were rapidly emerging. He learned to read and speak it, not very accurately but fluently, and he wrote it without much facility of penmanship, as may be seen from such bits of his script as survive.

He thought of himself as a Frenchman. Like most men of genius, he derived more from his mother than his father. Though he may never have crossed the Alps, he was always dreaming of doing so. There lay France; there was his spiritual home. He was the Little Frenchman. His favorite tongue was French, and this he always used when he was more than usually happy and wished to express the ebullient joyousness of his nature. Yet even of French he had imperfect mastery, being more facile than correct.

From this Provençal mother of his, Francis learned not only French—not the French of the North but that southern dialect that was so much nearer Latin and, therefore, Italian—but also French poetry. Lady Pica was probably a good deal better educated than were most of the burghers' wives in Assisi, and in the case of a well-brought-up woman of that time gentility showed itself not so much in formal learning as by refinement and sensitiveness, particularly to poetry, however much its production was virtually a masculine preserve.

The love lyrics of the Provençal troubadours had overtones of a sort that we must suppose escaped Francis. Beautiful as many of them were, they also often had immoral implications. The "courtly love" that was now beginning to be systematized was essentially a system of adulterous love. When closely examined it is seen, in its total separation of love from marriage, to be profoundly cynical, and its cynicism to touch a still more profound pessimism. It was connected with that despairing Manichaeism which was threatening so many of the intellectuals of the Christian world.

The troubadours were affected by this Manichaeism, though they were little concerned, being poets, to give it philosophical expression. Several of the most notable of these poets had left Provence at this time because of the opposition that was arising to the Albigensian mode of thought and life, and they had found a home in Italy, a country in whose knightly circles poetry was highly esteemed, but whose language was not yet sufficiently developed to produce much poetry of its own. Bernart de Ventadour, Peire Vidal, Cadenet, and Raimbaut de Vaquières, among others, all found Italian patrons. Fortunately their songs were heard only in the castles of the nobles and did not reach the mass of the people.

Peter Bernardone was not a man interested in poetry, or even in ideas, though it was often men like him, traders between one country and another, who served as carriers for more than bales of goods. Italy was being affected by Catharist ideas, and we hear of a podesta of Assisi in 1203—Giraldo di Gilberto—who was a heretic, but he probably was an exception. Francis not only remained untouched by such things but was even unconscious that they existed. Even in poisonous flowers he saw only their beauty.

Francis, as we can see from the frequent references he made to epic poetry, was more deeply stirred by that than by amatory lyrics. It was the poetry of chivalry that appealed most strongly to his own chivalrous spirit. His whole life was to be a kind of *chanson de geste*. Other matters passed safely over his head, though it remains something of a wonder that he escaped unscathed. Only the ennobling influence of the grand stories about Arthur and Charlemagne and Roland operated in his case. There was nothing —if we except the first preachy pages of Celano's first *Life*—to lead anybody to suppose that there was ever any harm in young Francis Bernardone, however much he may have exposed himself to danger. It is psychologically impossible to imagine that there could have been, at any time, any evil in one whose natural disposition was so sweet and sunny and fastidious. The most that can be said is that by degrees he might have coarsened and hardened. In so far as there were external safeguards, Lady Pica must be credited with having provided them. And she, by stimulating his love of poetry, was unconsciously preparing him for his special work of bringing the world back to Christian joy. It was a work that only a poet could have done, or rather one who was at the same moment a saint as well as a poet. He had begun by wandering the streets of Assisi at midnight singing love songs with his boon companions; he ended with his "Canticle of the Creatures," all of them joining him in a cumulative praise of God.

Yet he was a very unusual sort of poet—one of the type that we have been sickened with hearing about in cant phrases, the poet who lives his poetry rather than writes it. But most cant is, after all, the carapace of truth; and for once a poet really did appear who lived poetry instead of writing much of it. Francis translated his dreams into action.

That there was in him this appetite of action was the salvation of his youth. One gets glimpses of him being suddenly struck immobile by an idea, but immediately he proceeds to put it into application. As he appeared to those who knew him as he was growing into manhood, he was a brisk young businessman, conspicuously good at the work at which he had joined his father in boyhood, even if he offset his ability to make money with a still greater ability for spending it. He went from his father's shop to his own lavish banquets. But what dreams he had were those of chivalry. His notion of being a knight —and nothing did he want more than to be a knight—was to be at the forefront of a heroic battle, not reclining in ladies' silken chambers. While measuring cloth he saw himself in shining armor.

Peter Bernardone was disposed to encourage this in his son. Being a snob—a snob much more than a miser—he felt that his son's ambitions redounded to his own glory. He grumbled at times over the amount of money that Francis spent among his friends, but he made no attempt to stop the spending. He was the kind of vulgar romantic who could rise no higher than that. Perhaps almost as much as Lady Pica he unwittingly prepared the way for Francis's career. Rather in admiration than in complaint he would say, "One would think you were the son of a great prince!" That Francis threw money around showed that there was plenty of money to spend. It advertised the business and therefore brought in business. The popular Francis was able to reach wealthy young men outside of Peter's own circle. Even the lending of money to these young men was not such bad business. They usually repaid their debts in one way or another. Even when they did not, there was some satisfaction to Peter Bernardone's self-esteem. Though he hoped that when his son's exuberant follies had run their course he would settle down to being a solid merchant, he could also hope that if Francis really was able to carry out his idea of becoming a knight, another kind of fortune would be made. In either case Peter was willing to humor Francis.

All this tended to remove Francis from the bourgeois standards which would have been normal to one in his not particularly elevated rank in society. The puffy and absurd ambitions of a purse-proud father served to open a door of a gold brighter than Peter could imagine. He was helping to develop a son whose special mission would be to deny nearly everything for which Peter Bernardone stood.

How much of this Lady Pica understood it is impossible to say. She was a good woman, though she may not have been notably intelligent. It was enough that she regarded with mild scorn the pomposity and gross competence of her husband and that she perceived that her son had something in him that his father (and the rest of Assisi) never suspected. It was from her that Francis derived not only his taste for poetry and his romantic temperament but his feeling that there were more important things to do in life than to make money.

"He seemed," says Celano, "to all as if born of other parents than those from whom he was said to have sprung." Some people were struck by the noble bearing and the courteous manners of the youth; others thought of him as a gay reveler who probably would come to no very good end. To all Lady Pica would say, "How think you that this son of mine will turn out?" Without waiting for them to answer, she would assure them, "He will become a man of God." The Franciscan legend enforces this with a story of how she had been made certain of this by divine inspiration while praying, perhaps with the boy kneeling by her side, at the tiny half-ruined chapel of the Little Portion, or St. Mary of the Angels, which stood in a wood near Assisi.

It was that chapel that was destined to be the center of the work Francis was to do.

MASTER OF THE REVELS

We have a description of Francis as he was when about forty by one who knew him then. It is the Francis we think of, the friar in a much patched gray-brown habit of coarse material, barefoot and girt with a cord. By that time he had grown a sparse black beard. Yet he was even slimmer than he had been in his youth, for he was worn by his austerities. His movements were so quick that he seemed to run when he walked. He gave one the impression of being as light and free as a bird.

It is also clear from what Celano says, listing his details with the bluntness of a catalogue, that Francis was not very handsome: slight, rather undersized, round of head, with a long straight nose that was a trifle too prominent, a low forehead, eyes dark and bright, ears standing out somewhat but fortunately small, thin lips, and a swarthy complexion. The picture is far from prepossessing. Not only did he lack good looks, he struck one at first glance as insignificant.

That this was so, however, makes it all the clearer that his charm must have been immense. Those dark eyes of his were bright with candor and affection and a good will that was boundless and simple. Except for such times as he had an air of melancholy (and that, too, was attractive), he was radiant in his joy. People also noticed that there was nothing about him that was not delicate and refined; this shone in his face and was materialized in his thin fingers and his small bare feet. Though he might appear undistinguished, everybody became conscious almost immediately that this utterly unself-conscious man was the most remarkable personality they had ever encountered.

A good deal of this was no doubt due to his aura of sanctity, something quite unmistakable. This he did not have when he was a very young man, though he was even then notable for his gentle and courteous manner. It may, however, have been because he was painfully aware of having slight physical attractiveness that in his early days he did his best to offset what he lacked in form and feature by dressing more sumptuously than anyone else in Assisi. The well to do of the Middle Ages decked themselves out in rich bravery, though less so than did the men and women of the Renaissance; but Francis made himself conspicuous not only by the splendor of his attire but by going in for the fantastic and the bizarre. In order to emphasize his taffetas and velvets, he had these materials empaneled with stuff that, by contrast, was rather drab and poor. So far from being afraid of bright colors, he made them clash and explode upon him. When he strutted down the street he burst upon the eyes like a sudden rainbow.

"A burgher's son!" the envious would growl when they saw him.

"It shows," would come the answer, equally envious, "that our Bernardone is rich."

"Verily that is what it is designed to show," concluded the appraisal.

Sometimes the criticism was even more severe. "Our Little Frenchman has his parti-colored minstrel's dress this evening," would be the comment.

"Then he is on his way to another of his feasts."

"And you and I will be wakened at midnight by the drunken songs of Francis and his friends."

"Yes, and young Bernardone as the Lord of Misrule parading at their head when they come from the inn and stagger home."

Yet Francis was no Lord of Misrule, though he certainly was the Master of the Revels for the roistering young men of Assisi. Many of the remarks made about him were spitefully exaggerated. Some of his companions might get a little tipsy, but this was the ebullience of youth, and their gay hilarity did not require much stimulation from wine; nor have the Italians ever indulged in the gross guzzling of northern peoples. Though the generous Francis did not fail to provide plenty of wine at the banquets he gave, he and his friends gathered to jest and sing and spout poetry rather than to drink. It was all very harmless. But it did sometimes annoy more staid and older folk, or those who were not invited. There was enough ostentation to justify those who called the youth in the minstrel's dress a clown.

Those who attended the festive occasions could have enlightened the critics, though some of Francis's companions were disposed to criticize him for a different reason. They came to notice that he whitened as though he were a maid at any unseemly word. Occasionally one of the company would attempt this by way of a prank to see its effect upon their host. "Shall I sing that song about the innkeeper's daughter of Todi?" would be a whispered question.

"Nay, not that song," would come the answer. "You know that it would but make Francis sad and silent. Why spoil his joy and our own?"

Less and less such songs and jests were heard. They would be a discourtesy to so very courteous a host. Even those who laughed at Francis behind his back for being so fastidious had no wish to dampen the spirits of one whose merriment was the soul of their own enjoyment.

Fastidiousness and refinement give no permanent safeguard to good behavior, but they can at least delay the contagion of the world's slow stain. Already working in Francis were other forces about which he said nothing—all through his life he was reserved about his secret thoughts—and these, unsuspected as yet even by himself, pointed to another goal. He was not especially pious, but he did go on meditative walks, and these sometimes led to that little ruined chapel where rumor had it that angel voices could be heard singing. Whether or not he ever heard them, any mention of the love of God sent a thrill of tenderness through him. It was hardly more as yet than a poet's sensitiveness to beauty, part of that romantic temperament of his that made him so tinglingly responsive to music and lovely lilting verse, and that made him dream—dream even while he was measuring scarlet cloth for some stout rich woman—of winning fame as a warrior. Yet it was a side of his nature which, though undeveloped up to now, would seek for deeper satisfactions than are to be found in a convivial poetry society or in the flaunting of expensive finery.

About his dreams of being a knight—about those particular dreams least of all—he did not often speak. He was aware that he would have been mocked for such an ambition. It was much safer and much more plausible to talk of hoping to be a famous poet. But to him it did not seem absurd to picture himself charging with a lance on horseback or swinging a sword. Only when he had dismounted did he become conscious that it would be better not to tell of his fantasies, lest they bring derision upon him. He knew he would be told, "Alas, poor Francis, your heart is stronger than your arm! Best keep to your lute and your lyrics."

Then, too, there were moments when he was uneasily aware that his popularity had an edge that could be turned against himself. He was sure that he was liked, but he could not be sure that he was really liked as much as his friends told him. They gathered round him because he gave good dinners and because he lent money. The lesser nobles of the city, even they did not disdain to borrow money from him, being certain that the openhanded Francis would lend when others might refuse. Oh, they knew that he was really a glad giver, but they also were able to take some advantage of the fact that he had, as it were, to bolster his position among them in this way. He was almost accepted by them as one of themselves because his mother was *Lady* Pica; at the same time they did not forget, or forget to make him remember, that his father was only a cloth merchant. There was a patronizing air about these vulgar sprigs of aristocracy when they took his gold or when they paid it back, as they sometimes did; and one might catch a scornful glint in their eyes.

There was something else of which the young men who were Francis's boon companions may have now and then caught a glimpse, try as he did to conceal it. Francis was not only liberal to his friends, he was also liberal to the poor. His personal extravagances were not so great that he could plead, as his friends did, that he had nothing left for those in need; toward the needy he was equally extravagant. That was not the way of the gilded youth of Assisi, and they wondered, setting it down to an affability so eccentric that it extended even to those from whom he could look for no return. They did not understand that it went a great deal deeper than that.

One day there came to the Bernardone warehouse a beggar. Francis looked up from the work with which he was busy, a look of annoyance momentarily flitting over his face. It was a bad time to be interrupted.

The poor old man cried, "Give me something, for the love of God!" For the love of God! That was a conjuration Francis could not resist. He instantly made a resolve: never, never would he refuse anyone who asked for alms for the love of God. Putting his hand in the till, he scooped out most of what he found there. The beggar, dazed by his good luck, went out calling down heaven's blessings upon him.

After the man had gone, Francis fell into one of his brown studies. His thoughts ran: "Since you are bountiful and courteous toward those from whom you receive nothing but a passing and empty liking, it is fitting that you should be courteous and bountiful toward God, who is himself most bountiful in rewarding his poor. Had this man asked you for something in the name of a count or baron, you would have given what he asked. How much more, then, should you do it for the King of Kings and the Lord of all."

He was so glad that he had given to this man; caught off guard at a moment when he was preoccupied, he had almost returned an irritable refusal. From that time on he gave more freely than ever; and the more he gave, the more he was asked to give, for the beggars took advantage of him in their own fashion, but for much the same reason as did those friends of his for whom his purse was always open. Often he would be accosted when he was on his solitary rides or walks by professional vagrants who knew his habits. Then, if he happened to have no money upon him, he used to lead the beggar to some secluded spot and take off his own shirt.

He would go home furtively, hoping that his alms would not be heard of. He knew what his father would say. Peter Bernardone was willing enough that Francis should spend money on his rich friends. Even when grumbling, "One would think you were the son of a lord, not of a merchant," he was secretly proud of his son's extravagance. It flaunted in the face of the world that this merchant was richer than many a lord. But Peter did not approve of the giving of more than a copper coin or a crust of bread to a beggar. "Idle scamp, begone!" was the greeting such a man got from him. But Pica, turning over her son's clothes and often finding some of them missing, guessed where they had gone. She grew increasingly sure that this son of hers, this reckless spendthrift, would turn out to be a man of God. Though as yet the young Francis had no inkling of what his special vocation was to be, for all his thoughts still ran upon chivalry and poetry, it is permissible to see in his cheerfulness and generosity—even in the pleasure he took in good company—the natural basis upon which the grace of God was to build.

We hear of a strange figure who appeared in the streets of Assisi about this time. Those who remembered this man in later years thought of him as a kind of John the Baptist to Francis. He was generally accounted a simpleton, though some believed him taught of God; and he did nothing except greet passers-by with, "Peace and good! Peace and good!" Nothing, that is, except in the case of Francis. Whenever he met that gorgeously dressed young fellow, he used to take off his cloak and spread it before his feet. "Here is one," he used to declare, "who will one day do great deeds and be worthy of all honor."

Francis thought so too. Yet one fancies that his courtesy and his sense of humor forbade him to use this odd creature's cloak as a carpet. He was a coxcomb but not enough of a coxcomb for that. When the crowd laughed at the spectacle, Francis gave his smile and deprecatingly waved away the honor, but there was in his inmost heart a conviction that the simpleton was not as simple as he appeared to be. Yes, he, Francis Bernardone, *was* going to do great deeds. He would win fame as a poet, and the world would ring with his exploits at arms.

KNIGHT-ERRANT

Like so many of the Italian communes, Assisi was a turbulent place, having not only its factions but also its quarrels with neighboring cities, and the relations between Pope and Emperor, in which each side made an attempt to use the smaller units, served to keep everything uneasy.

The fall of the house of Hohenstaufen was still some distance off, but already we can see that the Emperors were losing their effective power south of the Alps. Barbarossa had been driven to come to terms with what he considered his Italian possessions. Henry VI had succeeded in regaining part of what had been lost, but upon his death the new Pope, the great Innocent III, who began to reign when Francis was sixteen, insisted so successfully upon the prerogatives of the Church that he found himself powerful enough to demand that Conrad of Lutzen, who had been made Duke of Spoleto and Count of Assisi by Barbarossa, should appear at Narni to hand over his authority to the papal delegates. This, Conrad, an amiable enough tyrant who had hanged the unruly with high good humor on the Collis Infernis and had obtained the local nickname of "Whimsical One", very meekly did. The moment he departed, the Assisians, wild with joy, rushed upon the castle on Santa Rosso and with shouts of "Liberty and the Pope!" tore it down completely.

They exulted to see the hated Germans depart, but they did not want the castle occupied by the papal forces. As they knew that this would happen unless they acted promptly, they braved the threatened interdict and used the stones of the demolished castle for the building of an extended city wall which they hoped would make them safe against their powerful rivals of Perugia, and also any punishment the Pope's forces might inflict. As nearly everybody there must have taken a hand in this operation, so quickly was everything done, Francis probably assisted and acquired at this time that skill in masonry, elementary though it no doubt was, which was later put by him to a very different use.

It was a precarious security that Assisi obtained. Hardly a year had passed before the commune sought to enforce its authority over the local nobles. When some of these resisted, the citizens razed their strongholds as enthusiastically as they had already razed Conrad's *rocca*. The result was that these nobles sought refuge in Perugia and egged on that city to declare war on Assisi.

Francis now received a taste of that soldiering for which he craved. It was only a taste, and not a very pleasant one, but at least it was something. Marching in the Assisian ranks, he fought in the battle at the bridge of San Giovanni at the Tiber north of Perugia, and there he was taken prisoner.

For over a year he was incarcerated in the Palace of the Captain of the People in Perugia, until a treaty of peace was signed in November 1203. Under this, the nobles of the Assisian territory who had sided with Perugia—most of them Germans—were permitted to return, and though they did not regain all their former power, they were at least powerful enough to join with dissident anti-clerical elements in the city in electing a heretic as podesta. Most of the lesser nobility, being of Italian blood, had thrown in their lot with the people; it was with these knights and not with the men-at-arms that Francis was imprisoned. The wealth of his father and the shadowy aristocracy of his mother gained him that much consideration; so also did his fine manners and courtly bearing.

Far from being downcast by that dreary year, he seems, on the contrary, to have been stimulated by the fact that he had fought in a battle, even though it had been on the losing side. And his association with his aristocratic fellow captives increased his longing for a life of chivalry. The way he endured his fate did him far more credit than that in which the Assisian knights accepted theirs. He danced and sang so gaily that many of them thought he must be insane. Again he managed to charm his companions, and as he received supplies of money from home, he was able to give little feasts even in captivity. When one of the knights made himself unbearable to the others by his arrogance and savage ill-humor, Francis continued to be his cheerful friend. He did this so successfully that he brought him round to a better frame of mind. Then the other knights took him into their good graces again.

They still continued to regard Francis as a bit touched in the head because he made so light of his imprisonment. They wondered still more when, upon their reproving him for this, they got the answer, "Do not marvel that I can exult. The day will come when I shall be worshiped by the whole world." Sanctity was not, so far, part of his ambitions; he was thinking merely of military glory.

We may smile at the boyish boast, but we should not smile too much. Francis felt his genius stirring within him and was sure that he would be famous. He had confidence in his star, though he did not see it otherwise than dimly and confusedly. In 1203 he was not very far from the start of his unique career.

Upon being released, the first thing he did, naturally enough, was to go back to his round of feasts with his friends. As he now had to make up for lost time, and as prison had told upon his health, he became ill.

His illness proved to be of a salutary sort, for at this time there began a vague dissatisfaction with his former mode of life and a vague longing for something better. When at last he was well enough to go out, worn by the effects of his fever and leaning upon a stick, his first thought was to go to the nearest city gate, the Porta Nuova, and to gaze upon the landscape he loved. That, he felt sure, would help to restore him.

Never was he so disappointed. There, indeed, was the lovely familiar landscape: the plain full of vineyards, poppies in the wheat, the road that led to Foligno, and the road up Mount Subasio. Spring was in flower. To his astonishment, he found that he no longer had any relish for what he saw. He remembered that he had enjoyed that beauty and wondered why he no longer did so. He had supposed that it could never fail to stir his heart. Shocked that what he

saw awakened so little response in him, he returned home, now leaning more heavily on his stick. The poet in him seemed to be dead;
the saint had not yet come alive. It was only that he had not recovered so completely as he had thought.

At this point, Thomas of Celano spreads on his unction a bit thick.
As he was himself a poet, he should have known better than to say
that Francis felt that the lovers of nature's loveliness were fools, or
that from "that hour he began to despise himself and in some sort
to hold in contempt what he had admired and loved before." Our
good Thomas, once he starts moralizing, is all too apt to administer
a horse doctor's dose. Francis's momentary distaste was not a sign
of grace but merely of lack of health; his delight in the beauty of
nature was not only to return but to be increased a hundredfold,
deriving from sanctity a deeper insight. Although Francis was the
very last man in the world to regard depression of spirits as a good
sign, perhaps in this instance it did mark an empty moment of
transition. Sabatier's phrase is worth remembering: his was the
solitude of a great soul in which there is no altar.

He got well. Soon afterwards an opportunity for knightly glory
occurred of a much more brilliant sort than a petty quarrel between
two small Italian cities. This time there was war on a larger scale in
which great issues were involved. The kingdom of Sicily had come
to Henry VI through Constance, the heiress of the Norman king.
But their son Frederick (afterwards the Emperor) was the ward
of the Pope, and the Pope was resisting the pretensions to the
guardianship of Markwald, who had the support of the German
nobles. It was a phase of the conflict between the papal and imperial
authority which, though theoretically regarded as being each su-
preme in its own domain and (again theoretically) inconceivably in
opposition, were in actual fact continually clashing. Especially was
this the case in Italy, where they overlapped, and where the temporal dominion of the papacy often proved to be almost the only
support of local liberty.

At first, the war had gone steadily against the popular party,
headed by Innocent. But now Walter of Brienne had been put in
command against the Germans and had defeated them at Capua
and Cannae. And Count Gentile—perhaps one of those who had
been in prison with Francis in Perugia—was raising a force to serve

under Walter in the South. He had been sufficiently impressed with the fiery spirit of Francis to overlook his not very robust frame and, therefore, willingly consented to accept him as squire, with the promise of knighthood as soon as he had proved his prowess in the field.

Francis now felt that his heaven-sent chance had come. He had always been certain that it would, but he had not looked for it so soon. And perhaps it had caught him in what was not the most propitious moment, as he may still have been somewhat weak from his long illness. If one must look for pathological explanations of what followed, possibly they may be found here. At all events, he was wildly excited and went round elatedly telling everybody, "I know I shall be a great prince." He was still, it will be seen, a good deal of a boaster.

To prepare for the expedition, Francis bought very costly equipment—the brightest and best of armor, the most delicately tempered of swords, enriched in the hilt, a long lance, and an excellent horse. Without any complaint, Peter Bernardone footed a bill which we may be sure was unnecessarily large. The merchant wanted his son to cut a splendid figure and considered that the outlay would bring returns. Poor Peter Bernardone, though in everything he did there was a love of the ostentatious, had come to believe that this mettlesome son of his was now going to achieve something. Little as he understood Francis, he dimly perceived that he was a rather remarkable person. His heart swelled when he saw that others were also impressed.

Fame Francis did win, a fame greater than that of any man of his time, a fame hardly surpassed by any man in history. Yet the very first thing he did must have seemed completely crazy to everybody who knew him, and most of all to his father. He gave away all of his expensive equipment. It was to a poor knight whose name we do not know. We do not even know whether Francis had ever seen him before, though he may have been one of those imprisoned with him in Perugia. That he was in shabby clothes and in dented armor was enough for Francis. Looking at this knight, he was ashamed that a seasoned warrior should have such poor accouterment while he, who had so far not fleshed his sword, should have all that money could buy.

He went up to the man at once and said, "Your horse, sir, is not good, and your——"

"What is that to you?" the knight returned coldly, thinking that he was being twitted.

"Then take mine, sir."

This time the knight thought that he was being ridiculed. Poor he might be, but there was surely no need for this wealthy young man, a mere squire, to stress a comparison already glaring enough.

But Francis had dismounted and was holding the bridle of his own charger with one hand and the bridle of the other sorry steed with the other. He was in a position where the knight could have struck him in the face with his mailed fist, but who could strike that bright upturned face, so full of kindness, so simple in its affection, so innocently eager to be of service? As they talked, it became evident that Francis would take the exchange of horses and arms he was proposing as an immense favor. He was not offering a courtesy but asking one, a courtesy that could not be refused. In the end the exchange was agreed upon.

It is easy to imagine how disgusted Peter Bernardone was when he heard of this transaction. He appears to have been a man of ungovernable rages, but even the most equable of souls might be pardoned for being angry when he saw a small fortune thrown away on the whim of a senseless moment. As we hear nothing about any explosion because of this episode, perhaps the honest burgher managed to bottle up his disappointment, and the others that followed it, until their accumulation was too much for him. We should remember this and put it down on the credit side of that ledger he loved so much when we come to the other incidents, a long series of absurdities, that culminated in a final breach between father and son.

What made the gift to the knight so strange was that it happened the day after Francis had had a dream. The dream was induced by his excitement at the prospect of riding to war in the train of Count Gentile. In the dream he saw himself in the familiar warehouse, but instead of bales and bolts of cloth it was hung with saddles and swords and lances and shields. As all the shields were emblazoned with a cross, this would indicate that he looked upon the enterprise as a crusade. All his exploits had to have the most romantic significance. Then the place melted away and enlarged into a great palace. There was a beauteous bride there, his bride. A voice was telling him that all these things were his, these were the munitions of war with which he was to furnish the knights under his command.

When he awoke, he felt all the more sure because of his dream that his expedition to Apulia near the heel of the Italian boot was going to be more glorious than even he had imagined. In spite of this, when he met the knight later in the day, he gave away his horse and equipment. It was fantastic folly, it was folly of the sort that he was to commit over and over again for the rest of his life; that is, if it was folly at all. Inflamed though his mind was—inflamed as never before—with visions of glory, a profound instinct told him that there was something more glorious still. A crisis had come, and he knew that he must not hesitate. Eagerly he took off the grand armor of which he had been so proud and laced on himself the poor knight's armor instead.

Yet he did not give up his visions of glory. It was, however, in a thoughtful mood that a day or so later he rode rather bedraggled into Spoleto, the first stage of the march toward Apulia.

It was as far as he ever got.

There he had another dream, though as recorded this was something that may have happened in the shadowy state between dream and waking. He heard a Voice, but he saw nobody. The Voice asked, "Do you wish to go to Apulia to the war?"

Francis answered, "Yes, that is my whole purpose."

Again the Voice spoke, "Francis, who can do better for you—the lord, or the servant?"

The answer was prompt, "The lord."

Another question came, "Why, then, are you seeking the servant instead of the lord?"

By this time, Francis was broad awake. He sat up in his bed and looked around him. There was nobody there. Then he understood. "Lord," he cried, "what wouldst Thou have me to do?"

Then the Unseen Speaker told him, "Return to the place of your birth, and there you will be told what you are to do. It may be that you will have to give your dream a meaning that you do not yet understand."

That night he could sleep no more. Though the command meant an end of his visions of knightly service as he had imagined them, he was now assured that it meant that something still greater lay ahead for him.

As soon as dawn broke he rode back to Assisi, radiant with joy.

BEGGAR IN TAFFETA

What could Francis say when he got home? His father growled disgustedly, "I do not marvel that you left your count. Small wonder that he sent you back! Who would wish for a knight in such poor arms?"

Francis assured his father that he had returned of his own free will.

"Nor is that a marvel. Who would not be ashamed to ride to war on such a steed and with such arms? And I gave you the best that my good gold could buy!"

That was undeniable. Francis let his father's supposition stand for want of a more convincing answer.

The jeering questions of his friends were harder to bear. A few of them were now riding south with Count Gentile, though none of them had so magnificent equipment as had been given Francis. All the youth of Assisi had envied him; it was too much to expect that they should not make sport of him now to gain their revenge. Francis received it all with a smiling face, and they could see that he was not merely pretending to be pleased with himself, though why this could be passed their comprehension. His bearing and his countenance showed that he really did believe that something wonderful had happened to him, but as to what this was he did not offer any explanation. Instead, he spoke as in riddles, hinting at marvels but revealing nothing. In spite of all his candor he was, as they had discovered, addicted to a secretive reserve.

He did, however, give out some kind of a story. "I am going to do mighty and noble deeds here in Assisi," was what he said. Well, that was a touch of his well-known boastfulness, so everybody thought. What were the deeds that *could* be done in Assisi? What except to go back to the humdrum routine of the warehouse?

"Francis must be crazy," one man said to another.

"He was always a little crazy," was the retort.

"Yes, but never before like this. Ever since he was a boy, he told us of how he wanted to be a knight. How uplifted he was when the count took him into his service! Then he gave away all the splendid things he had. And now he comes home."

"Ah, but you forget that he is going to do noble and mighty deeds in Assisi."

The comment brought a roar of laughter from all the band of youths.

Francis now created another mystery. Perhaps he did this of set purpose, for he had a good deal of canniness in his disposition. He began to haunt a cave nearby, taking with him a friend to whom he confided that there was a great treasure hidden there. With that as a lure this friend went willingly, though far less willingly he was made to stay outside.

"Why cannot I come in too?" he demanded.

"Because you must watch and give warning should anybody approach."

While the friend guarded the entrance, Francis went into the darkness, and there he spent hours in prayer. When he came out, it was with a face haggard and drawn from spiritual struggle. The friend inferred that the treasure had not been found.

Who was this friend? It has been conjectured that it may have been the man afterwards famous (and infamous) under the name of Elias of Cortona. If so, it is strange that Thomas of Celano does not mention this fact. He wrote his *Vita Prima* while Brother Elias was head of the Franciscan Order and is careful to praise him several times in that book. And from all that we know of Elias, it is not easy to believe that so forceful a character would have been content to do all the watching while Francis did all the searching.

A treasure *was* found in that cave, though it was not the kind of treasure that anybody in Assisi but Francis would have regarded as such. God was found in the silence.

More than that we do not know. Francis never told anybody about it except in enigmatic riddles. What we may suppose is that he humbled his heart before God and raised up his heart to God. The definite commission from heaven had not yet come. All that is clear is that Francis was already forming, in however dim a fashion, the ideal that was to govern his life. He was seeking perfection, and he was beginning to see that, for him, perfection must mean the abnegation of everything.

So little inkling did his friends have about what was going on in Francis's mind that they tried to draw him back to his old gay life. He might be crazy, but he was still a good fellow—and he had a rich father. They thought it would help to restore him to his former self if they could get him to have a little distraction. They had some fears for his sanity, with all this talk about great and noble deeds to be performed in Assisi and a treasure in a cave. This time they were careful not to suggest that he provide them with a feast; they would all contribute to what would be a very special occasion. He was merely to spend the money that was collected and to make the arrangements. They knew Francis and that he would probably provide, as usual, a good deal out of his own pocket.

Francis was no longer in the mood for that sort of thing, but, in spite of his meditations, he did not like to appear unmindful of good-fellowship or to be taxed with stinginess. He seemed to enter into the plans for this great banquet with enthusiasm. Although his friends did not know it, this was to be his last party, his farewell to the world.

Of all his feasts this turned out to be the most sumptuous. In the end Francis did, as was expected, foot the larger part of the bill himself. In his gayest and most charming mood, he presided, dressed in his richest and most fantastic clothes. When the company came out of the inn, he emerged last, carrying in his hand the wand that marked him as the Master of the Revels. All were singing loudly except Francis, and he dropped behind, farther and farther away.

Suddenly he stood stock-still, almost in an ecstasy, his heart filled with the sweetness of God. He could neither speak nor move; as he said afterward, he could not have moved just then had he been pricked all over with knives. He saw nothing; he heard nothing; he was conscious only of the heavenly sweetness.

His comrades chanced to turn round and saw him there, rooted to the spot, he whom they had been accustomed to have strutting along arm in arm with them, singing at the top of his voice. Seeing him, they were afraid, and thought him ill or even dying, though none of them had seen a dying man look like that before. They spoke to him, and at first he did not reply. When they saw that he was abstracted, they began to banter him, hoping to draw him back to their revels in that way. One of them at last said, "About what were you thinking so deeply that you stayed behind?"

Another answered for Francis, "Oh, what *would* he be thinking of except the bride he is about to take? Tell us who she is, Francis."

At that he seemed to come to himself and said in a loud voice, "You have spoken truly. I *am* thinking of the Bride I shall take— One nobler and richer and more beautiful than any of you have seen."

By now the whole company had clustered around, and at his words—all in keeping with his other boasts about the great deeds he was going to do—they burst into mocking laughter. They were sure that it was not so, for any gossip of that sort would have already reached them. It was just one more proof that he was becoming mentally deranged. Not one of them had any idea as to what Bride he had in mind.

His moodiness descended upon him again, and they could get no more out of him. After a while they got tired of the fun they were poking at this queer fellow who made no response, and who was so different from the gay, carefree Francis they had known in the past, or even from the man who had glittered in their midst earlier that evening. Shrugging their shoulders, they drifted off.

Francis was left alone under the summer night.

This was not quite his last banquet, though it was the last he ever had with his roistering companions. It was at that moment that he became, if not entirely freed from the vanities of the world and everything that he had formerly loved, at least able to see them to be but vanities. He saw himself as he was, and Christ in his beauty. All his thoughts now ran upon how best to serve his Lord.

Just what he had to do had not been shown him, but it had been promised by that Voice at Spoleto that this would be shown. Meanwhile he tried to occupy himself as before in his father's shop, keeping aloof from his former boon companions.

He had feasts of a different kind. Some of these were secret feasts, when the sweetness that had swept over him that night would sweep over him again, but there were more public feasts as well. Now he would set the table in his house as though expecting a number of his friends. As soon as everything had been made ready, he would bring in a company of beggars. His father was away on one of his trips, or Francis could not have done this. Lady Pica, kind and indulgent though she was, might have objected had he invited all the riffraff from the streets to sit at her spotless table. So Francis went no further than to call them to the door and hand out the meat and bread and fruit and wine. They went away laden, crowds of them; his mother wondered and mildly protested against this new eccentricity of her son.

Even this was not enough for Francis. He was already sharing with the poor, but he was longing to be not merely their benefactor but one of them. He wished to know how it felt to be a beggar himself.

In order to make this experiment, he went to Rome. Nobody would know him there, so he would pass unnoticed. At the same time, he could make this the occasion of a religious pilgrimage. Very likely his ideas were a little confused, and he could not have said just why he went, unless he had a vague idea that in Rome he might encounter some very holy man who would be able to enlighten him in his perplexities. More probably he thought it would be as well to begin his career—he was now sure that it was about to begin—by praying at the tombs of the Apostles. What he was about to do was intended as a decisive sign of his submission to the Catholic Church.

He went straight to St. Peter's. Other pilgrims were crowding in, each, according to custom, making a small offering at the tomb, throwing in a coin through the grated window. Francis could not but observe how small these offerings were, so when he came to the window he almost emptied his purse. Gold and silver fell with a clang on the marble floor, and everybody stared at him. In this was possibly a touch of his old boastfulness and a desire to show off. But it may also be that he thought that, as he was about to become completely poor, this was the spot to begin.

When he came out of the cathedral, he found a crowd of beggars at the door. He had little to give them except the clothes he wore. The time was near at hand when he would do precisely that, but that time had not quite arrived. What he was doing just then was only an experiment. He would keep his fine clothes; he flinched from the thought of going home in beggar's rags. Instead, he drew one of the crowd of beggars aside and suggested the loan of his rags for the day. "See," Francis told him, "I will give you this silver coin. You come to an inn and stay there until I return. I will pay for your food and drink, and I will take my own clothes at the end of the day." Francis was now glad that he had kept a few coins back. The money he offered was much more than the man was likely to make on St. Peter's porch, so he willingly agreed. It was Francis who sat there for the rest of that day, at last a beggar among beggars.

Francis begged in French. That he did this showed that he was very happy, for though his French was far from perfect, he always used it at moments of exaltation. This time, however, he may have used French as a further means of disguise; it would make him appear a stranger from a foreign land. Begging was something new to him, and, while it gave him a sense of exaltation, it also caused him some embarrassment. Not for some while was he able to rid himself of that feeling.

How long did Francis stay at Rome? The records do not say. But as he had gone there only with the object of making an experiment, we may suppose that one day would have sufficed. He was never given to lingering over anything unnecessarily. It is not a great distance from Rome to Assisi on a good horse. His father was away. Nobody may have noticed his absence except his mother, and she may have thought that he had gone to a neighboring town on business.

A KISS FOR A LEPER

So far Francis had said nothing to anybody as to what was in his mind, with the exception of Guido the Bishop of Assisi, though even to the bishop he did not tell everything. If it comes to that, he was as yet far from decided himself, except on the single point that he was to be dedicated to religion. The bishop may have been his confessor. It has even been suggested that about this time the bishop gave Francis minor orders, so as to give him ecclesiastical standing. Be that as it may, Guido certainly showed himself a friend to Francis in the events that were soon to occur.

This point should be stressed, because some of Francis's modern biographers, in particular Paul Sabatier, choose to represent Francis, if not exactly in conflict with ecclesiastical authority, at least hampered by ecclesiastical officials who were out of sympathy with his ideas. The truth is actually the reverse of this. Officials of every sort are all too prone to be very officious, so that one would expect the dignitaries of the Church to have been much more guarded than they were. It would not have been surprising if they had been suspicious or even hostile. They were nothing of the kind. Though they may have sometimes been puzzled by Francis or doubtful of the practicability of what he proposed, he was given an extraordinarily free hand.

It is probably safe to say that if a Francis of Assisi arose today there would be a considerable degree of reserve in his regard. The reason for this is that after a number of unfortunate experiences with hairbrain enthusiasts, the ecclesiastical organization has grown cautious; and the rules governing such a case as his are now more clearly defined and stringent. This is, upon the whole, very much to the good. Yet even today it is often surprising how much latitude is given to innovators.

As Macaulay has pointed out, the Catholic Church has always understood how to make the best use of enthusiasts. It does not expect to find very many of them. Nor does it believe that enthusiasm, as such, is necessarily admirable, for it can be misguided. The Church knows that most of the world's work has to be performed by dull and commonplace men, but it also knows that the most valuable work of all can only be done by men who are aflame. It found such a man in Francis of Assisi.

Yet his career might have ended, almost as soon as it began, had not Francis found, first in his bishop and then in the very highest officials of the Church, the sympathy and support he needed. Though they may not always have been perfect, it would be a falsification of his story not to point out that it was these that made his work possible at all.

Bishop Guido was not a saint. Knowing the Bernardones as he did, he might well be pardoned had he dealt a little highhandedly with a young man of whose escapades, innocent though they were, he must have been fully informed. He had heard the loud singing in the streets at midnight. He may have wondered in the beginning how genuine the conversion of this mercurial and impulsive fellow was. He had, however, a conviction as to Francis's sincerity and enough good sense not to treat his former eccentricities too seriously. His mind was even elastic enough to be tolerant of what may have been more perplexing to him, the Franciscan mode of sanctity. In spite of a natural disposition to irascibility, he showed himself fatherly.

The form that Francis's eccentricity took shortly after his return from Rome was an unaccountable interest in the lepers.

It is hard for us to realize what the situation was then. It is perhaps enough to say here that at that time there were about nineteen thousand leper hospitals in Europe. Indeed, the beginnings of an organized hospital system may be traced to the need of providing for these unfortunates. For them there was no hope. They had to be consigned to these small leper houses, where they were regarded as legally dead but were looked after, usually in a rather haphazard style, by several religious orders founded for this special work.

The lepers' exclusion from the rest of the community, however, was not absolute. They were permitted to wander at large at certain times in the year, though even then only when wearing a distinctive dress and beating a clapper to warn people of their approach. There was some theoretical pity for them and also a kind of reverence, as for those who, like Christ, in the prophecy of Isaiah, had been smitten of God and afflicted. Alms were given to them by the charitably inclined, but spasmodically and in insufficient quantities. Everybody took good care to keep out of their way.

So it had been with Francis himself. If he was fastidious with regard to vice, so was he also with regard to disease—especially this, the most loathsome of all diseases. Whenever he had occasion to pass the leper hospital of San Salvatore delle Parenti in the open country near Assisi, he would, even when he caught sight of it two miles away, close his nostrils in disgust. This was due, of course, to imagination on his part. There is a faint and disagreeable smell emitted by lepers, but it does not carry very far. That Francis put his fingers to his nose is the measure of his horror.

It was this horror that he now set himself to conquer. That he did so proved to be the decisive moment of his conversion.

He had been praying at the chapel of St. Mary of the Angels, the Little Portion—this ruinous shrine hidden in the woods was a favorite haunt of his—and an answer had come to him, spoken audibly as before at Spoleto or, more probably, heard only in his heart. The words he heard were these: "Francis, all those things that you have loved after the flesh, and have desired to have, you must now despise and hate, if you would do My will. Then the things that before seemed sweet and delightful shall become unbearable to you and bitter, and from those that you once loathed you shall drink sweetness and delight without measure."

After that hour of prayer and the answer he had received, Francis untethered his horse and began riding back to Assisi. He came out of the Portiuncula wood, and there the country was completely open, not even a hedge or a boulder or a bush on either side of the white, dusty road. Nothing was in sight but a leper who dragged himself along, coming slowly toward Francis. For a moment disgust and horror rose in him and by force of habit his hand began to lift itself toward his nose to shut off a stench that had not yet come to him. Then he told himself, "You are not a knight of Christ if you are unable to conquer yourself." He knew that this was somehow a great moment, the crisis of a battle, when one man's cowardice may imperil the entire issue. No, he would be loyal and true.

With a firm grip on his bridle reins—by this he felt he was getting a grip on himself—he rode forward steadily, not increasing speed but not diminishing it either. He heard the warning clapper, and he noticed that the man was drawing to the side of the road to give him room to pass without danger of contamination. At this, disgust again all but overwhelmed him, and for an instant he felt dizzy.

As he drew level with the poor putrefying wretch, Francis leaped from his horse. His first intention had been to do as he had formerly done and toss the man a coin; instead he ran to him and took the diseased body in his arms. A face eaten away and swollen into the aspect of a lion gazed at him; in the eyes was a look of astonishment. He put a kiss upon the hands, upon which there were only stumps of fingers, pressing into them all the money he had in the wallet at his girdle. And upon that shapeless mouth he put a kiss.

We do not know what was said. We do not know whether anything was said. A compassion so enveloping hardly needed words, and Francis's heart may have been so full that he was unable to speak. He got on his horse again and rode toward Assisi, while the leper shambled off along the road in the opposite direction.

When he had ridden a hundred paces, something made Francis swing his body round in the saddle and look back. There was the dusty road, and the fields were open on either side.

But there was no leper in sight.

It was characteristic of Francis not to be content with a dramatic incident. After that encounter he went nearly every day to the lazar house. There the lepers were always waiting for him, knowing that he brought alms, knowing that he also brought love. These visits would have been sickening to him had he not, at a stroke, conquered himself, for there was multiplication and diversity of deformity, the only thing common to all being the stench. These men were closely packed into a few rooms, ill cared for; and the nauseating odors always hung heavy there.

He soon discovered that these wretches, for whom few did anything at all, were exacting of those who tried to help them. Nobody had ever kissed their rotting hands before; yet those hands snatched without thanks at what he gave.

Nor was it only money and food that he brought. Girt with a towel, he used to wipe their sores and wash them and then bind them up as best he could, listening all the time to querulous complaints or, at best, getting nothing in return save a sullen silence.

His compassionate human heart, his poet's imagination, understood that their ingratitude must be pardoned. For these men the whole world had turned into suffering and loathing of themselves and their fellows. They knew, but only as a kind of abstract proposition, that there was a world outside their fetid cells. They themselves had once been of that world—how many millions and millions of years ago! Now they watched their hands and feet crumble and waited bitterly for death. Theirs was the death before death comes.

Their language, a railing obscenity that cursed high heaven, was that of the damned in hell. From the bottom of his heart Francis pitied them, not only for their physical state but much more because of their inconsolable souls. Gently he tried while dressing their wounds to bring some solace to their hearts by speaking of God, and sometimes he did succeed in touching some almost dried up spring into a trickle of life. He realized how hard it must be for them to bring home to themselves the truth of which he spoke, that God's love followed them even there, that by the bearing of these ills they could come all the more surely to the vision of God's face.

After a while he was welcomed, at least by some there, more for the compassion in his face and in his voice than for the gifts of money and food he brought. They listened to him now without blaspheming, and he was rewarded when he caught a gleam of joy in the eyes that formerly had glared out from their leonine faces. To himself he kept murmuring, "In all men I must see Christ, but most of all in these men. They are the very image of Christ in His sufferings." There were times when a natural revulsion still made such a reminder necessary.

It was to Christ himself that Francis felt he was bringing relief: Christ the leper, Christ crucified, the man of sorrows acquainted with grief. At the thought the tears flowed down from his eyes upon the feet he was bandaging. Then the tears of the leper would flow.

No longer was it necessary that Christ should appear as on that first day, for Christ was in his heart, an ineffable sweetness, an enveloping peace.

By now Francis could have been giving little, if any, attention to his father's cloth business. Even his time for prayer must have been diminished, now that he was paying so many visits to the lazar house. When he did go to his cave, it was not likely that his unnamed companion was with him any longer, for nobody would have wanted to go on with Francis afterward to the nauseating lepers. Moreover, the hidden treasure, which had been an inducement to his friend, had now been found. Instead of haggard and worn, he emerged into the bright light afterwards with a light upon his countenance that seemed dazzling. As he rode home, he sang words of his own making to a tune of his own.

He had told his former friends that he was going to do, there in Assisi, noble and mighty deeds. They had laughed at him for this brag, and he could smile at himself now. Yet it was true: he had become the knight of Christ.

Already in his care for the lepers he had found his vocation, or what was always to be an important part of it. He had not so much as thought of a band of men who would go throughout the world preaching. Not yet had he begun to preach at all, except for the words he whispered to those poor lepers whom he always addressed as "Fellow Christians," but this was to be to the end of his life an aspect of his special mission.

Nor did he ever lose another part of his vocation, the first and most important part of all: the life of prayer, the spirit of the mystic. He was often to wonder whether he should not give up everything else to yield himself utterly to the sweetness of union with God. He managed to the end to combine the two modes of the religious life, contemplation of the divine and help for the human. Though he was sure that there was still more to come, that all of God's purpose for him was not revealed as yet, he waited for this in a radiant serenity.

With his compassion for the poor and suffering went—indeed, this was its origin—a compassion for the poor Christ, the suffering Christ, as Francis often called him. One day he was walking in the wood that surrounded the chapel of St. Mary of the Angels, meditating upon the passion of our Lord. He was so overcome that he was sobbing and shaken with his sobs. Just then another man of devout life—others beside himself used to go occasionally to that little chapel where the angel voices were heard—saw him weeping and ran up to him in alarm.

"Are you ill," he asked, "or have you some great sorrow?"

"Aye," Francis told him, "I have a great grief. I weep because of what My Lord Jesus Christ endured upon the cross. For him I ought not to be ashamed to go mourning through the whole world."

At this his tears burst forth again. And the other man, likewise moved, wept with him.

THE CALL COMES

The chapel of Our Lady of the Angels, with its equally charming name of the Little Portion, was only one of two such half-ruined little chapels that Francis loved to frequent. Another almost as dear to him was that named for St. Damian. Like the other it was the property of the Camaldolese Benedictines of Mount Subasio. It did not have the same antiquity as the Portiuncula, which was erected in 352 by pilgrims returning from the Holy Land; yet it was very old and, according to tradition, was built by St. Benedict himself, a fact which, if true, gave it special sanctity. Both places had this in common: they were suitable for retired prayer, and they were simple and poor. Both also eventually passed into Francis's hands and were to play a big part in his story.

St. Damian's was almost completely devoid of decoration except for a Byzantine crucifix, which may still be seen at Assisi, though now in the church of the Poor Clares. It is no very great work of art, but it has, in spite of its archaic stiffness, a certain realism. By this it conveyed a deep feeling for the sufferings of Christ. For that reason perhaps as much as for any other, Francis chose the stone flags below it as a favorite spot for contemplation. There he would kneel, erect, for hours at a time.

One day he heard the Voice speaking again. This time he reached the point of ecstasy, which was often to happen to him again but had never happened to him before. Many times already he had felt a sense of pervading sweetness, a consciousness of the Divine Presence; this was, of course, a mystical state, though not one of the highest degree. Now kneeling at the foot of the crucifix, he was completely drawn out of himself and lost all consciousness except of God.

From the cross Christ spoke to him. "Francis," the Voice came, "do you not see that My house is being destroyed? Go therefore and repair it."

Astonished and trembling, Francis made answer, "Gladly will I do it, O Lord."

He took Christ's words in the most literal sense. He could see that the neglected chapel was badly in need of restoration, so he accepted the task laid upon him as being simply that of bringing stones and mortar and setting to work. Not for an instant did he imagine that the commission could be wider than that. Indeed, though the field of his labor was soon to widen to enclose the last limits of the earth, he never ceased to believe, as in the case of the lepers, that the local obligation was also his. He never ceased to be greatly concerned about the rebuilding and care of dilapidated churches.

From that hour the stigmata of Christ's wounds were imprinted upon his heart. Many years were to elapse before they became visible in his flesh. That could happen only because he had prepared for this by living a crucified life.

That hour was also a decisive stage in his vocation. It opened before him only by degrees, but by accepting the commission to renovate St. Damian's he also accepted everything else that was involved.

He went out of the chapel and found an old priest sitting in the sun. A priest in residence was more than the Portiuncula had, though now and then Mass was said there, probably by one of the Benedictine Fathers from Mount Subasio. The priest at St. Damian's may have been a Benedictine, too. More likely he was a secular, too infirm for regular parish work, who lived there as a pensioner of the abbey. Francis went up to him and kissed his hands, telling him that he meant to strengthen the walls that seemed about to fall. As a start, because at that moment he could not set to work with his masonry, and because it did not seem to have occurred to him just yet that he would have to do the repairing with his own not very skilled hands, he handed him what money he had with him and said, "Messer, with this buy oil for the lamp. It should always be kept burning before the altar."

Before the old priest could recover from his astonishment, Francis had ridden away.

The following day Francis did what has seemed to many a very strange and not quite justifiable thing. It must be remembered that he had worked with his father as a partner in his business for several years, and that he had always been free to spend money without question, even if Peter Bernardone had sometimes grumbled a little over his extravagance. Francis must be pardoned for not being able to distinguish very clearly what was his father's and what was his own. At worst he acted in impulsive thoughtlessness when he put some bales of cloth on a horse and sold it, along with the horse, for which he had no further use, at Foligno.

It may be presumed that, excited though his mind was, he had some misgivings about this transaction, and that that was why he went to Foligno. At any rate, that was the impression he must have given. In this, however, he may merely have had bad luck; possibly he chose Foligno for no other reason than that it was the most important city in Umbria from a business point of view, and he had a customer there. Obviously, he could not have imagined that the affair would not come to light, for Foligno was only ten miles away. What must be said is that Francis had acted inadvisedly but in good faith. Most unluckily he had done something that could be represented as not being strictly honest: he had given his father a weapon against him.

When this deal had been closed, Francis wanted to get rid of the money as soon as possible. He intended never to touch any kind of coin again. Never again do we hear of his having done so, except for a dramatic moment a couple of years later, when he was to give it away by the handfuls. To this smart young businessman, this reckless spendthrift, money had become, quite literally, filthy lucre.

He had not thought so far about doing the work at St. Damian's himself. His idea was to give the priest the money he had obtained at Foligno and let him see to the necessary rebuilding. However, on his way to St. Damian's he evidently made some preparations about this, for his eager habit was never to delay about anything. Out of the proceeds of the scarlet cloth and the horse he bought some stone. He bought it from a priest named Sylvester, a rather older man than himself related to the Scifi family, whose head was the Count of Sasso Rosso. Francis knew him to be rather sharp in his business dealings, rather keen for his gain; but he also knew that Sylvester had some stone available. For the last time Francis appears as a businessman.

"Ah," he said, approaching the priest, being careful to ignore the stone blocks lying in the yard, "I see, Messer Sylvester, that you have your little cousin here."

A golden-haired child of twelve was walking there, playing with a little dog. It ran up to Francis at once, and the child smiled at him. He had known her since she was a baby, for, though the Scifi had a castle outside the city, they also had a town house where they lived most of the time, and this was within a stone's throw of where the Bernardones lived. In a small place like Assisi everybody knew everybody else. Count Favorino dei Scifi and Lady Ortolana, the girl's parents, must often have been in his father's shop, and Francis, who moved in circles higher than his own rank in society, would have been likely to have included the Scifi in his own circle of friends.

The priest returned, "Yes, Francis, well is she named, this little Shining One. *Chiara,* that is the right name for her."

"It is the right name indeed," Francis agreed. He did not wish to introduce the subject of the stone directly himself, so he let Sylvester do it.

The priest soon came around to it. "A wool merchant may not be likely to know who wants to buy stone, Francis. But it is going cheap; and it is good stone."

Francis laughed. "He must be a shrewd trader who gets the best of it in a bargain with you, Messer Sylvester! But I know something about stone. I helped in the building of the city wall."

"I had forgotten that. Yes, you know many things that a cloth merchant does not usually know. Then you will know that this is good stone."

"But what do you call cheap?"

Sylvester named his price. Yes, it was cheap enough.

"But you would not cheat a brother priest," Francis twinkled at him.

Sylvester smiled back genially. "I would not cheat even you, Francis, though everyone knows you are rich."

Francis let that pass. It would spoil everything if he told Sylvester that now he was poor, making himself poor. So he said only, "Then I might buy it from you."

"*You*, Francis! What would you do with stone?"

"I might buy it for the poor priest at St. Damian's. Could you get a carter to take it there?"

Francis dipped into his purse and paid the agreed-upon sum. He saluted Sylvester, smiled at the shining Clare. Then he went on to St. Damian's.

When Francis emptied his purse there, the priest was frightened. He was also a little puzzled and a little annoyed. This heap of gold —Francis must be making game of him! Yesterday there was that money for the oil and now this! He was probably playing one of his pranks. Yet that smiling, candid face could not be suspected of being the mask of any unmannerly trick played upon an old man. The priest, more reassured, asked, "But how did you get it, Francis?"

Willingly enough Francis told him. "And I have some stone coming for you soon," he added.

The old man pondered this. He had heard some reports of how Peter Bernardone was protesting against the new way his son was spending money. He did not wish to involve himself there or run any danger of antagonizing a man as powerful in the community as was the rich cloth merchant. The priest could see that here the father might have a real ground for complaint against his son. It would not do for him to take any money obtained in this way. It was different with the stone, as that had already been bought and paid for. The priest knew Sylvester well enough to know that he would never repay money he had already received.

He answered after a little thought, "The stone you have bought, that perchance I may take. But if I take this money you offer, your father will be angry with me. No, I dare not take it."

"Then will you let me stay with you here while I work upon the walls of your church?" Francis had vaguely thought of asking to be allowed to do that, but he had not thought until that moment of doing the work himself.

Again the priest pondered. Then he agreed, "That, Francis, you may do. But I cannot accept this money."

"I cannot make you take it, messer," returned Francis, "but neither can you make me keep it." He threw it on a broad window ledge of the chapel. "Money and I are no longer friends."

When Peter Bernardone came home, he asked Lady Pica, "Where is that young fool, our son? What has he been doing now?"

Pica answered that she had heard that he had been staying for some days with the chaplain of St. Damian's.

"And the business?" he roared. "Has he not been going to fairs with the cloth?"

"Peter," she answered, "he did go out last week with a horse laden with cloth. More than that I do not know. I have not seen him since."

"I came in good time! I shall go at once to find him. He is up to some new folly, I warrant you." Off he went in a great rage.

He did not find Francis, for Bernardone's son had prepared for this. In the priest's house was a recess in a wall, which is still shown, and in this Francis hid himself. The priest was too terrified to tell the furious man where his son was.

"But my money, my money!" Bernardone yelled, after a fruitless search. "Where is my money?"

"He did leave some money here. See, messer, he tried to give it to me, but I would not accept it. I know where it is. Come with me." He showed him where it lay on the dusty window sill. That would show him that the priest was quite guiltless.

"Do you know where he got this money?"

"He said something about Foligno."

"Hah, so it was *there* that he sold my horse and my good scarlet cloth!"

He strode off, still angry with his son but a little mollified that he had got his money back.

Peter Bernardone had not counted the money in the priest's presence, but he did count it after he got home. Then his lips pursed and his brows gathered in thought.

"Your son, Pica," he told his wife, speaking slowly, "is a fool. That all the world knows for truth. But it is also the truth that this son of mine is a good trader. He knows the value of that cloth. And he knows the value of that horse. He might give a thing away for nothing, as he did to that knight, as he does to his dear beggars. But he would not sell a thing below its right price."

"Nor above it," put in Lady Pica sharply.

He gave her a swift look but did not pursue that subject. "The priest said Francis had been to Foligno," he said, switching to another track. "I also will go to Foligno. This very day. Perchance I shall hear more about your son's doings."

She did not comment on that. Instead she said quietly, "Son of mine he is, Peter. And your son also. Yet there are many who might find that last a hard thing to believe."

At this Peter stamped out of the house and rode to Foligno.

DISGUSTED FATHER

The inquiries Peter Bernardone made at Foligno gave him a grain or two of satisfaction. He discovered that the cloth had been sold at a good price, not too much but also not too little. The horse dealer in the market place admitted that he had bought the horse. "But," he added, "a few more such deals and I and my children starve."

"When that day comes, I shall give a feast," growled Bernardone. "Tell me the price you paid."

The dealer told him and got a grunted, "You and your children will not starve yet. But the price is not too bad. Will you swear that you are telling the truth?"

"No need for me to swear, messer. Think you that I would buy a horse without a bill of sale? Look, the price is on it. And I gave your son a receipt."

"But where is my son?"

"That is more than I can tell you."

Peter always plumed himself on his shrewdness. As he turned the matter over in his mind, he discovered a little comfort in it. True that the price Francis had received for the cloth and the horse was less than the money that had been found lying on the window sill. This showed that some of the money had been kept back. But it also showed that Francis was not quite a fool. He might still make a good merchant. A cudgel about his shoulders might knock some sense into him yet.

Peter Bernardone went to St. Damian's again to question the priest. Again Francis hid from his father.

Bernardone brutally demanded of the priest, "Did you not take some of the money?"

"Nay, I took none. It is all there."

"It is *not* all there. Some of it is missing."

The priest was a mild old man with little stomach for a quarrel, but there were limits to what he would endure. "Messer," he said, "did you not find the money lying on the window sill?"

"I found *some* of it there, yes, Messer Priest."

"Then know that I am too poor a man to leave money lying in such a place. Were I a thief I would hide it well."

"That I believe to be no lie. Perchance you have concealed it where you have concealed my son. Or is *he* the thief?"

Again the mild old man spoke with a touch of spirit, *"That,* Messer, never will I believe."

The records speak of Francis remaining in hiding at St. Damian's for a month. So long a time is unlikely, but it was at least several days before Francis mustered enough courage to go into Assisi. He meant to go to his father and explain. He knew that he would get a stormy welcome, but it could not be avoided forever. It would be better to go without too much delay.

The scene was stormier than he had expected. As he went along the city streets, a jeering crowd collected. Assisi had long believed him to be crazy; now Assisi knew that he must be. People had heard about the lepers; they had heard about the horse and the money in Foligno. These were but the more recent instances of his fantastic behavior. This time one glance at Francis was enough to tell everybody that he was deranged. He came along bedraggled and with hair uncut, beard unshorn, yet smiling—idiotically it seemed—toward his father's shop. That he should go there at all after what he had done was proof positive that he had lost his wits. Several stones were thrown at him by mischievous boys, and one cut his cheek open. He still went on smiling and talking to himself. A rope was suddenly jerked taut before him, and he fell into the mud. He picked himself up, his fine clothes in rags and filthy, and smiled again.

Peter Bernardone was enraged. If Francis must come home, why must he come in this way, to be the laughingstock of the town? It was not to rescue Francis that Peter rushed out of his shop but to vent his anger. He dragged him into the house and used the cudgel freely. Not a word of explanation would he listen to. "Tell me, where is my money? Give me back my money, you thief! Where is the money you have stolen?" When Francis tried to talk to him, he only got another blow from the cudgel and another shrieked question for an answer to which Bernardone would not wait. He was thrown into the cellar, beaten almost into insensibility, as a good way of teaching him sense. Then his father, having locked the door, left him to ponder over his foolishness.

"Cannot you be calm, Peter?" Lady Pica asked. "You have given Francis no chance to speak."

"He shall have his chance when I take him before the city consuls. Let him tell *them* what he has done with my money."

There was no arguing with this angry man. He had to go away that afternoon for a day or two. Pica was glad of the opportunity to have Francis to herself. She was sure that, however things seemed, he had done no wrong. Of course he had acted foolishly, in that impulsive way of his. If she could have a quiet talk with him, she thought she could make him see this. Then he might stop going to the lepers and giving money away by handfuls. When Peter came back, perhaps he would be in a better frame of mind. That would surely be true if he had made some money. She decided to say nothing that might irritate him further.

When Peter had gone, she went down to the cellar.

"See, dear Francis mine," she said, "I am not locking the door. Nor will your mother beat you. I have brought you some food and some wine. Eat and drink and tell me what you may have to tell."

He told of what he had done and something also of what he intended to do. When he said that henceforth he meant to live according to the Gospel, she cried, "But Francis, are we not all Christians?"

"Yes, my mother, and you are a good Christian. But I must live like Christ. I am now the knight of Christ."

He explained as best he could, but she really did not understand. She did see that he had got the idea not merely that he must be kind to the poor and the lepers, but that he himself must live as one of the poor.

"That is how Christ lived, mother," he told her.

She still did not understand. "But, Francis," she sobbed, "you say I am a good Christian. Do I have to live in what you call the poverty of Our Lord and His Blessed Mother?"

He shook his head and smiled. "No, Mother. He has not called *you* to that life."

"Do *you* have to live it like that? One who is poor may accept poverty as the will of God for him. So also should one who is sick. But must we *make* ourselves sick and poor?"

"I must make myself poor, Mother, to be like Christ." It was the only answer she could get.

She knew that if he talked to his father like that on his return, there would be more cudgelings; if a blow should fall on her son's head he might get killed. There was only one thing for her to say, "Francis, your father is an angry man. He must not find you here. Go away quickly and hide. Go a long way off."

She pressed money upon him but he refused it.

"Money is always useful, my son," she said.

"Not to me," came his reply. "To me money is only a danger."

Francis did go away, but this time he did not hide. The beating he had received from his father should have made him fear Peter more than ever; it did not have that effect at all. Instead it emboldened him. He saw now that the knight of Christ must show courage. When Peter Bernardone, having vented his rage against Madonna Pica, went again to St. Damian's a few days afterward, Francis did not scuttle into the secret closet in the wall but came out to meet him. He admitted everything: the exact sums he had obtained at Foligno (and these tallied with what Bernardone had already heard) and his expenditure of some of it to buy stone. Peter had recovered the main part of it from the window sill; the amount that he was actually out was not very large.

It was, however, large enough for a charge to be laid against Francis before the consuls of Assisi.

Just what was in Peter Bernardone's mind is uncertain; he may have had no very clear idea himself. He was accusing Francis of insanity in language that was hardly that of a sane man. At one moment he was shouting, "Madman!" and the next, "Thief!" Yet in his rage he could not have really wished to put his son into the city jail. What was probably in his mind was to force repentance, after which he would always have had an instrument for compelling good behavior (as Bernardone understood it) or, if that failed, making things so hot for Francis that he would be glad to go elsewhere. He was not to stay there and bring disgrace upon the family. If the worst came to the worst, and Francis persisted in his folly, the charge that could now be brought might serve to oblige him to renounce his rights as eldest son and his share in the business.

Peter turned for redress to the city authorities. When they sent a summons to Francis, he calmly handed it back and told the warrant officer, "I do not admit the jurisdiction of the court. I am now one dedicated to the service of God."

It is very doubtful whether Francis could have claimed the benefit of clergy, for, though it is possible that Bishop Guido had privately given him minor orders, there is no indication that this had happened, and it is inherently unlikely. Nor was Francis the member of any religious order or even a hermit in any recognizable fashion.

Although the consuls could not see upon what Francis based his claim—one that any rascal could make and so bring all law to a standstill—they did not believe, even from what Bernardone himself had told them, that Francis had been guilty of any dishonesty. In any event they feared that they would only get embroiled with the bishop if they took this matter into their hands. There was already quite enough conflict between the ecclesiastical and civic authorities for them to wish not to stir up any more, especially over so trivial and doubtful an issue. They discussed the matter in the council chamber of the Palazzo Publico and then, calling Bernardone in again, advised him to take the question to the bishop's court, as it appeared to fall under its jurisdiction and not theirs. To calm down the angry father, a man important enough in the commune for them to wish not to offend him, they gave him this assurance: "The bishop will see that you get your rights. He is a wise man. Punishment coming from him would do more good than punishment coming from us. The wits of this son of yours have been turned by religion; the bishop is the one best able to bring him to his senses."

Peter Bernardone allowed himself to be persuaded. Thinking things over, he came to the conclusion that less drastic action would serve as well. Bishop Guido would surely tell Francis to stop spending money—money that did not belong to him—on doing things that were none of his business, like repairing churches. Francis would surely listen to the bishop. Peter did not really wish to press things so far as to demand a renunciation by Francis of his birthright. The money in this particular instance was of small consequence. Francis had spent much more at other times. It was merely that Peter could now bring a charge that might frighten his son and so restore the foolish young man to his senses.

The bishop's court issued its summons. At once Francis answered, "Unto the Lord Bishop I will gladly go, for he is the father and the lord of souls."

Into the court there crowded as many people as possible. What could be better sport than an irate father and a crazy son? The crowd was looking for something amusing. Instead, it got something dramatic.

A case in which the facts were not under dispute could be disposed of quickly. "Francis, you sold this horse of your father's?" "For how much?" "And some bales of cloth?" "For how much?" "What did you do with the money?" "Have you any of it left?"

The bishop's verdict was a mild reproof of Francis, though it may have had a second edge in a suggestion that Peter Bernardone was not quite beyond reproach in his business methods. There was probably some sharp practice of which everybody knew, and Bishop Guido may have been hinting at this. But he could hardly approve of Francis's conduct at Foligno. Nor could he have failed to have some sympathy with Peter. It was obvious that the man felt outraged that, after all his openhandedness with Francis, he should have had this return of ingratitude and disobedience. This incident was the culmination of a long series of follies. The bishop saw that Peter's pride in his eldest son, a pride that was vulgarly self-centered, had turned to an incensed bitterness. In delivering judgment he tried to hold the scales even.

The first part of the judgment was in Peter's favor. Guido turned to Francis and said, "Your father is sore vexed against you and offended. Now therefore, if you desire to be the servant of God, give him back what property you have, as perhaps it was obtained by improper means." He paused, to allow what irony there was in that rebuke to Francis to sink into Peter's mind. Then, continuing to address Francis, he went on, "God does not want you to use in the work of the Church money that is going to make your father sin through anger. This will abate when you make restitution." He paused again and with a fatherly look at Francis said, "But have faith in the Lord, my son, and play the man and fear not. He Himself will be your helper, and will give in abundance whatever is needful for the work of His Church."

The words indicate clearly that the bishop knew of at least some part of what was in Francis's mind. Not only did he sympathize with it, he was encouraging him in his intention of divesting himself of all that he possessed and of trusting himself to Providence. On the small point of the immediate issue he upheld Peter Bernardone, and he could not do otherwise; on the much larger issue he was upholding Francis. One gets a hint that he had had a private talk with Francis prior to the public hearing of the case.

It was now that the dramatic scene occurred. Though the bishop knew that Francis would not contest his solution of the problem and was not only willing but eager to renounce his inheritance, he was not prepared for what happened. Francis answered, "My lord, with a light heart I give him back not only the money that belongs to him, but also my clothes." There and then he began to take them off, every stitch, except a loincloth of sacking that he had put on in preparation for this stripping of himself. Everything that might be considered as having been bought with his father's money was thrown to the floor. It was a sign that his renunciation was absolute.

Then Francis spoke again in the clear, resonant voice, developed by singing but rather surprising in one of so slight a build. It startled those who heard it and gave an impression of power not otherwise very evident. He said, "Let everybody listen and understand: until now I have called Peter Bernardone my father, but because I purpose to serve the Lord, I give him back the money over which he was vexed, and all the clothes I ever had of him. For now I desire to say only 'Our Father who art in heaven,' not, 'My father, Peter Bernardone.'"

The spectators gasped. At a stroke their sympathies, which until that moment had been with the father, went to the son. When they saw the enraged Bernardone, in the bitterness of his heart, gathering up all the clothes that Francis had thrown off, they were indignant.

Yet as we look back upon the scene, we must feel some pity for the stricken father. He had won his point, but at what a cost of public humiliation! What was there for him to do but pick up the garments from the floor and go out? He had been made to look a fool, though all the justice, he felt, was on his side.

It was a scene that might easily have turned into farce. But one does not laugh at such passionate sincerity. The spectators were in tears, as over the nakedness of Francis was thrown the cope of the bishop.

Guido cleared the court and took Francis into an adjoining room, while the curious crowd waited outside. The bishop could not allow him to leave there with nothing on, but Francis would accept only a discarded tunic that had belonged to Guido's gardener.

He emerged at last by a side door. On the tattered garment he was wearing he had made a large cross in chalk; it was the sign of his knighthood. As he walked swiftly toward the open fields beyond Assisi, his head was lifted high and he was singing loudly in French.

THE HERALD OF THE GREAT KING

It was late March or early April; spring was in the sky and the first blossoms on tree and bush. The fields were already alive, dotted here and there with budding poppies. And on the slopes of the hills, above the groves of olive, the vines festooned their trellises. It was as one of the choirs of birds that Francis sang.

He went out over the hills toward Gubbio, below the height of Mount Subasio toward the gorge of the Chiascio, crossing the stream by an old Roman bridge where the poplars were waking to new life. For him it was new life, too—a sense of liberation such as he had never known before.

The clean air, full of sudden little breezes that carried the sweetness of the flowers, the sight of the plain with its farms and copses of oaks, with the rugged mountains beyond, whose hollows still held snow that was blue in the shadows—all this might have inspired a poet to song. Though these seemed to be joy visible, they were not the cause of Francis's joy. He was poor now—and free.

He reached out his arms to draw everything to his breast—clouds and mountains and all. It was in his breast that that fountain of joy flowed sparkling like the Chiaggio River in the sunlight, seen by him as he reached the point where the road began to decline towards Gubbio. Now as never before he felt himself the son of God, directly and utterly dependent upon Him. That gave him a new sense of kinship with all created things, with the blooms in the fields, the birds in the air, the very dust of the road. "Brothers!" he cried, "Sisters!"

He had come to a dark wood, and he was going through it with steps even lighter and quicker than usual, almost in a dance, when fierce, dark men rushed at him from behind trees. They cut off his escape, though he would have attempted none. As they glowered at him, he smiled at them.

"Who are you?" the leader of the band of robbers demanded,

looking at his scarecrow tatters and thinking himself cheated that here was nothing worth the taking. "Tell me, who are you?" It was perhaps fortunate for Francis that he was in rags, for his life might have been taken along with his good clothes. It puzzled them that he stood before them without the faintest trace of fear, rather with a happy good will. A beggar, and yet the tone of his voice showed that he was well-bred.

Who *was* he? The question, coming so unexpectedly, suddenly showed Francis who he really was. He had not thought of this before, but now he saw it plain. He answered, "I'm a herald of the Great King."

"A herald of the Great King! Listen to him!" cried the leader of the bandits. And they laughed, but because of their laughter they were able to spare him. The worst they did was to push him headlong down a bank into a ditch full of half-melted snow.

"Lie there," they shouted down at him with ferocious geniality, "Lie there, lout, you herald of God!" They went back into the woods roaring at their jest.

This seems to have happened somewhere near the little town of Caprignone, about two thirds of the distance from Assisi to Gubbio. But Francis did not go on to Gubbio that day. His clothes were soaked through, the rags being further torn as he rolled down the bank through bushes and the protruding roots of trees, so he retraced his steps a little to the Benedictine priory of Santa Maria della Rocca. Francis had heard that the Benedictines were hospitable people, that hospitality, in fact, was part of their Rule. They could be counted upon to give him something to eat and a night's lodging and, surely, something to wear.

He did get something to eat: a bowl of soup; and he was lodged in a barn, like a tramp. Even to get this much he had to work in the kitchen scouring pots. But nobody offered him any clothes, though they saw how badly he needed them. He was still too new to this kind of life to make so much as a hinted request. Years later, after Francis had become famous, the prior apologized for this treatment. No doubt it was not he who had been responsible but some uncouth lay brother.

Francis stayed there several days, hoping all the time that his rags would be noticed and that he would be given something to wear.

When he saw that this was not going to happen, he decided to continue his journey as he was. At Gubbio he had a friend. From him he would be certain to get something to cover himself against the air which was still cold.

A tatterdemalion in bare feet, he climbed the steep cobbled streets of Gubbio to the house of his friend, Federigo Spadalunga. Francis was a bit embarrassed at having to present himself in this condition. The last time Federigo had seen him, he had been not merely a young man of fashion but the one who set the fashion for the wealthy youths of Umbria. Still, there was nothing but to go as he was.

"Francis!" Federigo exclaimed, hardly recognizing in this scarecrow the fantastic exquisite of the past. "Francis, what has happened to you?"

"You know me then? I did not know whether you would."

"You are shivering, Francis. Let me give you some wine."

"No wine. Just a piece of bread, if you will."

He told some part of his story to the wide-eyed, wondering young man. Poverty? The Gospel? It was all beyond Federigo Spadalunga. To his own mind he tried to explain this as a result of the encounter with the bandits.

"You are fortunate to be alive, Francis," he said. "We have heard of that band of men. They have killed several travelers."

"Yes," Francis agreed. "Brother Robbers *were* something less than courteous. Now with your bread would you in courtesy give me some clothes to wear?"

Federigo brought out several gowns, all of good, warm stuff. Each was rejected by Francis. "No, I cannot wear that. That is not what I want. Nor that. It would not be fitting for a knight of Christ."

It was only now, during this process of elimination, that he began to see what *would* be suitable for his future life. His friend's clothes were not. Never again would he wear anything like these.

"But you cannot go home in anything else!" Federigo protested.

"I am not going home any more. What is it a hermit wears? That is what I mean to be now. A tunic such as our peasants have— that is what would do." It was, not a habit, nor even a uniform, merely a serviceable frieze robe that could be worn in all weathers, having a hood.

Federigo did not have any garment that precisely answered this description, but he managed to find an old cloak that he used to wear for hunting. He held it up for inspection.

"That will do," Francis told him. "I can remove some of its folds. And if you will give me a needle and some thread . . . A cloth merchant knows something of their use," he said with a smile. "I can turn it into what I want."

He accepted also a shirt and a pair of stout shoes and a leather belt. Though already well-worn, he saw that they still had several more years' wear in them. They were to be all the clothes he had for several years.

"I pray you to let me give you something better," Federigo said. But Francis would only say, "Nothing could be better for me than these. I take them thankfully as your alms. You have given them to God."

Francis then went back to St. Damian's, where so far he had hardly started the work of renovation that Christ had told him to do. At the very outset he had been interrupted, but now he would be secure, sure that nobody would trouble him again. From the destitute what could be taken? He was now safe in his poverty. All that had happened during the last few days—except for his having given away all that he possessed—was that he now had clothes more appropriate for his new manner of life. That life itself, though, was simply a continuation of the one he had already begun to lead before being summoned to the bishop's court.

The old priest at St. Damian's was glad to see him there again. He had heard some strange stories, and he feared that some harm had come to Francis. Now he was going to get a mason who asked no wages, and who even provided his own stone. What little food he would need would come from the kitchen garden. It was an agreeable arrangement to both. Francis was happy in his work and prayer, and the lonely old man had a charming and lively companion.

Only very rarely did Francis go into Assisi. When he did, people noticed that he walked along chanting the praises of God. If anyone spoke to him, he answered courteously but without showing any of his former willingness to get into conversation. People saw that he was happy, though he looked preoccupied. He had ceased to excite much wonder. After that scene in the bishop's court every-thing else seemed uninteresting. He could be ignored or taken for granted as a religious eccentric. Though it was admitted that Assisi had never seen anybody quite so odd as Francis, still it had seen eccentrics before. There were those who continued to think him mad, but there were a few who were moved almost to tears when they remembered what an extravagant young scapegrace he had been and saw him as he now was. It was with awe that such people perceived that he seemed to be positively intoxicated with the love of God.

Francis never again went to his father's house. He was completely detached from his past.

CHURCH BUILDER

When oil was needed for the lamp at St. Damian's, Francis had to beg for it. It had not been too hard to beg on the porch of St. Peter's in Rome, for there he had been unknown. It was a very different matter when he had to turn beggar in Assisi. Yet he would not ask for money or ever accept money. He would ask for the oil itself. Already he had made a rule for himself not to handle coin. That was all over for him forever.

He picked out a friend for this purpose, a friend who was sure to have oil and who would be sure to give it—the easiest initial effort in what was to him a most distasteful task. When Francis got to his house, he saw his friend sitting outside playing dice with some com-panions. At once he got so embarrassed that he almost turned away. He did, in fact, go up the street before he had the courage to retrace his steps. This time he stopped and said before them all, "Could you give me some oil?"

They stared at him and some of them tittered. Francis continued simply, "I had intended to come in when I passed before, but I was ashamed. That shame was wrong, as I am asking for God. It is the lamp at St. Damian's that needs oil."

He spoke in French. His former companions had sung Provençal songs at their convivial gatherings, there being little Italian poetry available. To them Francis's use of French may have seemed a tactful reminder of former days. Although Francis usually used French only when he was specially happy, this time his use of it may have been to hide his own confusion. Some of that dice-playing group may not have known French and so would not have known that he was begging.

This seems to have been the first time Francis had begged for anything, except for that hour or two in Rome and for the clothes at Gubbio. The begging was to proceed by definite stages, each more humiliating than the last. The sensitive and fastidious Francis did not overcome his shame at a single stroke.

The next necessity was stone for his building operations. When he had used up what he had bought from the priest Sylvester, he had no means of obtaining any more—no means except that of going out and asking for it. Perhaps he did turn to Sylvester again and was refused. He may have had the reply, "Why do you come to me again? I gave you a bargain. A day or two later, if I had only waited, I could have sold that stone for a lot more. No, Francis, I do not owe you anything; I think it is you who owe me something."

Stone fortunately was yielded in abundance in the Umbrian hills. Even most of the poor houses were constructed of stone as far as the first story, with wood used above, if at all. Many people had blocks of stone lying in their back yards, kept for possible repairs. Some of this, Francis thought, they could spare. So he went through the streets—again with a rather ingenious method of approach—singsonging, this time in Italian so that everybody would be able to understand, a doggerel rhyme:

> Anyone who gives a stone,
> A reward shall have for one.
> Anyone who gives me two,
> Two rewards shall have as due.
> Add to that—and then shall he
> Three rewards receive for three.

Some people laughed at him, but some people also gave, even some of those who laughed. Not always did they limit themselves to three blocks of stone. Every one of these the frail Francis had to hoist upon his back and carry painfully down to St. Damian's himself.

The method was, like so much about Francis, both humorous and practical. It got results, not stone in great quantities—that was not necessary and, indeed, would have been too much for Francis to handle—but stone in sufficiency. It was a small instance of his individualistic style, soon to be exercised on a much wider scale. He had been a businessman and a successful one, except for his inability to keep a grip on the money he made. Though his subsequent career showed that he had no relish for the details of organization, he must at least be credited with an astounding faculty for setting things in operation in the shortest space of time.

Nevertheless that part of his development was still several years off. In his simplicity and modesty he had in his head just then no plan larger than that of doing what he had been told to do by Christ speaking from the Byzantine crucifix, to go and build up His church. Only later did it dawn on him that what was meant was "Church" spelled with a capital.

He got all the stone he needed, and if it came in slowly, he was in no hurry. Not all the day was spent in work; he prayed a good deal, and he continued his visits to the lepers. His masonry was at the start somewhat amateurish. Though he had gained some slight knowledge by helping in his youth in the building of the city wall, after the castle was destroyed, the shaping of stones for the little chapel called for a higher degree of skill. He had to chisel each block before he fitted it into place, and every block had to be carried down to St. Damian's from the city, a distance of two miles over rough roads.

Perhaps, too, he now and then obtained some assistance in that back-breaking toil. One of the early accounts of this period tells of his calling to people (whether to the local peasants or the people of Assisi is not clear), "Come and help me in the work of the church of St. Damian's!" He added, "It shall be a convent of ladies, by whose good report and life Our Heavenly Father shall be glorified in the Universal Church." If he did make in that public fashion a prophecy that was so completely fulfilled, it shows that already his eyes swept a wide horizon, and that even while keeping to a small job in hand, he was conscious that it would lead to something very big.

Yet as Celano points out, the humility of Francis was externalized by the fact that at St. Damian's he did no more than prop up walls that were about to fall, and that he thought of laying no new foundations. For him Christ was the sole foundation. It was on that that he built and so was saved from drifting like so many of the reformers of his time into schism with the Catholic Church. Odd as he often appeared to be, odd to the point of eccentricity, he was firmly anchored to the center: never did it enter his head to be anything but a most affectionately loyal Catholic. This highly original man, the open-air saint, had an unbounded reverence for the very fabric of churches and for all ecclesiastical authority. Whatever else he was, he was not a potential Protestant, born before due time.

Francis stuck to his work at St. Damian's. Though this went slowly, he was able, before embarking on the enterprises which were to be his main work, to renovate two other local chapels that needed repairs. His was the simple day-by-day task done without hurry, without anxiety, without any formulation of far-reaching plans, whatever inkling he may have had of greater things ahead. For those he was content to wait until the summons came.

This laborer was assuredly worthy of his hire. All that he got for it was lodging and a few poor meals from the priest at St. Damian's. We hear of this good man getting rather worried about his unpaid mason, who looked so frail and seemed to be attempting what was far beyond his strength. He therefore began to provide Francis with little extra delicacies.

Whatever these were, they alarmed Francis. He began to think of himself as living in the lap of luxury. That, he decided, would never do. His detachment was to be complete; never would he be beholden to anybody. He was not living in poverty, at any rate not absolute poverty. So one day he announced, "From now on I am going out to beg for my food." He took a beggar's bowl and set out for Assisi.

Most impulsive men—and nobody was as impulsive as Francis—are addicted to doing strange things; and many people will regard Francis's behavior in this matter as so strange as to be all but incomprehensible. But Francis differed from other impulsive men in one very important particular: where they, as is open to observation, are usually unstable, Francis never deviated from his course. The instant he saw what he believed to be right, he proceeded to do it and never left off doing it. He shot like an arrow from the bow to the target ahead.

With him, begging called for a great effort of will that constantly had to be renewed. The greatest effort of all was that of the first day. It was hard enough to ask people for blocks of stone with which he might repair St. Damian's, and it was also hard to ask for oil with which to replenish the chapel light. This, however, was begging of an impersonal sort, for an object that everybody recognized to be good and from which he could not be suspected of deriving any personal profit. Begging for his own food was something very different, done among people all of whom were aware that it was not in the least necessary, that he had only to ask his father's pardon to have a comfortable home. They were also aware that, even if he did not wish to do that, he would be given his board by the priest at St. Damian's. He therefore cut a somewhat ridiculous figure in the eyes of Assisi. There were also people who resented this unnecessary begging, as it made him, on however trifling a scale, a charge upon the community.

Francis understood this perfectly, and it called for immense courage to go out as he did. Nevertheless from house to house he went, thankfully accepting whatever scraps of food he was given: a few cabbage leaves, a crust of bread, the tail of a fish, some olives, the parts of meat that were not usually eaten, and the dregs of the soup kettle. At the end of the day he looked at the disgusting assortment of odds and ends, and merely looking at it was almost enough to make him vomit. He was one who had once feasted delicately. Even at St. Damian's, though the food was plain and meager, it was at least decent. But this horrible, nauseating mixture. . . . !

For a moment he thought he could never bring himself to eat what a dog might have spurned. But he dipped his fingers into the mess, and as he began to eat, he felt that never in his life had he tasted anything so delicious. From that time forward he feasted every day upon such fare. Now indeed was he the Knight of Poverty.

As to what the Bernardone family, with the exception of the father, thought about Francis we have very little information. Madonna Pica is not mentioned again by the first biographers, but as she had never approved of her husband's harshness, we may suppose that she visited Francis from time to time at St. Damian's. If her husband had forbidden her having any further relations with her son—and even of that Peter seems to have been capable—she probably disregarded what he said, though she may have been obliged to keep her visits secret. Francis had two younger brothers, but these are no more than mentioned and play no part in his story. One of them, Angelo, appears, however, for a moment later on in command of a company of the local militia. There are one or two passing references to him in the city documents that suggest that he was a bit of a snob, perhaps all the more so by way of counterbalancing the behavior of a brother who had disgraced them all.

Now we catch sight of this Angelo kneeling at Mass in one of the Assisi churches just behind Francis. He saw that his hermit's garb was already stained by hard work on the walls of St. Damian's, so he said to his companion in a whisper that was intended to be heard, "Go and ask Francis to sell you a pennyworth of his sweat."

Francis could have pretended not to hear, but he was not that sort of man. He turned round and whispered back, "I am going to sell it right dear to my Lord."

Angelo's gibe hurt nobody and represented no more than rough brotherly banter. His father's attitude was much worse. He never got over his anger and shame, which were all the greater because of the pride he had had in Francis, and because of whatever kind of love it was that he was capable of giving. Though Francis never went to the shop, now and then his father would chance upon him in the street. Whenever Peter saw him begging, he took this as a personal affront. Just as he had formerly been puffed up at the sight of Francis's extravagance, so now he was humiliated to the dust.

A sensible man, or even any man with social sense, would have hidden his grief and shame. Not so Peter. Whenever he encountered Francis he would curse him. It became one of the local sports to bring the two together.

Francis met this situation in a highly original way. He knew that it was impossible to soften his father's heart, but he did not want his father to give this unseemly exhibition in public. So he found a venerable-looking old beggar named Albert and said to him, "If you will come with me, I will give you half the alms I get when I am begging."

Albert blinked at him with rheumy eyes. He had observed that Francis was obtaining far more than any other local beggar, as some people gave to him not only out of pity but in admiration. He took his stick up from the pavement where he had been squatting and said eagerly, "Yes, I will go with you—gladly. You said you will give me half?"

"Half—or more," Francis assured him. "But listen to what you are to do. Whenever we meet my father and he starts to curse me, I will kneel down and say to you, 'Bless me, my father,' and you must make the sign of the cross over me and bless me in his stead."

At the next meeting with his father, as soon as Peter began to shout his curses, Francis and Albert carried through their little performance. Then Francis said to Peter, "You see that God has given me a father to bless me, and to offset your curses."

This shamed Peter somewhat, and bystanders who considered that he had already made enough of a fool of himself told him so quite bluntly. After that the curses stopped. We do not hear of him again in any way, good or bad.

FIRST DISCIPLES

We are all too likely to think of his first disciples as coming to Francis very soon after he had finally decided to live the life of poverty. Actually he lived alone, except for the companionship of the old priest at St. Damian's, for two full years, from the spring of 1207 to the spring of 1209. Though we now and then get intimations that he divined that wider activities lay ahead, he did not make the slightest attempt to press forward of his own accord. During those two years he lived what was simply a life of penance and prayer, and this was the preparation for what was to come and was always to remain its basis. Never once had he thought of looking for any followers or of founding anything. When eventually he did obtain disciples, it was not because he set out to look for them, though later he did sometimes issue a call to a particular man; it was because his disciples sought him out.

All that time he had gone on quietly, with no plans beyond that of the day's work; this was only the repairing of St. Damian's and, when that was finished, two other little chapels, St. Mary of the Angels and St. Peter's. In this there was nothing exciting: it was simply the laborious dragging down of blocks of stone from Assisi, or wherever else they could be obtained, and plodding and very monotonous toil. There was no question of things happening with dazzling rapidity or of a splendid spontaneity. Later, it is true, there was plenty of both, but not at this stage.

Having completed what needed to be done at St. Damian's, Francis went to live, for the sake of more complete retirement and solitude, in the woods near the chapel of the Little Portion, otherwise known as St. Mary of the Angels. It was a place that had long been dear to him, and it was to become the center of his work. Here, as there was no priest's house, Francis made himself a hut of branches and leaves and lived like one of the denizens of the surrounding woods.

Somebody seems to have stayed there with him for a short while. It may have been the old beggar Albert, or it may have been somebody else, possibly a homeless waif to whom Francis gave temporary shelter. He would not have refused that, for, great as was his love of solitude, his charity had no bounds and he was the most sociable of hermits. Whoever the guest was, he soon fell away and his name has been forgotten. He cannot properly be considered one of the disciples, whatever may have been his own vague ideas about that. The time for disciples had not yet come; first there was needed a crystallization of plan and a commission.

If St. Benedict really did build the Portiuncula, as tradition tells, he must have designed the little chapel in a prophetic spirit, for the two doors are disproportionately large, wide enough to admit many people at the same time. And who can say that there was not some prophetic insight in the mind of Francis in making his selection of the place depend in part upon those doors? They were certainly needed when the Portiuncula became, as it still is, one of the chief shrines of the Christian world. Celano gives as Francis's reason for going there the fact that it was revealed to him that among all the churches built in her honor the Blessed Virgin had for this one a special affection. All men now have for it a special affection because of its association with Francis.

So far he had made no attempt to preach, though he did some-times speak to such few people as he encountered of the love of God and was often heard singing his joyous songs of praise. By now Assisi had grown tolerant of him, or at least indifferent. The novelty he had provided had worn off, and people had found things to talk about other than his eccentricities. Though he was still sometimes derided, there were several men who were observing him closely, unknown to him, and they were becoming more and more im-pressed. Two of them in fact, both men of some prominence, were already meditating throwing in their lot with him.

First, however, Francis was unconsciously preparing himself for their coming. Until that had been completed, he would not have known what to do with disciples, for his own mode of life had not yet received its final form. This it received on the feast of St. Mat-thias the Apostle, February 24, 1209. And in an unmistakable way.

Mass was occasionally said at the Portiuncula, no doubt by one of the Benedictines from Mount Subasio, to which abbey it formed a dependency. We may further infer that this priest was a Bene-dictine from the fact that the average secular of those days would hardly have been capable of giving the exposition of the Gospel of the Day that Francis asked for and received when Mass was over.

The Gospel that was read out is not the one that belongs to this Mass as it appears in modern missals. At that time the passage given was that from St. Matthew's gospel in which Christ commissioned the Twelve. Nothing could have been more to the point or have more deeply stirred Francis: "As you go, preach, saying the king-dom of heaven is at hand." There it was, the Lord's direct command, taken by Francis as applying to himself. "Provide neither gold nor silver nor brass in your purses, nor scrip for your journey, neither two coats, neither shoes, nor yet staves." These passages, so unequiv-ocal, Francis accepted in the most literal and personal sense.

Yet before he dared do so, he felt he should consult the priest and ask him to explain the words. Francis, the dutiful Catholic, was afraid of laying a stress upon their sense greater than they could bear. The Benedictine may not have been informed that this eager and tremulously excited young man proposed to carry out these injunctions to the letter. Had he known what was in the mind of Francis, he might have explained poverty in the Benedictine sense as the surrender of all personal ownership to the group and not as a total divestment. He might even have said that these instructions were for a particular set of men on a particular occasion, and that they did not apply to all apostles. Had this happened, it may be that the Franciscan enthusiasm would have taken a different form. In that event the world would have lost the spectacle of an ideal which, however impracticable it has proved to be in its absolute application, has yet remained as an ideal and, as such, has been of immense practical value. The priest answered Francis's question, "And *that* was how Our Lord sent out His Apostles?" in the only possible way, "Yes, Francis, that was how He sent them out."

Francis now had his program. He cried, "This is what I have been seeking; this is what my heart yearns for."

Already he had been living in poverty; but he now saw that there remained things to do if he were to bring himself into perfect accord with his commission. The hermit's dress that he had been wearing, after a few simplifications had been effected, still served. The Franciscan habit was, after all, very similar to the ordinary peasant's garb. He discarded his belt as a luxury and girt himself with a rope instead. He laid aside the staff he had been accustomed to carry and henceforth went barefoot.

As there were a few details in his practice, austere though this already was, that he had to remove, so also there were a few details that he now had to add. "When you come into a house, salute it. And if the house be worthy, let your peace come upon it." It was at this time that he adopted the salutation, "The Lord give you peace!" Something like it he had heard from the queer character who had appeared a few years before in Assisi greeting all he met with, "Peace and good!" Not until Francis heard this in the Gospel did he make the salutation his own. When now he went into Assisi, a stranger figure than ever, people noticed that his face looked as though he were always gazing into the heavens.

He now began to preach. Yet even now it was hardly more than the giving of earnest little admonitions to such knots of men and women who would stop and listen. A few peasants resting after their lunch in the fields, a band of wide-eyed children, some idlers in an Assisi square—these were his audiences. He was later to discover extraordinary oratorical powers in himself (if oratory consists in being able to make a deep impression upon one's hearers); he was even to exercise powers of control over birds and animals, while using scarcely a trace more of deliberate art with them than he did with human beings. Vast crowds were to hang enthralled upon his words, both in churches and open spaces. But at this stage his preaching was no more than a little conversation addressed to small groups. It was something not unknown at this time in other parts of Europe, where a good deal of lay preaching, some of it of a dubious sort, was common, but it was something quite new in the experience of Assisi. Though scoffers were still in the majority, there were others who were touched and a few who were stirred to their depths.

It was about two months after St. Matthias's Day that Francis obtained, almost simultaneously, his first two disciples.

The honor of being the very first must go to Bernard da Quintavalle. He was a wealthy man, as the standards of Assisian wealth went, a magistrate, of a reserved and sober nature. Nobody thought of him as being enthusiastic, and his manner of approach was cautious before he finally committed himself to the plans of a man a good ten years younger than himself. He was probably quite the last man among them who the Assisians expected would act as he did. He was destined to be one of the notable mystics of the Franciscan Order, not one of its directive forces. He was one of that little group of select intimates who kept alive, long after Francis was dead, the Franciscan ideal in its primitive purity.

Bernard had been watching Francis for at least two years, noticing how cheerfully he bore derision and how constant he was. He began to say to himself, "It cannot be but that this brother has abundant grace from God."

There is, however, a good deal of difference between thinking that and following one's thought through to its last implications. It was just this that the sobersided Bernard proposed doing, on condition that he could be quite sure. So one day he invited Francis to stay with him overnight, and, though he could have provided another room for him in his large house, he arranged that his guest should sleep in the same room with him. There he always kept a night light burning.

Francis, when bedtime came, threw himself on the couch that had been assigned to him and pretended to sleep. As soon as he thought that his host was fast asleep—Bernard for verisimilitude was emitting a few snores—Francis got up and, kneeling in the middle of the floor, began to pray.

This was not ordinary prayer: Francis knelt there saying nothing but "My God! My God!" And so he stayed, while Bernard watched and listened, until the first streak of dawn. Only then did he get into bed, lest he be discovered.

Such prayer settled Bernard's mind. He said to Francis later that morning, "Brother Francis, I am fully determined in my heart to leave the world and to follow you in whatever you shall bid me to do."

At this Francis was taken aback. He was not looking for followers or perhaps had not even supposed that he was going to get any. So he told his friend, "Bernard, what you are saying is very difficult. In such a matter we must seek counsel of Our Lord Jesus Christ and ask him to show us his will and how we are to bring it to pass. Let us go to the bishop's house and hear Mass in his chapel. And let us do this also—afterward we shall open the missal three times, begging God that we shall find our path made plain to us."

Bernard had led up to this by asking, "If one had received from a master property entrusted to him, and had possessed it for a long time, but now no longer wanted it, what would be the best way to act?"

Francis had a prompt answer, "Give it back to him who had bestowed it."

To this Bernard said, "My case is this: all that I own of earthly possessions I have received from my Lord."

It was then that Francis gave answer that they should seek the direction from the Gospel itself.

They heard Mass at the church of St. Nicholas, after which they remained in prayer until Tierce had been said. Then they approached the priest and asked him to open the missal three times and read what he came across. The priest did so and, after making the sign of the cross, read out: "If thou wilt be perfect, sell all that thou hast, and give to the poor and follow me." He opened it again and read: "Take nothing for your journey, neither staves, nor scrip, neither bread nor money." At the third opening of the missal he read: "If any man will come after me, let him deny himself and take up his cross and follow me."

It was the answer to Bernard's question. Francis turned to him and another man who was with them and said, "My Brothers, this is our life and our rule—and that of all who shall wish to join our company. Go therefore and fulfill what you have heard."

The other man who had joined them that morning was of a rather different type than Bernard. He was Peter Cathanii, a canon of the cathedral chapter by virtue of being a doctor of laws and, as such, the legal adviser to the canons. He was, however, a layman. On the way to Mass, Bernard had said, "I have a friend who is of my own mind. Let him come with us and hear the Lord's will." Francis willingly agreed, and so it was this prudent lawyer of well-established position became the second of Francis's disciples, only an inch behind Bernard himself.

A few days later, as soon as Bernard had been able to sell all that he owned, he went with Francis to the square in front of St. George's Church to give away the money his possessions had brought in. A crowd at once gathered with outstretched hands, and right and left, with superb carelessness, Francis distributed Bernard's money. We never hear of him so much as touching coin again.

At that moment who should come up but the priest Sylvester from whom Francis had bought, two years previously, the stone he had used in the renovation of St. Damian's. He could not ask for money as one of the poor, but he had, he considered, a claim on other grounds. Pushing up to the front he said to Francis, "I did not get a very good price for those blocks of stone. Am I not entitled to some of this money?"

Francis did not argue the point. Instead he dipped his hands into Bernard's bag and pulled out handfuls of gold. Thrusting the money upon Sylvester he said, "You shall have your money, Messer!" Then at the startled and somewhat abashed priest he shot, "Is it enough? Are you satisfied?"

Before the year was out Sylvester had become a Franciscan. The

surly and grudging miser rose to be one of the great contemplatives
of the Order.

The three men, Francis and Bernard and Peter, went off to live
at the Portiuncula, occupying at first the hut of branches and leaves
that Francis had had, but afterward each man had his own little hut.
Though as the years went by the structure of such huts was slightly
improved, they were never anything much more than huts, having
no sale value and constituting no claim to possession. They merely
served to give a minimum of protection against the sun and the rain.

A few days later they were working at the leper hospital, for
Francis lost no time in taking his new associates to the performance
of a charity so dear to him. It was apparently there that the third
disciple found Francis.

He was a young man named Giles, shrewd, sturdy both in body
and disposition, and one of the famous "characters" of the Order.
He would have lived and died inconspicuous had he not become a
Franciscan. As he did become one, his natural talents found a
stimulation and an outlet they would have lacked elsewhere. There
are many stories about him that show him to have been a wit of a
racy and even an acidulous kind, though it is also clear that his
spiritual insight was even more admired.

His admission to the little band occurred on St. George's Day,
April 23. He did not know just where he would find Francis as he
had no settled habitation, but after having gone to the Portiuncula
and not finding Francis there, Giles had gone in the direction of the
leper hospital of San Salvatore. He knew this much about Francis:
that he was to be caught only on the wing.

As Giles came to the crossroads he was unsure which path he
ought to take, so he stopped where he was and prayed that God
would direct him. A moment later Francis himself came out of the
wood.

Immediately Giles knelt on the ground, crying, "For the love of
God, Brother Francis, take me as one of your companions."

Francis went up to him and gazed intently into his face. Seeing
there what he hoped to find, an evident love of God, he answered,
"Brother most dear, God has shown himself exceeding gracious to
you. If the Emperor were to come to Assisi and desire to make a

man a knight or his private chamberlain, ought not that man to be very glad? Then how much more should you rejoice that God has chosen you out to be his knight and his dearly loved servant, to observe the perfection of the Holy Gospel? Be steadfast in the vocation to which you are called."

With that he took Giles at once to Bernard and Peter to introduce him with, "Look what a good new Brother Our Lord has sent us! Let us rejoice in him and eat together now in charity."

Not now nor, in fact, until ten years later was there any formal novitiate among the Franciscans. The moment Francis had accepted a man, he was as much a member of the Brotherhood as Francis himself. All the first six disciples had the right of receiving men into the Order, a right also possessed, of course, by the heads of the various provinces as soon as these came to be created. But in 1209 there *was* no Order, or any organization; nor does anything of the kind appear to have been thought of as yet. Francis did not consider himself a religious superior but only a man who had had an inspiration from God. Anyone who had the same idea and wished to be his companion was welcome.

Even so, he was already giving those who joined him a kind of offhand testing. As Bernard de Quintavalle had made sure of Francis by watching him at night before deciding to follow him, as Peter Cathanii had also come to Francis because of what he had observed, so Francis, as we have seen, put to them a few searching questions and then made the way they received the three passages chosen by lot from the Gospel a test of their spiritual disposition. It was, of course, a means of guidance for them as a group, but it was also an individual sifting. There had probably been some disillusionment already in the case of the unnamed man who had lived with him for a while. Francis had no wish to encumber himself with those whose enthusiasm was likely to evaporate as suddenly as it had sprung up.

His testing of Giles was not obvious, perhaps not even calculated. It was not the less revealing because it came quite naturally from a chance happening. After the four men had eaten their frugal meal, Francis took Giles with him to Assisi to get cloth for the habit he was to wear. As he had no money to buy this, presumably he had a friend there from whom it could be obtained for nothing. It is possible that Madonna Pica could always find some remnant of rough brown-gray frieze that she was only too willing to give Francis when her husband was out of the way.

As they climbed up the road toward Assisi the two men encountered a poor woman, one of those beggars with which Italy swarmed. Though many of them were imposters, Francis would never question the reality of their poverty or refuse any plea for alms. When one or two of his later followers did so they were severely reprimanded and made to ask abject apology of those whom they had subjected to doubt.

"For the love of God, an alms!" It was the formula all such beggars used, and it was irresistible to Francis. But as he had nothing to give the woman, he turned to Giles. "Brother," he said, "for the love of God give your mantle to this poor woman."

Off it came in an instant. Brother Giles had proved himself. His Franciscan heart seemed to fly straight up to heaven in its joy.

FIRST PREACHING

So far there had been no real preaching, nor was there to be any until Francis had obtained permission for this the following year from the Pope. But now that he had obtained associates in his work, there was something that was rather like preaching, and it was carried farther afield than the districts round Assisi. Usually, though, it was still only a few words of encouragement or admonition or exhortation, a bit of comfort dropped here, an act of kindness done there. What was never heard from Francis then or at any time was anything even faintly resembling reproof, still less denunciation. It was this that set him completely apart from all the self-appointed lay preachers who were springing up in various parts of Europe. A good share of these denunciations were directed against the clergy, usually on account of their wealth and avarice, though the overwhelming mass of the clergy were as poor as might reasonably be expected of them. It is all too evident that the priest at St. Damian's did not have enough money to buy oil for the chapel lamp, let alone keep the place in proper repair.

What we hear of Francis's preaching at this time amounts to this: the substance of his discourses was, "Love and fear God, and do penance for your sins." After Francis had spoken, Brother Giles would tell the little audience, "Do what Brother Francis tells you, for what he has told you is true." Giles of the tart tongue could doubtless have said more, but Francis restrained him. Or it may be that Giles had not as yet discovered his vein of sardonic wit.

As the company now consisted of four men, they felt themselves to be, at least potentially, an army. Already Francis felt in his bones that his work was going to stretch far beyond the home territory, much as there was to do there. They went beyond the borders of Umbria so as to survey their future field and its possibilities. They went in twos because that was how Christ had sent out his Apostles. Francis took Peter Cathanii as his companion, going to the March of Ancona, while Bernard and Giles went on the road toward Florence.

Assisi had jeered at Francis, though it had come to take him for granted enough to ignore him. But now that the Brothers went among strangers, derision was again their portion. Nor is this surprising; they did look very odd in their rough patched habits, bound with a rope, and their bare feet. Celano describes them as being thought animals rather than human beings, and the Three Companions write of uplandish men, or wild men from the woods. Sometimes a prankster would shove dice into the hands of the Brothers and invite them to play—these Brothers who did not have the smallest coin about them! Others would amuse themselves by running up behind them and taking the poor Franciscans by their hoods and thus hoisting them, as though by halters, onto their own backs. Boys threw stones at their scarecrow figures.

It was when this happened that they exhibited, not for the first time but for the first time in this particular way, that solicitude for one another that was so conspicuous a mark of their charity. As the stones, and worse than stones, flew, first one of the Brothers and then the other would place himself on the side of the road where he could best protect his companion from these missiles.

Singing, quite as much as preaching, was a feature of this mission, as it was on many later occasions. There were some Latin hymns, still understandable to most of the people; and we may suppose that Francis taught them some of the ditties he had composed in Italian. His French songs would hardly have been of much use among the peasantry.

They slept wherever they could: in barns with the peasants they helped in the fields, asking from the farmer only a night's shelter on the hay and a little food, or in a chance cave, or on the floor of a leper hospital, or even under a hedge. They were quite indifferent to their lodgings, except that they praised God all the more when these were poor and then slept the more soundly in His love. Things of this sort did not trouble those for whom, when they were at home, the very maximum of comfort was a heap of straw spread over with a few rags. A log or a block of stone did not make a very soft pillow, but they never got anything better.

As to just what adventures Francis and Peter had we have no record. It seems to have been forgotten in the story which Bernard and Giles brought back. As that is typical of the Franciscan experiences, and as it was remembered mainly because it was taken as an exceptionally fortunate outcome of what had begun to seem a predicament, it may be supposed that the other two fared rather worse.

In Florence the two Brothers went about looking for some place where they could sleep that night but could find none. At last they came to a house that had an oven on the porch. Then they said to one another, "Here we may be able to take shelter." The mistress of the house refused to receive these two queer-looking men, so they meekly asked, "Well, may we for this night lie near your oven?"

That she could hardly refuse; often enough other vagrants had crawled up to its heat without asking permission or without her knowing, except for the signs her visitors left of their having been there.

"Oh, sleep there, if you must!" she said grudgingly and slammed the door in their faces.

When her husband came home he saw what he took to be tramps

on his porch, huddled for warmth near the stove, so he asked his wife, "Why have you given those rascals shelter?"

She answered, "I would not let them into the house. Where they are they can steal nothing, unless it is some of the wood. And they won't be able to eat that!"

"I am not going to have them on my porch," he said angrily, so he went out and drove them away. They could do no better for themselves than creep as close to the oven as possible without actually going on the porch. Yet there they felt that they were kept warmer by Divine Love, covered only by the shelter of Lady Poverty, than they would have been in beds of down.

At dawn they went to a neighboring church for Mass. As it happened, the woman of the house went there too, being pious in her own fashion despite her lack of charity. There she saw the two vagabonds to whom her husband had objected praying devoutly. She was impressed by that. Still more was she impressed when a man she knew, who was giving alms to such poor people as he saw there, went up to her tramps and offered them some money, only to have it refused.

She listened to the conversation.

"Why do you, who are poor," the man asked, "not take my alms like the rest?"

Brother Bernard answered, "It is true that we are poor, but to us poverty is not a hard thing, as it is to the other poor, because by the grace of God we have made ourselves poor of our own accord."

Wondering at this, the man asked, "Did you once have possessions?"

Bernard replied, speaking mainly for himself, for he had been a rich man, whereas Giles, though he may have been a fairly prosperous peasant, could hardly have had a great deal, "Yes, once we were rich, but for the love of God we have given all that we had to the poor."

Now the woman of the oven went up to the Brothers and said, "I see that I have done you a wrong. Gladly will I receive you as guests in my house."

To this Bernard made the courteous answer, "The Lord repay you for your good will."

It was the charitable man, however, who obtained them as guests, perhaps because he knew the woman's husband too well not to be afraid that the Brothers might still meet with churlishness at his hands. It may be, too, that some such idea was in the minds of the Brothers themselves. So they accepted his offer when he told them, "You would not take the money I offered, but behold a lodging made ready for you by the Lord! Stay with me as long as you wish."

It was with him that they did stay for the rest of the time they spent in Florence, all that time edifying everybody both by their behavior and their words. Charitable though he was before, that man became more charitable than ever. He was typical of thousands of such people, women as well as men, who obtained first a loose and than a closer and more formal attachment to the incipient order.

Simplicity of spirit was, even more than poverty, the distinguishing Franciscan mark. At this time circumstances compelled a bare simplicity even in the material means of the Brothers' devotions. Sometimes they were unable to do better than nail or tie two pieces of wood together in the form of a cross and kneel before this to say their prayers. Often they did not have even as much as that. Then they had to single out and fasten their eyes upon two crossed timbers in a barn or some twigs in a hedge that might seem roughly to resemble a cross. As they had as yet no service books, they could not say the Office of the Church. They contented themselves with a number of Our Fathers. The tender fervor with which they said these prayers, trying to time them in accord with the ecclesiastical hours, much more than made up for all else.

Francis taught them to follow his own custom, so that whenever they came upon a wayside crucifix or saw, though in the distance, a church campanile, they would kneel, facing in that direction, and say, "We adore thee, O Christ, and bless thee, in all thy churches throughout the world, because by thy holy cross thou hast redeemed the world." It was the cross, or rather the passion of Our Lord, that then and always was the center of Franciscan devotion.

From the outset Francis impressed upon them three things: that their lives were to be filled with prayer, prayer of the most withdrawn and inward sort; that this withdrawal was to repose upon an absolute poverty that freed their minds from all other considerations; and finally, that they were never to forget that they were apostles. He told them, "Dearest Brethren, let us consider our vocation, unto which God has called us in his mercy. This is not so much for our own salvation as for that of many, wherefore let us go through the world, admonishing all peoples both by example and by word to do penance and to be mindful of the commands of God. Fear not because you seem weak and despised, but with easy minds preach repentance in a simple way, trusting in the Lord, who hath overcome the world. By his Spirit he speaks through you, and in you, to admonish all men to turn to him and keep his commandments. You will find some men who are faithful, gentle, and gracious; but there will be others, and these the greater number, that are faithless, proud, and blasphemous, who will revile and oppose you. Fasten it therefore in your hearts to bear all things patiently and humbly."

Though every member of this first group of four, including Francis himself, found it difficult to keep in perfect balance the active life of preaching and the withdrawn life of contemplation, it was this that was the Franciscan ideal. Later, when the number of the Brothers had increased, some of them—notably Bernard and Giles—spent long periods in lonely hermitages where they did nothing but pray. This prayer was always considered as being the nourishment of those who preached and preaching as being of no avail without such prayers and those of the preachers themselves.

It was about this time that Francis withdrew for a period of prayer to a cave high above Poggio Bustone. There, abasing himself in spirit, he said over and over again, "God be merciful to me, a sinner!" and he received an assurance from heaven that his sins had all been forgiven and that his salvation was certain. It is true that even after this he did from time to time experience depression, which once or twice went as far as temptations to despair; but, except for such brief interludes of darkness, his life was ever afterward lived in a light serene and clear and joyous. He did, in fact, now seem to be caught up above himself and wholly absorbed in this light. As a result the horizon of his mind was enlarged and a prophetic gift descended upon him. After this experience he was changed into another man.

Rejoicing, he returned from Poggio Bustone in the Rietine valley to the companions he had left to the north at the Little Portion. He was able to tell them now, "Take courage, beloved, and be not sad because you are so few. Nor let my simplicity or your own dismay you, for the Lord has shown me that we shall be a great multitude and go out to the ends of the earth. It is for your profit that I tell you this, for I would gladly keep silence. I have seen a great multitude of men coming to us. Frenchmen are coming, Spaniards are hastening, Germans and Englishmen running, and a multitude of diverse other tongues."

Though the first foreigner did not come for a while, from Umbria, mostly from Assisi itself, other men began to arrive, though in just what order is uncertain. One was a man named Morico, one of the Order of the Crucigeri who were in charge of the leper hospital of San Salvatore. Another was a knight from Rieti named Angelo Tancredi. He had decided to be a Knight of Poverty instead and was to be among the closest of Francis's personal friends. Two others were Sabbatino, of whom we do not hear much, and John da Capella. As he eventually fell away and ended as a suicide, there was a disposition among some of the Franciscan chroniclers, eager as they were to trace parallels between Christ and Francis, to see in him the Judas of their first twelve. The parallel was made all the more perfect by their remembrance of how Francis had obtained Brother Angelo. In the glow of happiness he felt about the promise of large numbers running to join him, he did what he had never done before and summoned him, in almost Our Lord's fashion of saying simply, "Come follow me." What Francis said to him, calling out in the open street, was, "Long enough have you worn the knight's belt and carried the spurs and the sword. The time has come for you to change that belt for a rope, your sword for the cross of Christ, the spurs for the dust of the road." Angelo Tancredi made an instant response and went on with Francis clothed in the brown habit.

Perhaps the most remarkable case of all among those of the first disciples was that of the priest Sylvester from whom Francis had bought stone for the restoration of St. Damian's, and who had afterward contrived to get some more money out of him when Brother Bernard was giving away to the poor all that he owned. For three nights in succession Sylvester had the same dream. In it he saw a dragon about to devour Assisi put to flight by Francis, from whose mouth there was a cross shining like gold that reached to the heavens. This decided him: he sought out Francis and joined his company, living for the rest of his life as a lover of poverty and conspicuous in the Brotherhood for his absorption in prayer. He was the first priest to join.

What Francis was doing was something very different from anything known before. Hermits were not uncommon, but Francis and his friends were not hermits, living as such only periodically in order to prepare themselves by solitary prayer for their preaching. It was to the people that they gave the fruits of their meditations. But still less were Francis and his companions monks or canons. For these it was necessary that there should be a settled abode, if they were to devote themselves to the performance of the liturgical offices of the Church. True, monks had occasionally been obliged by force of circumstances to undertake missionary enterprises, and most European countries—particularly England and Germany—had been brought to the Faith by Benedictine preachers. Yet the essence of the Benedictine life was that it should be lived in the cloister; and much as the abbeys had accomplished in more unsettled times by providing centers in the countryside where the arts of agriculture could be promoted, under new conditions, when the populace was flocking more and more into the towns, the monks had slight effect upon the people.

Not only that: the wealth that the monks had acquired, both by their own industry and the many endowments they had received, had cut off much of the influence they might have had. Even could they have gone out preaching, people would not have listened to them with much attention. Changed conditions were, in short, crying out for new methods, for men detached from every form of property, men with untrammeled mobility and therefore able to carry the Gospel to those unreached by the monks and also by a secular clergy who had too often become hardly more than ecclesiastical functionaries.

It was, however, not very easy to grasp the novel idea that Francis and his disciples were trying to put into action. Isolated hermits were tolerated, as there were never enough of them to constitute a problem, but the normal thing for those to do who wished to devote themselves to religion was to become monks or secular priests. Bishop Guido of Assisi had expected that Francis and these Brothers of his would eventually fall into the conventional pattern; when they failed to do so, he was, naturally enough, puzzled and also a little alarmed. He made, it should be noted, no attempt to stop them from preaching, and this he could very easily have forbidden. But he did say to Francis one day, "My son, this life of yours seems to me to be too hard and harsh. At the very least you should consent to accept property and provide yourself with some center for your work."

Francis smiled back at his kind but bewildered friend and said, "My lord, if we had possessions we should need arms with which to protect them."

The bishop was still puzzled. "Arms? Arms, Francis? Does every piece of property have to be defended with the sword?"

"Yes, my lord," Francis answered. "Sometimes it must be defended by the sword itself, as we see by the abbeys with their retainers. Yet always some sort of a sword is needed to protect riches, if not that of steel then that of the law. We do not want disputes and lawsuits such as would arise did we possess property. This would prevent us from loving God and our neighbors as we should, and also do harm to our neighbors. Therefore shall we live according to the poverty of the Gospel."

It was an answer that silenced the good bishop.

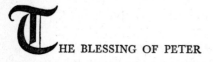

THE BLESSING OF PETER

Bishop Guido's advice was not merely a piece of generalized good sense; it was occasioned by a new situation. In Assisi the attitude toward Francis had shifted several times. At first it was mainly derisive. Then some admiration was mixed with the contempt. It was evident that Francis was sincere, and he might even be the saint some thought him. But it was one thing to have a single beggar going round with a bowl asking alms for the love of God, and quite another to have a number of people doing the same.

It was true that Bernard da Quintavalle and Peter Cathanii had distributed their property to the poor, and others of the Brothers also had had possessions to give. But only the poor had benefited, not the respectable citizens who afterward would have to support Bernard and Peter as well as Francis. Now almost every day it seemed that there was a new member for the Brotherhood, another mouth for Assisi to feed. Where could this be expected to end? There were growls being heard: "Yes, they have given up their own goods, but only in order that they may devour the goods of others instead."

The complaint was not very just, but what troubled the bishop was that, just or not, the complaint was being made. Yet actually the Brothers asked very little, even when they asked at all. Their ordinary means of livelihood was to work in the fields with the peasants and take whatever they were given in the form of food—but never any money. So they really were little charge to the community. But Assisi began to have visions of the whole place swarming with pious mendicants and was getting angry and even threatening violence. Bishop Guido had some reason to be troubled in mind.

Perhaps it was partly to relieve him of embarrassment and to avoid giving further offence to the city that for the time being Francis decided to move from the Portiuncula to a deserted shack at a place known only as Rivo Torto, or the Crooked Stream. The shack belonged to the leper hospital, and it may be that Morico's having come from those in charge of that little institution would account for their being permitted to use it, though one might imagine that the help Francis had given the lepers and was still giving them would be a sufficient reason. If one must look for still another, this may be found in the proximity of the shack to a number of caves on the mountainside. These, known as the *Carceri* (the prisons) afterward became one of the Franciscan hermitages.

To these caves the Brothers could withdraw during the day; they had much to think about now in addition to their ordinary devout meditations.

Francis by now had twelve disciples, and the missionary journeys they had already made showed that the fields were indeed white unto harvest. The world is always ready for the reaper who will put his sickle in. Francis had had his vision of thousands coming from all quarters to join him; he also had a vision of converting the whole world. Nothing less was his design; nothing less was his commission. And that came directly from God.

Just who these twelve men were is uncertain; still more so is the precise order of their admission into the Brotherhood. This may be due to some discrepancy in the spelling of the names in the lists, partial or complete, that have been given, or it may be due to there having been rival claimants for the honor of being among the first twelve. What matters is that Francis, having now obtained this number—that of the Apostles of Christ—felt that the moment had come for regularizing his position.

So far he had not written even the most fragmentary of rules. They had lived merely "according to the Gospel," finding all that they needed in the Gospel for St. Matthias's Day and the passages that had been read out to Francis and Bernard and Peter when they had attended Mass together. For anything else that was needed the day by day instructions given by Francis, as called forth by the necessities of the moment, sufficed. This would hardly be enough for presentation to the Roman authorities, and some thought and discussion had to be devoted to the case they were to present.

We hear of Francis's having made several rules at this time before deciding upon the one that should be presented for approval. In this he may have had the help of the trained canon lawyer Peter Cathanii. But, since in the end what was decided upon was, according to Celano, "written down simply and in few words,"—and this mainly the Gospel passages they had taken as their rule from the start—it would appear that the legalistic form that Peter surely would have suggested was discarded in favor of what Francis wished, a rule that was not of his making but that consisted of what Christ himself had said. The production of this rule—especially if it was recast several times—could hardly have been the work of a week or two.

While these discussions were going on the Brothers lived all huddled together so closely in the shack that Francis had to write each man's name in chalk on the wall so as to indicate just how much space was allotted to him. This, however, was not for the usual reason—that this or that man was claiming too much space—but rather because all of them were too likely to remain outside in solicitude for everybody else.

They not only had cramped quarters but their beds were the bare ground. As food was scarce, they often had to eat roots. Moreover Assisi was further off than from the Portiuncula—a good hour's walk away—and, in any event, Assisi was more or less closed to them for the time being. Yet none of them repined. On the contrary all of them rejoiced with Francis in their poverty, which grew more precious to them the greater it became. Only men who did rejoice would have been capable of holding out in such a situation. The knowledge that this was so gladdened Francis still further; it was a test for all of them. Any other novitiate was unnecessary for such men as these.

Francis was under no canonical obligation to seek Roman approval for the founding of a new religious order. Stringent regulations regarding this question were to come five years later at the Fourth Lateran Council. Then, though the founding of new orders was not specifically forbidden, all such orders were obliged to select one of the already existing rules. This meant in effect that the choice was narrowed down to the Rule of St. Benedict or the Rule of St. Augustine, though it was possible to embroider these with constitutions peculiar to the special needs of the new institute. In this matter Francis just barely escaped by approaching Rome when he did; his friend St. Dominic (as yet unknown to him) had to accept the Rule of St. Augustine.

It is, however, questionable whether Francis intended to found an "Order" in the usual sense. He did not even think of himself as formulating a "new" religious rule. All that he was attempting to do was to live according to the Gospel, that is, in the way he believed that Christ and His Mother and the Apostles had done. For this there was no need of any official sanction: how could the Pope refuse to approve what had been approved by Christ? What Francis was seeking was official permission to preach: his Rule was laid before the authorities as no more than an explanation of his manner of life and as a kind of guarantee of his orthodoxy. He may already have discovered that not every bishop was as sympathetic as was Guido to laymen preaching, even in the very simple and informal style the Brothers had used. He could see that his position might become untenable or at least that his activities might be restricted, unless he could point to the approval that he sought. Though it is at least questionable whether official permission to preach outside churches was required at this time, even when dogmatic matters were touched, there was always the possibility of the Inquisition taking action. The papal sanction would therefore be a safeguard for the friars.

If Francis did not consider that he was founding an order but rather giving impetus to a movement, he must have realised that the movement was likely to develop into an order. It would either do that or degenerate into an unorganized mass of cranks and tramps and irresponsibles. Even with the Rule it came perilously close to this. Whatever Francis may have thought, we may be quite sure that this was the view taken by the Pope and the cardinals. We can also be quite sure that there were many discussions and inquiries as to the Franciscan plans that do not appear in any of the records.

When they were ready with the Rule, Francis said to his twelve, "Let us go to our Mother, the Holy Roman Church, and make known to the Pope what God has begun to do through us, that we may continue as we have begun, according to His will and decree." It showed great confidence in God and also great confidence in the discernment of the authorities. But did it not also indicate—this is something that seems to have escaped nearly all the chroniclers and the commentators—a good deal of shrewdness on Francis's part? He was not obliged to do what he was about to do; but it was extremely fortunate for him that he did do it. Nor was it just a piece of luck, though luck entered into it; it was an instance of his canniness. Nor was it merely canniness; it reposed upon a submissive and humble spirit. That, finally, was the luckiest thing of all, and the most signal proof of his good sense.

For the journey to Rome Francis refused to act as superior. He had a moral ascendancy as the inspirer of the plan, and his word had been law; but all through his life he disliked to exercise authority except when this was unavoidable. There had to be somebody, of course, to decide such matters as where and when they were to take their meal and stop for the night; but it mattered little who this was, so long as it was not Francis. For him to have assumed a right to command might have seemed to be asserting a candidacy for the superiorship that would be established as soon as the rule had been approved. He wished to leave the choice unfettered. Accordingly he insisted that somebody else be chosen: "He shall be our captain to guide us, and as it were the Vicar of Christ." Bernard da Quintavalle was elected, probably for no other reason than that he was the first man to join Francis.

In this unassertive habit of his we find one of Francis's most charming characteristics. It serves to explain both his success as an inspirer of men and his lack of success as an organizer. Yet we must not assert too confidently any lack of success here: more capable men than he might have failed to win their ends, for they would have relied upon their cleverness. Finesse, too, might have been as ineffective as forcefulness, for these qualities would have been met by men who possessed them in abundance and who enjoyed their exercise. It was the sweetness and simplicity of Francis that proved irresistible.

Nevertheless sweet simplicity met a rebuff at the outset.

Francis went straight to the Lateran Palace and accosted Pope Innocent III as soon as he saw him. The authority of this story is open to some question as it comes from an insertion in St. Bonaventure's *Life* made by his successor. Yet it is not unlikely that the Pope thought this uncouth intruder a fanatic and bade him begone.

Whether or not Francis did start at that point, he now turned to Bishop Guido, as he discovered that the bishop was in Rome at this time. It was a natural thing to do and was what he should have done in the first instance. Guido was, not unnaturally, rather annoyed because he had not been consulted, and a little alarmed because he feared that the fact that Francis had come to Rome indicated that he was intending to transfer his activities from the Assisi district. As to that Bishop Guido was soon reassured, and any ruffled feelings he may have had were soothed by the explanation that the Brothers had been living at Rivo Torto and keeping out of Assisi. So far from being offended, Guido took Francis to a man who could do a great deal more for him than was possible for a mere local official. This man was the Cardinal John of St. Paul, Bishop of Sabina, of the illustrious Colonna family.

The cardinal suggested at first what any man in his position would have suggested, that the Brothers enter one of the established orders or, if that was not to their taste, that they live as hermits. When he found Francis resolute in his purpose of following poverty and of living the apostolic life, he proposed what would be, in his opinion, more practicable ways of achieving the same purpose. The purpose itself he admitted to be admirable, but he seriously doubted whether it could be carried out, whether the whole scheme would not prove too difficult.

Francis convinced him in the end, and in so wholehearted a fashion that not only did the cardinal take the cause of the Brothers in hand but he became the official protector of the Order. According to the Three Companions he even asked Francis that "henceforth he might be accounted as one of the Brethren." Perhaps this would make him the first Franciscan tertiary, though, of course, anything resembling the establishment of the third order had not as yet been thought of. Not to press that point too far, it might be safer to say that the cardinal looked upon this as a movement with which he wished to be associated, but not as an "Order" as that term was understood.

Now the cardinal went to the Pope on Francis's behalf, saying, "I have found a man of most perfect life, who is minded to live conformably with the Holy Gospel, and to observe in all things Gospel perfection. Through him, I believe, the Lord is minded to quicken throughout the world the faith of the Catholic Church."

Whether or not the story is to be believed that the Pope had already ejected Francis from his presence, he was now prepared to listen to him. He appointed an audience the next day. At this interview Francis told Innocent a parable, the point of which was that the Brethren were coming before the Pope as sons, hitherto unrecognized by their father. And it turned out that both men had had dreams at night.

Francis's dream, which he did not relate to the Pope, as it might have suggested a certain complacency and overassurance, was this: He was walking along a road when he came to a very tall, strong, and beautiful tree. As he stood beneath it, marveling at its height and loveliness, all of a sudden he found that he could touch its top. Not only that, he was able to bend it down easily to the ground. As he took Innocent III to be that tree, it would have been scarcely tactful to tell the Pope of his dream.

The Pope also may have kept his dream to himself at this stage. He had dreamed that he saw the church of St. John Lateran about to fall, and that a little man in a religious habit had held it up by setting his back to it. That little man he now recognized as the one standing before him.

This story has been rather full of dreams, though they tend to diminish from now on. That they occurred is something not too unlikely in the case of men whose minds were constantly preoccupied with a single idea. To the early biographers they had a supernatural significance, and, though we may be permitted to see a simpler psychological explanation, the possibility is not to be dismissed that dreams may be used for divine guidance in human perplexity.

What is not so easy to explain, except on the grounds that in some way or other an inspiration from heaven came to the minds of the Pope and his advisers, is the readiness they showed to support Francis in this very strange idea of his. Or, rather, this would be strange if Innocent III were merely the masterful ecclesiastical politician that many historians have represented him as being. That he was deeply engrossed in a great problem of statecraft—that of extending and consolidating the temporal power of the papacy against the pretensions of the Empire—is, of course, perfectly true. That makes it all the more astonishing that a statesman of this sort, a most remarkable organizer and administrator, should have been even momentarily interested in an unknown young man who came to him with a handful of followers from a small provincial city to ask his approval of a mode of life novel to the point of eccentricity.

It is not simply that the ecclesiastical authorities were men who, so one would have supposed, would have had no time to be bothered with what they might have been expected to regard as fantasies; they had good reason, based on past experience, to be distrustful of such plans as that of Francis. They exercised, it is true, a cautious reserve, but that is what they should have done. On the other hand, they gave him all the support he looked for and perhaps even more.

Let us note that the cardinal's argument with the Pope was not merely that they should make use of a movement which might, under proper direction, be of advantage to them, but that they dared not, as Christians, refuse to back Francis. "If we reject the petition of this poor man as a thing too hard and untried," Cardinal John said, "when his petition is that the pattern of the Gospel life be sanctioned for him, let us beware lest we stumble at the Gospel of Christ. For if any man says that in the observance of the Gospel there is contained aught that is untried, or contrary to reason, or impossible to observe, he is clearly seen to blaspheme against Christ, the Author of the Gospel."

To that apparently unanswerable argument Innocent might still have found an answer. He might have said, "That is true, my lord cardinal. But it is also true that we have seen other men who spoke as this Brother Francis does, and they afterward became heretics. With such men it is perchance not malice but lack of learning that led them into heresy. May it not be so with Brother Francis in his turn? For he also is an unlettered man."

In all likelihood the Pope did say something of the sort; if he did not we may be sure that some of the cardinals said it. The profession of poverty of an extreme sort was rather under suspicion. The Waldenses had professed it, and they had drifted into heresy, like the Catharists and the Albigensians (who also talked much of poverty) who had been heretics from the start. The preaching of poverty it would seem invariably proceeded to the denunciation of the wealthy among the clergy, and from that it was but a short step to denouncing the whole clerical body and the Church itself. Poverty had almost become, in fact, the war cry of the heretics.

Not only that: the practice of an extreme asceticism often reposed upon or engendered the Manichaean dualism that regarded all matter as essentially evil. From this there flowed either a hatred of life that among the "perfect" sometimes resulted in suicide as a means of liberation from the loathed body or, far more commonly, the grossest sexual promiscuity or perversion as things of no consequence. Dominic Guzman, a learned man with learned men as his associates, had had some success in his preaching in Languedoc, but in the end the Pope and the civil authorities had been obliged to combine to extirpate the Albigensians with the sword.

It is not to be wondered at that there was a good deal of uneasiness in the minds of the Roman authorities. Yet a much greater cause for wonder is that, in face of the facts of experience, they were willing to back Francis. It can only be explained by saying that they made a delicate and difficult distinction. Whatever the corruption of a Christian idea, the twisting it awry into heretical forms did not change the Christian idea itself. Practical men as they were, practical men as they had to be by virtue of their position, they did not cease to be idealists as well. In this case idealism was the most practical mode of approach to a problem much more complicated than this simple Brother Francis could imagine. Though they were prepared to use other weapons in defense of the Church, they perceived that there could be no weapon so effective as sanctity.

For the life of poverty, the uncompromising practice of the Gospel, there was a deep and true instinct among the mass of the people. Nor was it lacking even among the worldliest of the clergy, however little they might be prepared to carry it out themselves. Innocent III looked into the burning eyes of the frail young man who stood before him and recognized not only enthusiasm but humility. It was this humility that convinced him that Francis was to be trusted.

Yet he was cautious in his response. "My little children," he said to them with exquisite kindness, "this life of yours seems too hard and rough, for though we believe your fervor to be such that it would ill become us to doubt you, nevertheless we must have regard for those who shall follow after, lest this way of yours be too hard for them." He dismissed them by saying to Francis, "Go, my son, and pray God that he may reveal to you whether what you seek comes from his will, so that we, being assured of God's will, may accede unto your desires."

It was evident after that that Francis had won more than half his battle with the Pope.

In the end Innocent III approved the Franciscan Rule. His words at a later interview were: "Go, and the Lord be with you, Brethren, and as He shall deign to inspire you, preach repentance to all. And when the Lord Almighty shall multiply you in number and grace, you shall report it to me with joy, and I will grant you more than this and shall with more confidence entrust greater things to you."

The Pope's words call for a brief commentary. The approbation of the Rule was tentative and therefore not put in writing. But Innocent expected the Brotherhood to increase and develop in other ways; he had promised to do more for them when that happened. Meanwhile they were given permission to preach, but only to preach repentance; doctrinal subjects were excluded from their sermons. This was a wise and necessary safeguard to the inadvertent venting of heresy.

This permission to preach meant that they might now preach in churches and not, as hitherto, merely in the streets or the fields, though such preaching remained their ordinary mode. As a sign of this authorization the Brothers—none of whom was a priest, with the exception of Sylvester—were given the "narrow tonsure" by the Cardinal John of St. Paul. This would seem to indicate no more than minor orders, so Francis's diaconate—he never proceeded further—must have been conferred later, unless, as some say, it was the diaconate he received at this time. As the superior of the group —its minister-general, though that title was not yet used—he was authorized to appoint the preachers at his discretion.

About this preaching a further word needs to be said. Preaching was looked upon as one of the functions of the bishops, though many bishops rarely preached and no bishop, however energetic he was, could deliver sermons regularly in all the churches of his diocese. The average parish priest was considered unqualified for this office, for few of them had had any formal theological training, except for a little reading of theology under the direction of parish priests, who had in general been prepared for the ministry in much the same haphazard fashion. The majority of priests limited themselves to saying Mass and administering the sacraments. In the abbeys, of course, there were men of learning, but the monk, by his very profession, was cut off from more than an occasional sermon in the abbey church. Such attempts as had been made—as in the case of St. Norbert's foundation of the Premonstratensians—to combine the monastic life with preaching, came to very little, as the monasticism smothered the preaching.

Yet the need for preachers remained urgent. In the absence of others to do this work, unauthorized laymen had sprung up who had taken the preaching office upon themselves. These often preached heresy unwittingly or got involved in conflict with the ecclesiastical authorities. The fact that almost all such preachers were poor men created an association in the popular mind between preaching and poverty. So much was this the case that the Cistercian abbots who made the first attempt to convert the Albigenses were almost totally ineffectual because they went in their abbatial state. It was not until Dominic Guzman organized a group of preachers dedicated to poverty with a mobility impossible to monks (as these were attached to their abbeys), that any headway was made with this pressing problem.

We can see therefore that Innocent III had a comprehensive view of what was needed. He was not acting merely upon his intuitions or upon the impression the charming and selfless character of Francis made upon him—though, of course, his judgment of that character was a deciding factor. Innocent was acting with exact knowledge, such as nobody but he was in the position of possessing so fully, as to how to deal with a grave situation. He thought of the Dominican preachers as resisting speculative dangers and of the Franciscans as the preachers of repentance, the men who dealt with the moral aspects of the situation.

The appearance of these two orders, almost simultaneously, not only accorded with the Pope's statesmanlike program but served to crystallize and develop it farther. When two such instruments became providentially available, Innocent saw at once how to use them to the best advantage. At the time of the Fourth Lateran Council, only five years away, he issued orders to the bishops under severe penalties that they "provide suitable men, powerful in word and work, to exercise with fruitful result the office of preaching." Such an order would have been unavailing and would not have been issued, had it not been that the Church by that time had at its command the two orders of friars, the two groups of preachers.

The Pope therefore was acting with profound wisdom when, in dealing with these simple young men from Assisi, he trusted his intuitions and decided to commission them. It was nothing less than a stroke of genius on his part. It was also prudent of him not to commit himself too far. The approval of the Rule and the permission to preach was only tentative and not put in writing. Even so it amply sufficed.

What the Pope knew was, of course, unknown to Francis. He may even have been unaware that he had had recent forerunners, that in 1201 the Illuminati of Lombardy and in 1207 the Catholic Poor Men of Germany had received from Innocent permission to preach penance, though they were only laymen. Certainly Francis owed nothing to these forerunners, except in the sense that the permission he received may have been given all the more readily because of a precedent already created. But these other groups accomplished little and eventually passed from the scene without having made the least detraction from Francis's originality. As to that we must say that he believed with intense conviction that he and these men with him and the immense throng who, so he had been assured by divine revelation, were soon to join him had a direct commission from God himself to preach, and that they were to do this in the apostolic mode by practicing total poverty. He was, however, not quite alone in such a conviction. It was an idea that was in the air at that time.

The scene therefore in the Lateran Palace is that of Francis aflame with his enthusiasm and utter certitude before the great and wise Pope who saw in him and his companions men sent from God.

THE HUT BY THE WINDING STREAM

They left Rome in a state of wild excitement and delight. Passing through the Porta Salara they took the northern road that runs through the Campagna. This was the malarial Roman summer against which not even the Franciscans' joy and peace could be proof. Though they were not overcome by positive illness, by the end of the day they found themselves in a desolate place without food and utterly exhausted. They sank down by the side of the road and might have died had not a stranger appeared, seemingly out of nowhere, bringing them food. At this they wondered greatly and admonished one another to have greater trust in God's mercy. Here was an evident proof of the Providence to which they had confided themselves.

At the little village of Orte, where the beautiful Nera, rushing through its gorge, joins the Tiber, on one of the hillsides they found a cave formerly used by the Etruscans as a tomb. Such a dwelling, the most primitive of all and the only kind directly provided by God,

always greatly appealed to Francis. Apart from this, they were by
now too shattered to continue their journey. There they stayed,
as they thought, for a night.

Actually they remained there for fifteen days. At the very moment that they had received papal approbation for their apostolic
life and work, there came a kind of temptation, one that never
ceased to tempt Francis: it was that of the hermit's life. The cry
of *O solitudo beata! O sola beatitudo!* echoes for moments, at least,
in every sensitive spirit though few can surrender to it.

Nor could Francis do so, though he had begun as a hermit and
though he was to end very close to being one. His life of intense
activity was rooted not only in poverty but in a longing for complete
withdrawal from the world. The greatest sacrifice he was called
upon to make was not that of giving up his burgher prosperity, *that*
was easy and in many ways a relief; his greatest sacrifice was to give
himself to his fellow men. Several of the men with him, especially
Bernard and Giles and Sylvester and Angelo, felt almost as strongly
as he did this attraction to a life of solitary contemplation. The question was discussed among them as to whether they would not, after
all, do better to remain as they were than to go out preaching.

The temptation came, only to be resisted. Nor could there be other
than a serious misunderstanding of the Franciscan spirit to imagine
that the surrender was made grudgingly. Francis understood his
special vocation, even during those recurring hours when he was
overwhelmingly conscious of the sweetness and preciousness of a life
devoted solely to prayer.

It was accordingly the most difficult of all modes of life that was
accepted by Francis, that of combining activity and contemplation,
emulating at once Martha and Mary. It would be too much to say
that it had never been attempted before, many attempts had been
made by individuals; but this surely was the first time that it had
been made the basis of a religious order, even if Dominic in Languedoc was at that same moment conceiving a religious order along
much the same lines.

As to all this they soon became clear in their own minds. Moreover, they recognized that the charm of the place where they were
living was an inducement to their staying there. As soon as they
recognized this, they also knew it to be a temptation, as there was
another in the fact that by remaining in their cave they might

entangle themselves in a semblance of ownership. That, too, helped to decide them. They returned to the hut by the winding stream, Rivo Torto.

If there they lived in a solitude almost as great as that of Orte, it was only by way of preparation for their work. Assisi was not so far away that they could not return to preach and beg again in its streets, this time with the authorization of the Pope. And at Rivo Torto there could be no seeming claim to ownership, as the shack there belonged to the Crucigeri of the leper hospital and Francis was living in it only temporarily and on sufferance.

Remote though the place was, there must have been fields and vineyards not far away, for the Brothers were able to work at day labor, receiving some of the produce by way of hire. Never would they accept payment in money, but, of course, payment in kind was not only common enough at the time but an ordinary manner of payment.

By these means the Brothers might have provided fairly well for themselves had it not been part of the Franciscan spirit to accept a good deal less than might have been considered their due. Francis had the fastidiousness of a gentleman and had had more than enough in his father's shop of the driving of hard bargains. Even from the little they received he always made a point of giving away as alms everything left over from the bare minimum of their needs. He disliked finding himself at the end of one day with anything left over for the next. His trust in Providence had to be exercised from hour to hour.

The hovel into which they crowded together at night was bare of the slightest comfort. "My Brothers," Francis told them, "one ascends more quickly to heaven from a place like this than from a palace." Was their food rough? Then they heard: "Refresh yourselves, my Brothers, with the bread of tears, which is prayer." When cold weather came, against which they had no blankets, Francis assured them, "If through our yearning for the heavenly fatherland we become enkindled by its warmth, we can easily endure this bodily cold." They forgot all their privations in their joy. "Praise God, my dear Brothers, in all things and through all things. We must possess nothing that we may the more fully possess everything in the Lord."

In their new enthusiasm it would seem that some of the Brothers carried matters too far, so Francis was obliged to moderate their ascetic practices. Then he would say, "Brother Body should be sufficiently provided for, lest he be tempted to sloth, lest he weary in watching and prayer and so find occasion for murmuring. Then he might say, 'I am faint with hunger; I cannot bear the burden.' Due needs are to be allowed for. But if after eating sufficient food he should mutter, let him know that a lazy beast wants the spur, and that the goad waits a sluggish ass." In this respect alone did the deeds of Francis not correspond quite perfectly with his words, for he always subjected himself to much greater hardship than he thought fitting for others. When he had to explain this discrepancy he would say, "I have to treat myself more severely than you should, because I am a greater sinner than you."

From this period at Rivo Torto there came two stories that illustrate the kindliness and good sense Francis showed from the outset, even before experience had shown him what was best. One night in the hut a Brother woke groaning, "I am dying! I am dying!" All of them arose, very much alarmed, and a lamp was lit. Then Francis asked, "Who is it that is dying?" And the Brother answered, "It is I." When Francis asked, "Of what are you dying, Brother," he got the answer, "I am dying of hunger."

The situation was one that might have provoked a smile, for things could hardly have been as bad as all that. Instead of laughing, Francis ordered that food be set out, and, so that the "dying" Brother should not be put to shame, he ate with him himself, and so did the others. It was the sort of delicate kindness that was always characteristic of him.

When the little meal was finished Francis said to them, "My dearest, I bid each of you consider his nature, because though one among you may be able to sustain himself on less food, yet I do not wish that he who requires more food should imitate him. Instead let him give his body what it needs, so that it may serve his spirit." Then he added, "Just as we are bound to beware of superfluity in eating, as that harms both body and soul, so also—but even more —we must beware of too great abstinence. I therefore command all of you that—within the limits of our poverty—we satisfy the body according to its necessities."

A similar case—we hear that it was that of the priest Sylvester, one of the most recent recruits—gave another opportunity for exemplifying the sweet reasonableness of Franciscan asceticism. Francis noticed that the Brother's health was suffering from self-imposed penances. As they did not have any medicines, he cast about in his mind for another means of restoration. He thought, "If this Brother would eat some ripe grapes early in the morning, I believe it would do him some good."

This time he did not assemble the rest of the Brothers but quietly took Sylvester with him at dawn to a vineyard nearby. There the two ascetics ate grapes together after Francis had chosen a vine on which the grapes were specially fine. While they were eating, Sylvester was cured, and together they praised the Lord. It may be that the solicitude of Francis was even more beneficial than the grapes. To the end of his life Sylvester could never speak of that incident without tears.

There was a young Brother named Ricerio, who joined them about this time. He was of a noble family but had an oversensitive spirit. Somehow he got it into his head that Francis, whom he deeply admired and loved, was avoiding him. In his slightly morbid condition everything seemed to prove this. Francis was not unobservant. So one day he sent for Ricerio and, taking him off into the woods, said to him, "Do not let any temptations of this sort bother you, my son. You are most dear to me. I want you to know that you are even especially dear and have to the full my affection and intimacy. Come to me whenever you are in trouble, and let my friendship give you confidence to speak."

Ricerio was astonished at this penetration of his secret melancholy thoughts. Shy and diffident and young, he had been given a wonderful proof of the way Francis watched over those with him. He was greatly touched and very grateful. Not only was his distrust completely banished, from that day forth he showed a larger trust in the mercy of God that had led him to such a leader and friend.

Another incident of a different sort occurred while the Brothers were living at Rivo Torto. The Emperor Otto IV had been crowned at Rome in 1209 by Pope Innocent III and soon afterward tried to regain his lost power in Umbria. As part of this effort he appointed Dipold of Acerra Duke of Spoleto, with the authority that had been lacking since the ejection of Conrad the Whimsical. There was resistance to this, led by Perugia, with the result that an imperial army marched into Umbria. Otto himself arrived in the province. Upon hearing this, Francis—though he would not go to gaze on the chivalric trappings that had once so appealed to his romantic soul—sent one of the Brothers to the Emperor with a message. It was that his glory would endure but a short time. When an excommunication was pronounced on him by the Pope late in 1210 it was considered that the prophecy of Francis had been fulfilled.

It was while he was at Rivo Torto that Francis went out preaching for the first time in a formal way, in churches, as contrasted with his former brief and friendly admonishings of such passers-by as he encountered in field and market place. His first sermons were delivered at the church of St. George in Assisi, on the steps of which Bernard da Quintavalle had distributed his possessions to the poor. Very soon these sermons attracted so much attention that Bishop Guido and the canons of the cathedral asked him to preach there every Sunday at an early Mass. Until the Pope's approbation they could not do this, though it should be noted that the bishop did not raise the slightest objection to his open-air preaching, if preaching was what it really could be called. Though the bishop was not in the least obliged to give Francis such an invitation, the fact that he did so so very promptly is significant of his sympathy with Francis's aims.

It is very evident that the relations of Francis with the clergy, not only then but all through his life, were of the most cordial kind. One of his most strongly marked characteristics was his reverence for the priesthood—for their sacred office in such cases in which he could not approve their personal lives. Never would he listen to any word against even an unworthy priest. He told his followers that they should always bow when meeting a priest and kiss his hands. He went even further than this in his own practice, for if he was speaking to one of the clergy who was on horseback he would kiss not only his hands but the hoofs of his horse. "If I chanced to meet," he used to say, "at the same moment a saint from heaven and a poor priest, I would do honor to the priest first. I would cry, 'Oh, wait St. Lawrence, for this man's hands handle the Word of Life and possess something that is more than human!' "

The mode of many reformers of the time—including some who were saints but, of course, far more of those who were merely censorious and contentious people—was to denounce all that they considered amiss in society and the Church. That was never the way of Francis. If he did not permit any criticism of the clergy, neither would he permit any of the Brothers to judge harshly of the rich and luxurious among the laity. The Franciscan protest, such as it was, was to be made entirely by offering the world another manner of life. The very last thing Francis wished was to single out any person or any class for criticism. His message was that of peace with one's neighbor and of repentance toward God.

On Saturday nights he used to go to Assisi to stay with the canons of St. Rufino's cathedral. The greater part of these nights he spent in prayer. Neither then nor at any time in his life would he make any other preparation than this. It sometimes happened that when he went into the pulpit he found that he had nothing to say. Then, instead of saying that nothing at great length (which is the usual way), he merely gave the people his blessing and came down. That seems to have impressed them just as much as a sermon. They knew how burning his words were when he was inspired.

His fervent spirit imparted itself to those he left behind at Rivo Torto over these week ends. One Saturday night the Brethren were asleep in their shack, when suddenly all were awakened by a chariot of fire that came in and went from side to side in that tumble-down shelter. Over it was a ball of fire as dazzling as the sun. They concluded that it must be the soul of Francis, burning with love for God and for men.

We shall hear more about Francis's preaching later, but its fruits were immediate. Almost every week men went out from Assisi to seek Francis at Rivo Torto or in the woods surrounding the chapel of Little Portion, where some of them now had to live. And Sunday after Sunday, listening to him with a heart that sang, was a seventeen-year-old girl, the Lady Clare Scifi. Her story was to be closely entwined with his.

Francis and the Brothers—or such of them as could squeeze into a shelter too small even for the first twelve disciples—remained at Rivo Torto through the autumn of 1210 and the following winter. It became increasingly clear that they could not remain there much longer, and newcomers had to take shelter in the caves or in the woods. Yet they made no attempt to seek other quarters until they were forced to do so. It came about in this way. One day a boorish peasant drove his donkey into their wretched hut, shouting, "Get in here; this place will do for you!"

Francis would not dispute possession with this man. He regarded himself as being there only because nobody else wanted the place. So he merely got up from his knees and said, "I feel sure, Brothers, that God did not call us from the world to provide stabling for an ass or an inn-parlor for men!" He was deeply hurt at this piece of gratuitous rudeness, and yet he was perhaps glad that it had occurred, as it obliged him to look elsewhere for a place where they could be undisturbed in prayer.

THE LITTLE PORTION

The burden of the sermons by Francis, all of which opened with his salutation of peace, was that of peace and repentance. The effect was of a most practical kind and was almost instantaneous. On November 9, 1210, the upper and the lower classes of Assisi, officially designated the *Majores* and the *Minores*, agreed that, except with common consent, there should never be any alliance between Assisi and the Emperor or the Pope or any other city or personage. This ended, by signed treaty, the old factional fights and the domination by the wealthy that had been, in Assisi, as elsewhere, a very sad story. The peace now made was so firm that even the traitors of 1202, who since that time had been living in Perugia, were allowed to return home.

Too much need not be credited to Francis for bringing this about. The city had already shown that it did not wish to be drawn into either side of the papal-imperial quarrel, and it had seen enough of the antagonisms of rival cities. Men have always known that personal or public conflicts rarely bring anybody any benefit, and nevertheless they persist in engaging in these. Unless a positive love of peace is brought into their hearts, self-interest alone is rarely able to subdue their belligerent passions. Francis, as the inspirer of this peace, put a permanent mark upon Assisi. All through his life the advancement of the cause of peace was to be one of the distinguishing characteristics of his work.

The word *Minores* now provided him the name for his Brethren. Hitherto when asked who they were, they had said merely, "We are penitents from Assisi." Even when showing their Rule to the Pope they had not thought of any official designation for themselves. Now one day a Brother was reading the Rule aloud to the group, and when he came to the part that told how they were always to serve and never to take office over others but to be subject to all, the words *sint minores* flashed sudden light into Francis's mind. He held up his hand and stopped the reading. "I will," he said, "that this Brotherhood be called that of the Lesser Brethren, the Friars Minor." It was as such that they always spoke of themselves afterwards.

As Francis now had to find another center for his work, he went to Bishop Guido—which was the routine of ecclesiastical courtesy— to ask if he could suggest anything. Francis probably was aware that the bishop could do nothing except make the routine suggestion that he approach the canons of the cathedral. Neither they nor Guido were unsympathetic, as is shown by their having given him invitations to preach, but the housing of a group of lay evangelists such as these did present a problem. A church might possibly have been provided had they been prepared to become priests and to assume parochial duties. But, though there was nothing to prevent any of them receiving ordination, which Sylvester alone had, the very essence of their work was that it should be carried out in every direction and not be localized. A center was to be nothing more than a meeting-place after their excursions. Francis could not have been surprised when he was told that there was nothing that the ecclesiastical authorities could do for them.

He now turned to the Benedictines of Mount Subasio. Everything suggests that he had known from the outset that he would have to end by going to them, and that he had made his preliminary moves merely as a matter of form, for the early chronicles lay great stress on his very early certainty that the chapels of St. Damian and the Portiuncula would eventually be associated with his work.

Without any hesitation the Abbot of Mount Subasio offered to give him the Portiuncula.

Francis refused to accept it as a gift. What he did do was thankfully accept its use. As a sign that it was only *rented*, he punctiliously sent the abbot an annual basket of fish, receiving by way of receipt a flask of oil. We are also told that the abbot made one stipulation: it was that the chapel of the Portiuncula was to be, however widespread the Order eventually became, its main house. In this the abbot probably did not think of himself as making a serious prophecy; he was indulging in an amiable pleasantry. In any event, there was no need for him to lay down such a condition: for Francis the Portiuncula was the dearest and most sacred spot in Italy. Almost his last words to his sons were that, should they be driven from it by one door, they were to enter it again by another. Yet neither that place nor any other would he hold by either personal or communal ownership; even there they were to be pilgrims and strangers.

Paul Sabatier offers the suggestion that the Abbot of Mount Subasio was so quick to comply either because he realized that his monks were not very popular and he wished to do something to curry favor with an Assisi where Francis was now being received with enthusiasm, or else because he hoped that by befriending Francis he would annoy Bishop Guido. All this is entirely gratuitous. M. Sabatier's is the least rabid and most refined brand of anticlericalism, but never was there an anticlericalism so obstinate in its prepossessions. Surely the simpler explanation that the abbot had, like everybody else, good will toward Francis is much nearer the truth.

The Portiuncula was to be for Francis, and afterward for all Christendom, one of the greatest shrines. It is probably unique among such shrines in that the holy of holies is still that tiny chapel whose tottering walls the young Francis had carefully, if a bit clumsily, strengthened before he had any idea of the world-wide work ahead of him. Over his grave there now rises a gorgeous basilica, one often thought to be little in keeping with his life of simplicity and humility

and poverty. His spirit lives in the Portiuncula—there and at St.
Damian's.

In taking over the Little Portion, his only sign of appropriation
was a hedge built round a cluster of huts: the cloister beyond which
no secular person, man or woman, was allowed to pass. Within that
encircling hedge even the Brothers were expected to speak only of
God.

This chapel had always been regarded by the local peasantry as
holy, for people used to affirm that angel voices were heard in it.
Francis was to have a vision there of Christ and His Mother. In fact,
according to one story, it was this vision that prompted him to go
immediately to the Abbot of Mount Subasio and ask for this place.
An unnamed Brother also had a vision before his conversion. In this
he beheld a countless host of men, all of them blind but all with faces
upturned to heaven, kneeling round the chapel and stretching their
hands on high beseeching God's mercy and light. Suddenly a great
radiance did fall upon them, and they found their sight and, with
it, their salvation.

New men came to join Francis, among them four who constituted
what might almost be described, even as early as this, a new generation of Franciscans who were perhaps more "Franciscan" than any
of those who had previously joined, with the exception of Brother
Giles. These four were Leo and Juniper and Masseo and Rufino, all
quite different from one another but all full of the unmistakable
Franciscan fragrance and charm. Soon—too soon, many will think
—still another generation of Brothers will appear, the organizers and
builders of the Order. It would be not only ungenerous but undis-
cerning to disparage these, for without them the Franciscan idea
might have faded away as a beautiful dream. But it is also true that
the Franciscan idea would be nothing were it not a dream, a dream
to which practical men had to give more solid form. As they had
not yet arrived at this time, we may be permitted to gaze a while
longer entranced upon these early disciples.

Among that crowd of cowled faces only a few features are now to
be distinguished clearly, and in some of the later cases—those of
the efficient men—we do not see so much the man as the work he
performed. These other men, those whom we know as delightful
human beings, were all the companions of Francis himself, and

of them we shall hear more as his story progresses. Yet there may have been dozens as delightful about whom we hear nothing at all. All at this stage may perhaps be best treated not as individuals but as making up that first little group, living at the Portiuncula or making their first missionary journeys through Umbria. The engaging personal characteristics of some of them will be pictured later; at the moment these hardly appear. What we have now is the idyll of a band of Brothers, living as one, individually anonymous.

They lived in huts made of wood and wattles and mud, and though these were probably better built, being intended to endure for a few years, than the hut Francis had built for himself in the woods, they had hardly any greater value. Under their low eaves the Brothers slept on the bare ground or, at best, on a bag filled with straw. Even a few torn rags over such a couch were, says Celano, accounted as the comfort of a marriage bed. Others described these huts as being like the lairs of wild beasts.

They took little sleep, their abstinence here being as rigorous as that regarding food and drink. Lest they should have slumber insensibly steal over them while they were praying, some of them held themselves up by ropes or chains, or by a kind of wooden cage; thus they were sharply awakened if they dropped off to sleep. Though Francis tried to check this practice, they noticed that he rarely stretched himself out completely but dozed briefly in snatches, half sitting up.

To be completely poor, that provided all the austerity that any man might need and also his joy. Yet what was more important than poverty itself was its provision of interior detachment, for this, while removing all desire to rest in the material goods of the world, also brought a release from their tyranny. Poverty therefore was not looked upon as a hardship but as a privilege, a liberation. Nobody was ever so greedy of gold as Francis was of poverty. In this was the treasure that a man had hid in a field. Francis had found it now, and so was rich.

Yet he had no criticism for those who were unable to travel by his road. It was enough that *he* held up an ideal and proved that it could be attained. That idea was not of his inventing. His only originality was in his uncompromising practice. In this he showed himself very practical, for the ideal is one that appeals to all unvitiated hearts, however few wills have the resolution and courage needed for its complete acceptance. Philosophers all through the ages have known that they were speaking what would be recognized as axiomatic truth in asserting that man's happiness does not increase by increasing his wants but by diminishing them. What Francis did was to state this truth poetically and to bring it home to the heart as a primary fact of religion.

There was one condition for admission to the Brotherhood: "If thou wilt be perfect, sell all thou hast and give to the poor." When, as sometimes happened, a man was ready enough to divest himself of his belongings but wished to make his renunciation in favor of his relatives, Francis would not receive him. The possessions had to be given to the poor.

Yet he was not fanatical in the application of this rule. Thus we hear of a peasant named John, a simple and humble man who, finding Francis one day sweeping out a church—though he loved poverty he did not love dirt—said to him, "Give me the broom and let me do it." Afterward they sat on the church steps and John told Francis, "Brother, I have long wished to serve God, and especially after I heard about you. But I did not know where to find you. Now I wish to do whatever is pleasing to you."

When it came to giving away what he owned, he took Francis to the little farm he tended, where he lived with his father and mother and some younger brothers. Then he said, "Of our oxen I may claim one as my due for the many years I have served my family. This I will sell and give the money to the poor." Not unnaturally John's family, upon hearing this, raised such a lamentable outcry that Francis could not but pity them, seeing how poor they were. So he said, "Well, let us first eat together, and then I shall make you happy." At the end of the meal he told them, "You are sufficiently poor already, so I wish your son to return the ox to you."

Even such a concession may leave us with the feeling that Brother John's family suffered hardship in losing their chief breadwinner. But we must remember not only that the peasant life in its simplicity could, more easily than any other, sustain such a loss, but that by accepting poverty the Franciscans gave to the poor, working for them, helping them in all kinds of ways, encouraging them and —most important of all—setting free a flood of charity over the whole land. For every man who actually joined Francis, a hundred others were inspired by him to live not merely more justly but with a generosity that until then had never occurred to them.

The Brothers were so far from possessing anything except a single habit, and that usually patched and repatched, that Francis grew alarmed when one day a Brother remarked innocently, "I have just been looking for you in your cell."

"*My* cell!" Francis exclaimed. "I have no cell."

Never again would he enter that wretched hovel lest he seem to be claiming even that much as his own. "The world is our cell," he used to say, "Wherever we go we have our cell always with us. Brother Body is our cell; and our soul is the hermit." He never tired of quoting Our Lord's words: "The foxes have holes and the birds of the air their nests, but the Son of Man hath not where to lay His head." In that respect, as in others, he did his best to emulate Christ.

A poverty greater than his own—and this he did occasionally encounter—always seemed to rebuke him. It was his desire to be poorer than the poorest. At such times he would say to his companion, "This man's destitution has brought us great reproach, for we have chosen poverty as our riches, and lo! she shineth forth more clearly in him."

Similarly, when seeing a beggar, he would take off any article of clothing he could remove without leaving himself quite bare. Then he would say, "This we must return to its owner. For we have received it only as a loan until we found somebody poorer than ourselves." If anybody protested against what he was doing, the answer was, "I will not be a thief. For it would be counted a theft in us if we did not give to him who is more in need."

Nor were any suspicions to be entertained of the poor. Francis must have known that there were imposters and that sometimes beggars deliberately got themselves up in rags and even deformed themselves as part of the equipment of their profession. He might have admitted this as a generalized fact, but he felt that it would be most uncharitable to believe it of the person actually present. Even the suggestion that the pauper might not be poor in spirit met with indignant reprimand. To one of the friars who said something like that one day, he gave the order, "Make haste, put off your tunic, fall down at this man's feet and proclaim yourself guilty of speaking evil against him, and not only beg his pardon but ask him to pray for you. For you have sinned not only against him but against Christ. The poverty and infirmity of this man is, as it were, a mirror to us, in which we may see and pity the infirmity and poverty of Our Lord."

Francis made no attempt at all to distinguish between what are called deserving and undeserving cases. If in this he was far from being an enlightened sociologist, the essence of charity, after all, is giving upon the basis of need and not that of desert. Other men could make their careful calculations as to where their giving would do the most good; what he had to do was to waken the impulse to give. "I have," he would say, "only two mites to give—my body and my soul." Those he gave with open hands. And in this, because of the effect he had upon others, the impractical idealist showed himself the most practical of men.

If the begging of the Brothers does not appear "sociologically" very justifiable, it should be remembered that, of what they received, they usually gave away more than they kept. Furthermore, though begging was joyfully undertaken and regarded as the noblest form of poverty, it was only something that was fallen back upon when other means of sustaining their very simple life failed. Normally they expected to support themselves by the work of their own hands, each working at the trade he knew, those who did not know any trade when they entered the order—which would have applied to Bernard, the magistrate, Peter, the lawyer, and Angelo, the knight—having to learn one. Yet in the main theirs was unskilled work; all had to be handy men, ready to do any job that presented itself.

It is obvious that had Francis wished to found a co-operative society in which all pooled the profits of the work for the benefit of the group, the inevitable result for men living so frugally and industriously would have been prosperity. Nothing could have been further from his thoughts. "Sufficient unto the day" was his motto. Nothing was to be stored up. Even for their lay labor they commonly took much less than they were entitled to and at once distributed among the poor any surplus that there might be. Men who gave so lavishly out of their little were surely being no burden to society at such times when, work not being obtainable, they went out with their beggar's bowls.

As to this work of theirs, we know, from casual glimpses we catch, that Francis did some wood carving and that Juniper carried an awl

about him for mending shoes. As we get our fullest account of
Brother Giles in this matter, he may be taken as a good exemplification of the Franciscan mode of life. We hear of him at Brindisi bor-
rowing a pitcher and going through the streets as a water seller. At
Ancona afterward he made baskets from rushes and disposed of
them. He even made a living for a while by carrying the dead to
their graves. On one occasion he went to a forest to chop wood for
a woman at an agreed-upon price. When this woman, upon learning that he was a friar, offered him more than she had promised, he
handed it all back, saying, "My good woman, I do not wish the
vice of avarice to overcome me. Therefore I will take only what
you agreed to give." As she persisted in pressing the little more upon
him, this man threw overboard all the parsimonious habits of a
peasant and told her, "Now I will take only half what you said you
would give!" Giles would seldom work all day long, for he stipu-
lated that he must have time for prayer, and nobody was more punc-
tilious than he about observing the rule that he was not to be paid
in money but in food or some other commodity.

This abhorrence of money, which was regarded as a thing never
to be touched lest it be contaminating, must, of course, be understood in relation to the age. Money, the actual coins in circulation,
was in Francis's time coming to play a more important part than it
had before. Wealth was increasing and also the hunger for wealth.
As to this, Francis knew something by personal experience. In his
father's business he had seen how engrossed men could become in
the accumulation of coin. And, unlike our own times, when coin is
usually seen only in its smaller denominations and for all larger
amounts has to be symbolized by paper or by a row of figures in a
book, the material currency had an immense importance. It was not
so much the token of exchange as a concentration into mere metal
of goods earned by men's labor, or obtained by fraud, and laid
aside for future consumption. To Francis, therefore, it was the positive materialization of greed.

Now and then, it is true, under very exceptional circumstances and
if there were no other means for relieving the sick, he would permit
money to be accepted to buy what they urgently needed. Even this
concession he made most reluctantly. There were times when one of
the Brothers had taken a piece of money with this in mind; but
when Francis thought that the good purpose could be effected as

well without it, he ordered the culprit to pick up the coin with his mouth and deposit it on a dung hill.

Yet one would seriously misunderstand Francis if one should think of him as being rabid on the single point of poverty. A still greater mistake would be made if it should be supposed that, however fantastic his actions sometimes seemed, he believed that there was anything more evil about Brother Gold than about Sister Grass. The evil was all in the avaricious souls of men, who misused gold. So there could also be in the misuse of wheat, should one hoard it after a poor harvest to send up its price. Nobody was less likely than he to attribute to any material object anything except good. What he wished to free men from was their greed, and as he was addressing himself to the mass of the people—most of them sufficiently poor but most of them also caring more about their physical requirements than the good of their souls—he used the methods that we think of as characteristically "Franciscan."

In this he was a good pedagogue for simple-minded people. Certainly there was nothing in the least prim or pedantic about his teaching. Nor was there, perhaps, any conscious or calculated intention of teaching even when, on the principle of taking no thought for the morrow, he forbade Brother Cook to soften beans in water in preparation for the next day's meal. The cook had to wait until after Matins before he did this, as by that time the new day had officially begun. His wish was that the Brothers should never know what they would have for their next dinner or even be sure that they would have any dinner at all.

This love of poverty did not only bring the Brothers joy and liberation from care, but their trust in Providence was often apparently miraculously rewarded. Thomas of Celano says no more than simple truth in writing: "Not only all creation served this man of God at every nod; the providence of the Creator was at his disposal according to his own pleasure . . . Need and supply, desire and fulfillment were always one."

This is why Francis always rejoiced when he and the Brothers were reduced to beggary. The food received in alms was, for him, the bread of angels; and there was what he called the table of the Lord. Possibly there were men among the friars who plumed themselves upon their humility when they begged, who made out of begging a grim pharisaic exercise, but Francis and those like him took it simply and were even able to make of it an occasion of gaiety. Yet he did not forget how much against the grain it was when he went out begging the first time; neither did he forget the sweetness he had experienced when he ate his first bowl of broken odds and ends. He managed to impart his spirit to others, so that sometimes those who had gone out in quest of alms made a kind of humorous contest of it and displayed at the end of the day, like so many trophies, their crusts and carrots and cabbage stumps. If any were ashamed of this employment he did not blame them, so long as they did not, on that account, draw the foot back. Once at the Portiuncula when a Brother returned from Assisi with a bulging wallet of scraps, and Francis noticed that he was singing, he jumped up and ran to meet him, so pleased was he with such joy. Then, kissing the Brother's shoulder where the wallet had lain, he put the burden on his own shoulder. How often he used to tell them, "Many noble and learned men will join our company who will consider it an honor to beg for alms!" His axiom was: "The nobler my son is, the readier let him be to go."

It came to be observed that the wellborn and the refined and those of the "gentry" were usually the most ready to demean themselves in this matter. Nor is this very wonderful, for snobs are usually found among the comfortable and the respectable and those unsure of themselves. It was great good fortune for Francis—and for us— that he was not technically a "gentleman" and as such obliged to consider his position, but that he was at the same time a man with all the instincts of the gentleman. He was a poet and, as such, the equal of any aristocrat.

Being the kind of man he was, he was able to carry off successfully what nobody else would have dared to attempt. Some of the things he did were so startling as almost to seem scandalous. Thus he once ordered the very well-connected Brother Rufino, a member of the Scifi family, to go to the cathedral at Assisi wearing only his breeches and preach in this manner. It was a drastic method of dealing with Rufino, but apparently one that was necessary, for here was a man withdrawn in contemplation, having little or no taste for the apostolic life. He had to be shaken out of himself.

After having given this order, Francis thought, "Why do you, the son of Peter Bernardone, wretch as you are, command Brother Rufino, one of the nobles of Assisi, to exhibit himself like a madman? Go and do yourself what you order others to do." Upon this he stripped himself of his own habit and, followed by Brother Leo, who carried his habit and Rufino's, he hurried to the cathedral—thereby, of course, confirming the impression that an epidemic of insanity had broken out at the Portiuncula. Even the children were jeering and everybody's comment was, "Those fellows do so much penance that they have lost their wits!"

By piecing together the various accounts of this incident we find that Francis, as regards himself, did even more than he had imposed on Rufino, for he had Peter Cathanii drag him along with a rope round his neck, while another Brother was instructed to take a pan of ashes and throw them in his face when he went into the pulpit. Though the friar flinched from carrying out that part of his orders, the spectacle, even without it, was amazing enough. Francis began his sermon by saying, "You believe me to be a holy man. But I confess here publicly that while I was sick I ate meat and soup made with meat." There he stood, still shaking with the fever from which he had not quite recovered. And after the sermon he was dragged, still with the rope round his neck and still bare except for his breeches, to the Collis Infernis, the place just outside the city walls where criminals were hanged. At that spot he completed his denunciations of himself. At that spot now rises the great church in which his body lies.

All were astonished and overawed. Many were in tears at such a sight. The retiring and contemplative Rufino, doubtless much to his relief, seems to have been completely forgotten in the more sensational incidents that followed. He may even have got out of preaching his sermon.

ℭHE SHINING ONE

St. Clare of Assisi used to describe herself as the Little Plant of Francis. She meant by this that he put her where she was and fostered her development, and to that extent the description is accurate. It would be even more accurate, though one fears a touch of sentimentality, to say that she was his Little Flower. She, more than anybody else, was the purest exemplification of the Franciscan ideal. Only a woman could ever have been that, because only a woman could have been so completely withdrawn from the turbulent currents that were to cross Franciscan life, and only a woman could have shown Clare's delicacy, sympathy, and grace. Everyone came to feel that her name of the Shining One was appropriate, and Thomas of Celano in the first chapter of her life plays upon it in his Latin in a way that it would be impossible to reproduce in English.

On both sides she came of noble blood, her father being Favorino dei Scifi, Count of Sasso Rosso, the ruins of whose castle near Assisi may still be seen, and her mother Ortolana was of the Fiumi family of Sterpeto. Besides Clare, they had a son, who probably died young, an elder daughter, and three younger girls, Almata, Balbina, and Agnes, all of whom followed Clare's example. So in the end did her mother and her aunt. So even did Favorino, to the extent of becoming a Franciscan tertiary, though before that happened he figured in several tempestuous incidents.

Ortolana was evidently a pious woman, as we hear of her having made the arduous journey to the Holy Land, and doubtless Favorino himself was not unmindful of religion in his rough, soldierly fashion. He regarded it as fitting that his daughter should be charitable and devout, but he showed no understanding at all of the kind of life to which she felt herself called and so did his best to thwart her vocation. He probably would have allowed her to become a Benedictine nun had she wished, that being recognized as fitting for a wellborn lady; but he was puzzled by her simultaneous refusal of that safe harbor and the usual anchorage of marriage. He found her will stubborn, even when her ideas were not as yet very clear. So she managed to hold off all suitors until what was regarded then as the late age of seventeen. Her younger sister Agnes, who was fourteen, was acting more sensibly and had consented to be betrothed.

Clare as a child must often have seen Francis. Although, of course, she had always been fast asleep at the times of his nightly revels, she would have heard of them and had him pointed out to her as a rather "wild" young fellow. Since then she, like all who lived in Assisi, had heard of his other eccentricities, of so very different a kind, as a subject for gossip. To her these absurdities had not seemed very absurd, and she may have been inspired to perform her own charities by knowing of his. Hers far exceeded those of a Little Lady Bountiful, and she secretly added to them penances, including that of the wearing of a hair shirt, which were no doubt injudicious in a girl of her age.

She did, in fact, have quite early, however vaguely, the idea that she had been called to a special kind of life, though to outward appearances she was only an ordinary young lady of high rank with somewhat more than the ordinary feminine devoutness. It was not until she heard Francis preach at St. George's church and at the cathedral during the winter of 1210–11 that her mind became clear as to what it was to which she was really called. Her cousins Sylvester and Rufino had gone to join Francis, and, though as yet no women were Franciscans, Clare began to see that women as well as men might have open to them the life of perfection according to the Gospel, such as Francis proclaimed.

Some time in 1211 she went to see him in company with her aunt, Bona Guelfucci, and told him what was in her mind. It presented a problem, for obviously she was unable to live in all respects as did the friars. Regarding this, there are indications that Bishop Guido was consulted and that the plan finally decided upon had his approval.

On Palm Sunday, March 18, 1212, she attended High Mass at the cathedral, dressed for the last time in her richest attire and wearing her jewels. When the moment came for the people to advance to the altar rail to receive their palms, Clare was too overcome by emotion to leave her place. It was then that the bishop, noticing this, left his throne in the sanctuary and came down to her, carrying her palm. This was his way of encouraging her in the resolution she had made. She took it in that sense; those who witnessed it took it, according to the constitution of their minds, as an instance of the bishop's fatherly kindness or of special favor to the daughter of a rich and noble house.

Clare needed such encouragement, for what she was about to do was something so unheard-of that even a kind and sympathetic bishop might well have tried to dissuade her. Francis and his disciples could adopt absolute poverty and living by doing odd jobs or by begging; but how was this going to be possible to a woman, especially one who was completely alone?

But Clare Scifi, for all her gentleness, had a heroic will. That very night, according to plan, she crept out of her father's house accompanied by her aunt. She left by a small side door, of a kind that many houses had—one used only when a dead body was carried out. Though Clare's leaving in this way added to the danger of detection, it was a symbolic act and therefore had to be performed. She was obliged to remove with her own hands the timbers and blocks of stone with which the door was blocked up. She was sturdily built, and that night she had what seemed superhuman strength.

The Brothers at the Portiuncula were waiting for her in the dark woods, torches in their hands, and she was led at once into the tiny, dimly-lit chapel. There she laid aside her rich dress and put on the rough Franciscan habit and was girt with the Franciscan rope. She took off her shoes, to walk henceforth in sandals. Francis sheared off her long golden hair and laid it on the altar, and then and there she made her vows to him. As this was normally the function of a bishop, it must be supposed that Guido had delegated to Francis the necessary authority. Though not a priest, he was, in effect though not yet in name, the general of a religious order.

After this ceremony Clare was immediately escorted by the Brothers to the Benedictine convent near what is now Bastia. The nuns there had been notified in advance—surely by Bishop Guido—that she would arrive for temporary shelter among them.

The plans had been well laid. The secret, though shared by more than enough people to have given it away on every hand, was well kept. Everything went off without a hitch and with perfect timing.

Francis had expected, of course, that the Scifi family would protest, though he may have been surprised by the violence they showed. Count Favorino and his brothers demanded an interview with Clare and obtained it, but they found her firm against all their alternating threats and promises. Fearing that they might attempt a coup of their own, Francis decided that a safer refuge could be found in another Benedictine convent near by. If they attempted to carry her off by force from a convent she had already left, some of their fury might be spent. Rages as wild as these quickly subside, and Francis was giving the count a chance to recover his normal good humor.

Just then Agnes Scifi left her father's house and went to join Clare. It was about the most unpropitious moment she could have selected, as her going would, she knew, infuriate the count still further. But it may be that he was talking of marrying her out of hand, and that she was therefore obliged to act at once.

The attack now centered on Agnes, the younger and more pliable of the sisters. The Scifi could argue that she was as good as married and should not go back on her word. This time the count sent his brother Monaldo and a body of armed men to drag her home.

When the nuns at the convent saw weapons they were terrified. And they had reason to wonder whether, at least in the case of Agnes, the family was not to some extent justified. They made no attempt to protect her, so she was taken out weeping by her uncle and his men. Among these there may well have been the young man to whom Agnes was betrothed.

The poor child was frantic with fear. She resisted as well as she could, and they found that they had to carry her. The man who had her in his arms dropped her, saying, "She must have been fed lead all night by those nuns, she is so heavy!" Thomas of Celano assures us that even when they asked a number of men who were working in the fields to come and help lift her across a stream, they were unable to raise her at all. As he also says that she had been beaten and kicked by her captors and that her uncle drew a dagger with which he would have killed her had not his raised arm been paralyzed, we must suppose that, though violence was undoubtedly used, we have here an instance of the Celano exaggeration. There may have been, however, the brandishing of a dagger by way of scaring Agnes.

In her terror Agnes called, "Clare! Clare, come and help me! Come quickly, Clare!" At the time of the brief interview in the convent parlor Clare had been in her room, but the nuns would have rushed there as soon as Agnes was dragged away to relate what had happened. So Clare hastened down at once and had not far to go. She had already won her own battle and these men knew that she was not to be trifled with. Now with flashing eyes she said quietly, "Leave her alone! How dare you touch this child? She has given herself to God."

The whole group, and perhaps the bullying Uncle Monaldo in particular, were by now rather ashamed of themselves. The task they had imagined would be easy had unexpected difficulties. And if they succeeded in getting Agnes home, the bishop might excommunicate them all. They therefore let Agnes throw herself into the arms of Clare for protection. So, discomfited, they went back to Assisi. They were so thoroughly defeated that they made no attempt to stop the youngest of the Scifi girls from joining her sisters when she did so a few years later.

Francis had to provide for the group of women when it numbered, as it soon did, more than Clare and her sisters. They could remain with the Benedictine nuns only by becoming Benedictines themselves, which they did not want to do, or by becoming boarders, which to them would have seemed pointless. They were now part of the Franciscan community.

Yet they could not adopt the life of the friars. This would have been in those days quite impossible for women. The modern sisterhoods that conduct schools, orphanages, and hospitals and go out as foreign missionaries had not been thought of, and would indeed have been unthinkable. Though Clare some years later wished that she might go out to Morocco to spread Christ's gospel, she was well aware that this could only be a dream. Nevertheless, she was proposing to accept a poverty as absolute as that practised by Francis himself.

Francis, fortunately, was full of resources. He found her a location at St. Damian's, the small house attached to it being made into a convent. He turned for this again to the Benedictines of Mount Subasio, and again the Benedictines proved themselves his friends. As the Poor Ladies could not go out begging or do more than raise a few vegetables in their little garden and sew altar linens in their cells, he had to make himself responsible for their support by assigning one of the Brothers to beg on their behalf.

Their "privilege of poverty" was in some respects harder for them to maintain than it was for the friars. Their sanctity excited so much admiration among highly placed friends that these tried in every possible way to undermine its whole basis by getting them to accept a little property on which to maintain themselves. These ladies might live as ascetically as they wished, but their friends feared that poverty, in the Franciscan sense, was out of the question for them.

The most affectionate and solicitous of these friends was also the most exalted. We shall hear more about him later. He was the Cardinal Ugolino who, after having taken Clare and her nuns under his protection, rose to be Pope, in which position he was able to be even more useful to her. But his idea of doing her good did not at all coincide with her own. The time was to come when, upon his urging that he dispense her from her vow of complete poverty and allow the community to own property, he got the answer, "Holy Father, never will I consent to be dispensed from following Christ!" Her struggle for what she wanted lasted through the reigns of several Popes and did not, in fact, end until two days before her death, twenty-seven years after Francis had departed from this life, when at last her Rule was confirmed by the Holy See.

At first she had no formal Rule but only a brief formula of life. This was not detailed enough to lay before the Pope for approval, and, though she was regarded as a member of the Franciscan family, Francis would not presume to act as her official superior. Therefore, Cardinal Ugolino drew up for her in 1219 a Rule based on that of the Benedictines. Although this was tentatively accepted by her, as it was also by Francis, it did not satisfy them but was merely tolerated until Clare would obtain canonical approbation of the Rule she wished. She had a lifelong battle with the kindest and tenderest of friends before the privilege of poverty was finally secured by the confirmation of her Rule.

Her relations with the Popes were of an extraordinary character. When Gregory IX (the former Cardinal Ugolino), by way of forcing her hand, forbade the Sisters to receive the spiritual ministrations of the friars, she declared that, in that event, she would also renounce the material help they gave. Her words were: "If we have to do without spiritual bread, we can also go without bodily bread." In face of that threatened hunger strike, the Pope had to yield.

Yet when this same Pope was visiting her, she asked him to give the blessing on the meal in the refectory. To this Gregory answered, "Sister Clare, it is my wish that you bless these loaves and make upon them the sign of the cross of Christ, to whom you offer yourself in constant sacrifice." Falling on her knees, she said, "Pardon me, most Holy Father, for I should deserve to be greatly blamed if I, a poor woman, should presume to give this blessing in the presence of the Vicar of Christ." There was nothing for him to do but to put her under obedience to do what he asked. Whereupon she made the sign of the cross—and on each one of the little loaves that sign physically appeared.

When Pope Innocent IV visited her toward the end of her life, she insisted on kissing his foot, and, as she was ill in bed, he had to lift his foot on a stool beside her. When she asked his absolution, he returned, "Would to God, my daughter, that I had as little need of God's forgiveness as you!" She was a wonderful exemplification of the Franciscan spirit, with its union of perfect submission and perfect freedom.

She was made abbess in 1215, much against her will. Even in that dignity she refused to exempt herself from any of the menial duties her convent household needed to have performed. Not only would she take her share of the kitchen work and the waiting at table, but she made a special point of expressing her humility by washing the feet of the lay sisters, whose duties sometimes took them into Assisi. On these occasions, when she had finished the washing, she used to kiss their feet. One day one of these sisters, unwilling that the lady abbess should perform this office, tried to pull her foot away, with the result that she inadvertently kicked Clare in the face. Instead of crying out from the pain of the blow, the abbess merely smiled. And that time the foot got a longer kiss than usual, and on the sole. When all the nuns were asleep at night, Clare used to make the rounds of her little convent to visit each bed and make sure that each of her daughters had sufficient covering. She was indeed their tender mother.

Francis himself did not go in much for the working of miracles.

If these were necessary, he preferred to have them performed by Clare. So he used to send any of the Brothers who were sick to her to be blessed. We hear of one case in particular, that of a Brother Stephen who was insane. His mind was restored by Clare. Normally, however, it was not so much a question of anything supernatural but of nursing the Brothers who seemed to need something better than could be given by their own infirmarian. Francis himself in his last days was cared for by Clare in this way.

As might be expected of a woman of her high breeding, and one who, moreover, was a saint, she had a sensitiveness that gave her additional charm. It was this that made her enter so completely into the ideas of Francis and enabled her to give him, at such times as he needed it, the warm human sympathy he could not obtain elsewhere. In addition, there were about her the kind of pleasant human touches that soften the picture of her asceticism. She cultivated a tiny flower garden of her own, which is still kept as she used to keep it, with her favorite flowers, though it is now the Franciscan Fathers who occupy St. Damian's. And Thomas of Celano, who was very much a literary man and somewhat too addicted to flowery turns of phrase, is at pains to assure us that she greatly relished a polished sermon, though she was not "skilled in letters" and though she could also "seek for roses among wild thorns"—that is, endure inelegant discourses if their matter was good.

Her entering the Franciscan family called for immense resolution and courage. These qualities she showed every day of her life, but especially on two occasions when Frederick II's Saracen mercenaries were preparing assaults, the first time on the convent and the second, on Assisi itself. On one of these occasions she rose from her sickbed and, taking in her hands the pyx of silver and ivory containing the Blessed Sacrament, went to the window against which the scaling-ladder had been placed. From the pyx there came a voice, like that of a little child, promising her protection. The trembling nuns heard it too, and Clare told them, "I assure you, my daughters, that you shall suffer no harm; only place your trust in the Lord." The leading man on the ladder was so surprised by the sudden apparition of the veiled figure that he fell backward, and the others gave up the attack. The window at St. Damian's where this is said to have happened is still pointed out, and what is certainly the pyx that was kept in the little chapel adjoining Clare's room is preserved as a relic.

Hers was a daily mystical death. In addition, she almost daily expected her physical death. In the last year of Francis's life she fell ill and remained ill for the rest of the twenty-eight years of her life. She continued to govern her community and, even in illness, work at some small task, if it was only needlework done in bed.

Lying there, she was frequently swept heavenward in ecstasy. One Christmas night she lay grieving that she was too ill to go with her nuns to the chapel for the chanting of Matins. Instead, she began to meditate on the Holy Child, when suddenly she found herself transported to the great church Brother Elias had built over the bones of Francis. There she heard the friars' resonant voices singing to the organ music and saw the Christmas crib and the Bambino in his manger. When next morning the Sisters went to her she told them, "Blessed be Our Lord Jesus Christ! He, when you left me alone, did not abandon me. For by His grace I was present at the solemnities in the church of the friars." According to the *Fioretti* version of this story, she was even able, in that miraculous transportation of her body, to receive Holy Communion.

Her special devotion, as that of Francis, was to the sufferings of Our Lord. One Good Friday eve, while meditating on them, she was rapt sitting upright in bed, stock-still and oblivious of everything. So she remained until the following evening when a Sister came and lighted a candle and reminded her that Brother Francis had laid her under strict orders never to allow a whole twenty-four hours to pass without taking some food. At last she was roused enough to ask, "Why the candle? Is it not daylight?" When told that she had been like this the entire day, she said, "That was a long sleep. But what I much desired has at last been given me. But beware lest you tell anyone of this so long as I am alive."

Once Francis had made sure that she had reached the heights of spirituality, he did not wish her to depend on him too much. Though two of the Brothers were deputed to live beside St. Damian's, so that they could perform their sacred functions and also look after the Sisters' material needs—as this was part of the contract that Francis had made with Clare—he himself rarely went to see her, and less and less as time went on. Once he even complained, "The devil will yet give us Sisters instead of wives!"

At last Clare had to send begging him to come to her, and in this she was upheld by the Brothers at the Portiuncula. So Francis said, "Think not, dear Brothers, that I do not love these Ladies perfectly; for if it is a fault to cherish them in Christ, must it not be a still greater fault to have united them to Christ? But I am giving you an example. I do not wish any of you of his own accord to visit them, but I order that only reluctant men accept this office, and that only those who are spiritual and approved by long and worthy life be appointed to this service." He went rather grudgingly, and a strange scene followed.

Instead of any sermon, he merely spread ashes in a circle about himself and poured ashes over his head. Then he stood in silence while they, greatly perturbed, waited for him to speak. But all that he did was to intone the *Miserere,* after which he walked out without another word. This conduct was not very characteristic of the gentle and courteous Francis, but perhaps an excuse can be found in the fact that about this time he was passing through a period of black depression and discouragement. Even so, one fancies that he afterward relented enough to partake of their frugal meal.

What was far more like him was what happened at a time Clare and some of her nuns were visiting him at the Portiuncula. Then he caused the meal to be served on the bare floor, as was often his way. Before they began to eat he began to speak of God so sublimely that not only Francis and Clare but everybody there was rapt in ecstasy. Night fell upon them, and they sat there unmoving. The inhabitants of Assisi, like the peasants nearby, seeing a glow all over the Portiuncula, supposed that it had caught fire; so they ran toward it in crowds to try and save the place. But when they came where Francis and Clare were sitting they found all the poor buildings intact and the saints sitting on the ground in rapture before their untasted food, and over all there shone the fire of Divine Love.

The Lady Clare died two days after her Rule was ratified. With her were her sister Agnes, who had been separated from her for thirty years, serving as abbess in a convent near Florence. Leo, Angelo, and Juniper were also there, Brother Juniper with what Clare gaily called his "news from God." After giving her blessing to her weeping nuns—"I now give you all my blessing while living. I confirm it to you after my death"—she said, "Go forth in peace. For thou shalt have good company on the journey. Go forth. For He who created thee hath sanctified thee, and, protecting thee always, He hath loved thee with a tender love, even as a mother loves her child. Blessed be Thou, Lord God, who hast created me."

One of the Sisters asked her to whom she was speaking and got the answer, "I am speaking to my own happy soul." Another Sister saw at that moment a glorious vision: into the room there came a procession of virgins, all clad in white and all crowned with gold. Among them was one more beautiful than all the rest; her diadem was so resplendent that it turned the night into day. It was in the embrace of the Mother of God that the happy soul of Clare ascended to glory.

She died on August 11, 1253. Pope Innocent IV happened to be in Assisi at the time. At her funeral he did something that had never been done before and that has never been done since. When the friars began to chant the Office for the Dead and Requiem Mass, he made a sign for silence and ordered that instead the Office of Virgins and a High Mass of triumph be sung in honor of one he believed to be already in heaven. It was a kind of canonization, and the Pope would have made it formally such had not his cardinals begged him to let the ordinary process be instituted. At this the chief witness was the aunt in whose company Clare had fled from her father's house. Two years later the new Pope, Alexander IV, placed her among the saints. In the bull by which he did so, one that glowed not only for his admiration for a saint but his affection for a personal friend, he gave her the title of Princess of the Poor.

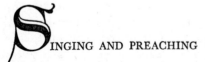

SINGING AND PREACHING

That strange figure, the Calabrian Abbot Joachim of Flora, who in some respects seems to have anticipated Francis and even to have prophesied his coming, wrote what may be taken as a description of the ideal Franciscan friar: "He should own nothing except his lyre." Francis began as a poet and ended as one, though during the years of his active life he appears to have been too busy living poetry to have felt much inclination to write it. A large part of his peculiar charm is that he approached people as one would expect a poet turned saint to do. He was a poet in his intense feeling for the totality and mystery of life. Because he was a poet he sang the Gospel rather than preached it.

The vast fund of stories that show his sense of kinship with all created things comes a little later, when he had reached the very fullness of his powers, which still required some development. But from the start we find him singing, usually in French, at moments of great joy. There were times all through his life when he heard a music inaudible to other ears. Then he would pick up a piece of wood from the ground and, drawing another stick over it as though it were a bow, would play as upon a violin, his ecstasy of joy often ending in a flood of tears.

This sort of thing was reserved for private. As for his French songs, they would have been of no use in carrying his message to unlettered peasants or even most city folk. Yet he found a way to use singing in his missions, and he would as often refer to his friars as the Jongleurs of God as he referred to them as the Knights of the Round Table. However much he changed after his conversion, he never ceased to be the gay and romantic Francis that Assisi had known in his youth.

We get a hint that there were now and then bits of improvised rhyme that were sung to tunes which the crowd all knew. Certainly there was the singing of the *laudi* of the kind that afterward was more elaborately utilized by the fourteenth century Franciscan, Jacopone da Todi, and also of those Latin hymns of the Church which, at the time, were sufficiently intelligible to everybody. The simplicity and earnestness and gay good humor created an impression that reminds one of the first days of the Salvation Army. Indeed, we know that General Booth and his associates stole more than one leaf out of the history of Franciscan and other Catholic missions.

It would seem that even on the part of the few priests in what was at this stage essentially a lay movement there was as yet no touching upon doctrine. The Pope's commission was that they should preach repentance. Therefore everything except practical considerations, and of these only such as were within the experience of their humble audiences, were left on one side.

Of Francis's own style of preaching we can say that it was altogether unstudied. He never prepared anything but, depending upon the inspiration of the moment, addressed himself with burning intensity to those before him. His whole body seemed to preach, and his gestures were vivacious and, perhaps, violent. Had it not been for his crystalline sincerity he might have struck people as absurd. Probably, too, it was not only in the famous sermon he was soon to deliver before the Pope and the cardinals that his feet danced while he spoke. His great dark eyes, full of fire and tenderness, seemed to look each person present through and through. He had a voice so resonant that it was startling, coming from so frail a man. It was fortunate that he had that asset of the orator, for his physical presence was not at all impressive, and what slight advantages he might have had in this respect were thrown away because of his appearing in a coarse habit patched with material still coarser, sackcloth that did not even match in color. Thrown away? No, perhaps before he had finished, people felt that his very lack of all external advantages gave him all the more force. The listeners forgot everything as soon as he began to speak, for these were words that came from the heart and went straight to the heart. He saw the largest concourse of people as one man, and to an audience of one he preached as though he had thousands there.

Afterward people could not always remember just what it was that Francis had said. The general effect remained, but there were no striking phrases, no highly original ideas that could be recalled. It was the personality of Francis that was the real sermon. The power of this preaching was tremendous, as we can see from the countless thousands it converted.

Though we have very few and very meager reports about things that Francis said in his addresses—and most of these concern his addresses to the Brothers, not those delivered on his missionary journeys—we may get some idea of his method from what amounts to a "broadcast" sermon, the long "Letter to all the Faithful" written some time after 1215. A typical passage runs: "You think to possess for long the vanities of this world, but you are deceived; for a day and an hour will come of which you think not and do not know and are ignorant of. The body grows feeble, death approaches, neighbors and friends come saying, 'Put your affairs in order.' And his wife and the children, neighbors and friends, make believe to weep. And looking, he sees them weeping and is moved by a bad emotion, and thinking within himself he says: 'Behold, I place my soul and my body and my all in your hands'. Verily, that man is cursed who confides and exposes his soul and body and all in such hands. Wherefore, the Lord says by the prophet: 'Cursed be the man that trusteth in man.' And at once they cause a priest to come and the priest says to him, 'Wilt thou do penance for thy sins?' He answers, 'I will.' 'Wilt thou from thy substance, as far as thou canst, satisfy for what thou hast done and for the things in which thou hast defrauded and deceived men?' He answers, 'No.' And the priest says: 'Why not?' 'Because I have put everything into the hands of my relatives and friends.' And he begins to lose the power of speech and this miserable man dies a bitter death.

"But let all know that wheresoever or howsoever a man may die in criminal sin, without satisfaction—when he could satisfy and did not satisfy—the devil snatches his soul from his body with such violence and anguish as no one can know except him who suffers it. And all talent and power, learning and wisdom that he thought to possess are taken from him. And his relatives and friends take to themselves his substance and divide it and say afterward: 'Cursed be his soul because he could have acquired and given us more than he did, and did not acquire it.' But the worms eat his body. And thus he loses soul and body in this short life and goes into hell, where he shall be tormented without end."

Probably Francis was not often so terrifying as that, but when he was, he had the shattering force that is given only to the gentle. The tone of that was one of commiseration, and was therefore overwhelming.

Such preaching shook his audiences to their roots. Yet prayer rather than preaching was relied on, and Francis used to say to his preachers, "Why do you boast of men converted, when it is my simple Brothers that have converted them by their prayers?" The preachers themselves had to pray more earnestly than they preached. His own preparation for preaching was prolonged prayer. No oratory was of any use unless the orator gave good example. There is a story of how Francis once went out to preach, taking with him a novice to whom he would seem to have wished to teach a lesson in his own dramatic fashion. They walked through the streets of the town, the novice expecting Francis to stop at every street corner and start to preach. But he took the novice home without having said a word. When the youth wanted to know, "What about your sermon?" Francis managed to convey that the sermon *had* been delivered—by their humble and recollected air.

He was greatly distressed when any friar sought elegance in speaking rather than earnestness. The love of souls could come only from love of God. "The preacher," Francis used to tell his Brothers, "should first draw in by secret prayer what he is afterward to pour forth in sacred discourses; he must rather grow hot within than utter cold words outwardly." He himself often completely withdrew for long periods from the crowds that thronged about him, and, in addition to the ordinary Lent, he sometimes observed three other such Lents in the course of a year. We hear of his having spent one of these alone in 1211 on a little island in the middle of Lake Trasimeno. There he lived in a kind of cave in a thicket of thorns, taking with him as his food for forty days two small loaves, of which one and a half were found uneaten when the boatman came for him on Holy Thursday.

He was now being venerated as a saint, so that when he entered a town the church bells would be rung and the whole population would go out to meet him, rejoicing, the children clapping their hands and carrying bunches of leaves and flowers in their hands. At first this annoyed him, but afterward he accepted it, a little to the scandal of one Brother who said to him, "Do you not see that the people are worshiping you? And you don't attempt to stop them but seem rather pleased with it!" To this Francis answered simply, "These people never do anything out of respect for Him whom they ought to worship." This distressed the Brother still more, until Francis said, "Look, Brother; this reverence paid to me I never take to myself, but I pass it all on to God. Thus the people benefit, for it is God whom they are worshiping, though they see him only in his creatures."

How thoroughly he meant this he proved at a certain occasion at Terni. After Francis had preached, the bishop told the congregation, "At this last hour God has enlightened the Church by this man, poor and despised, simple and unlettered; wherefore we are bound ever to praise the Lord, knowing that He has not dealt so with every nation." Upon hearing this, Francis fell at the bishop's feet, saying, "Truly, Lord Bishop, you have done me great honor! Where others deprive me of what is mine, you have kept them unharmed. Like a discerning man, you have separated the precious from the worthless, ascribing praise to God and worthlessness to me."

On the other hand, when the Bishop of Imola somewhat pompously told Francis, "Brother, I can do all the preaching needed here!" Francis, though he bowed humbly and went out without another word, soon returned.

"And what do you want now, Brother?" the bishop demanded.

He got the reply, "My Lord, when a father has driven his son out of one door, he comes in by another."

At once the bishop, completely charmed, gave Francis and the friars permission to preach anywhere in his diocese.

As all the journeys were made on foot, and as the Brothers were still few, they rarely went at first beyond the borders of Umbria. By degrees they pressed farther afield, to the north and south and the March of Ancona. Within two years after his obtaining his first disciples, Francis was dreaming of missions to the infidels.

Before he set out he went to Rome to obtain the Pope's blessing on this enterprise, and that having been readily given, Francis took ship at Ancona for the Holy Land. He meant to preach to the Saracens, conducting his own kind of crusade.

He did not get very far that time. The ship was driven by storms to Dalmatia, and as there he could find no ship that was sailing that year for Syria, there was nothing for it but to return home.

A difficulty arose. He had no money to pay his fare—how he had paid his fare to Dalmatia does not appear—so he went on board a ship with his companion by stealth as a stowaway. Stated thus baldly, the proceeding seems a bit reprehensible, but, as always, Francis managed to do something that more than justified his action. A friend had smuggled a considerable amount of food on board and had given this into the keeping of a member of the crew, telling him, "Give this to the poor men in hiding when they need it." So there was some connivance and possibly a substantial tip. When a new storm drove the ship out of its course and the food for the crew ran short, Francis came out of his hiding-place and put what he had at their disposal. Then all on board were glad that they had stow-aways among them, and attributed their escape from peril to the prayers of one whom they now considered a saint.

A second journey, this time to Spain where Francis intended to preach to the Moors, also failed. Francis fell ill and had to remain behind with a companion, while Bernard da Quintavalle and Giles made a pilgrimage to the shrine of St. James at Compostella. As there were only two of them, they made no attempt at evangelizing the infidels. Their cast of mind was contemplative rather than apostolic.

Though these efforts came to nothing, they were by no means without eventual fruit, for they marked the beginning of a revival of the missionary activities of Christendom. These, largely because the road to the east was blocked by Islam, were mainly confined to the not altogether edifying enterprises of the Teutonic Knights on the shores of the Baltic. The Crusades, moreover, had now given people the idea that the best—and indeed, the only—way of ex-tending Christendom was by means of the sword. Christians had al-most forgotten that there might be the possibility of conversion by other means. Francis had a world-wide vision from the outset and never thought of other modes than the preaching of peace and repentance. The new missionary impulse, therefore, begins with these unsuccessful journeys of his. He had failed, but he had not abandoned his idea.

On his way home to Assisi from Ancona other tokens of a great future met him. In one place, Ascoli, no less than thirty men in a group joined the Brotherhood. He therefore returned with a large recruitment of friars. On the way he had time to stop at San Sever-ino to preach at a convent. It was a ceremony of the clothing or profession of a novice, and this accounts for the presence there of a famous poet, who was one of her relatives. His name was William of Lisciano, and he had been crowned with the laurel by the Em-peror Henry VI and given by the people the name of the King of Verses. In Francis's story he is known as Brother Pacifico, for that is what he became the following day.

He had never seen Francis before and had been moving in circles where he was not likely to have heard much about him. While the

fervent little friar was preaching the eye of the poet saw two glitter-
ing crosses laid upon him, one going from his head to his feet, the
other across his breast. He was deeply moved by the discourse and
made up his mind to live a better life—at some future date. But
Francis had singled him out and spoke to him afterward. The
laureate was now unable to escape and felt impelled to say, "There
is no need to talk any more; let us come to deeds. Take me away
from men and restore me to the great Emperor!" He was the first
of many poets to join the Order, the best of whom in the time of
Francis was his first biographer, Thomas of Celano, the author
of the *Stabat Mater* and the *Dies Irae*. Before the first Franciscan
century was out, Dante had been clothed with the habit of the third
order.

The conversion of poets should not be very surprising. What was a
good deal more unusual was the conversion of a band of robbers.
At Monte Casale there were three bandits who were terrifying the
countryside. One day they turned up at the little house the friars
occupied there and demanded food. They were peremptorily sent
away by the guardian, who told them, "As men insolent and bold
you would devour even the alms bestowed on the servants of God.
Begone and do not come here again!"

When Francis heard of this he reproved the guardian, saying, "If
you will do as I tell you, I trust in the Lord that you shall gain
their souls. Go therefore and get some good bread and wine and carry
them to the wood where those robbers dwell and shout to them,
'Brother Thieves, come to us because we bring you good bread and
good wine.' Then they will come to you, and you must spread a cloth
upon the ground and serve them while they eat. But after the meal
you shall speak to them of God and ask them for His love to promise
you this much, that they will do no bodily violence to anyone. For
if you ask everything at once, they will not listen to you; but you will
find that they will willingly promise you this much, if you show
yourselves humble and charitable."

On the second day the guardian was to go again, this time adding
some eggs and cheese to the picnic. Now he was to say, after they
had eaten their meal, "Why do you live so hard and do so many evil
things? For these you will lose your souls unless you are converted
to God and serve the Lord."

The method worked as well as Francis had said, for some days later they not only gave up their evil course but sought him out and asked him to give them the Franciscan habit.

The *Fioretti* carries their story still further to tell us that, though two of the Brother Thieves died soon after becoming friars, the third lived on, practicing penance, until after Francis died. Shortly before his own death he had an extraordinary vision or dream in which he was shown, among other things, his godmother in hell. She told him, "My husband and I falsified the measures of grain we sold"; and this was why they were lost. But he himself was carried to the gates of heaven where St. Francis told the porter, "Let him in, for he is one of my Brothers." Then St. Francis, in the dream explaining the dream, told him that he had but eight days to live. His death came at the time foretold, and with it St. Francis himself to lead him to Paradise. The story is charming, but the *Fioretti* displays its embellishments by having Bernard and Giles with Francis in heaven. They lived on many years after the time when the last of the Brother Thieves left this wicked world. The account in the *Mirror of Perfection* does not contain these marvels, and is in other respects far more credible.

Along with Francis's tolerance and kindness toward others went a great severity toward himself. The food of the Brothers was always poor enough, yet he usually ate it uncooked or destroyed whatever tastiness it might have by pouring water or ashes over it. His explanation was that "Brother Ashes is chaste." Lest anyone should get the wrong impression, he used to tell the friars, "Beware of showing yourselves sullen and gloomy hypocrites. Instead, rejoice in the Lord and be merry."

His own asceticism was often humorous and not the less humble on that account. Once when sick, he had been told that he should eat some chicken. He marked his recovery by having himself dragged through the streets with a rope round his neck, the Brother who was leading him being ordered to call to the passers-by, "Behold the glutton who gorges on chicken when you think he is fasting!" When he was suffering from a disease of the stomach and the Brothers wanted to sew a piece of fox skin under his tunic, after a good deal of argument he consented, but only on condition that another piece be sewn on the outside. He would not appear before men other than he really was. Often he would exclaim, "If the Most High had given as much to a robber, he would be more thankful, Francis, than you!"

If he had occasion to reprimand any of the Brothers, he was as likely as not to show his remorse afterward by ordering that or another Brother to lay a penance upon him. Thus a rather simple-minded friar named James brought a badly ulcerated leper to the Portiuncula for a visit. Francis told him, "You ought not to lead out these Christians, as it is decent neither for you nor for them." Then, as the leper had heard this and, he feared, would be hurt, Francis demanded that he should have imposed on him the penance that he was going to ask for. It was that he and the leper eat out of the same dish. Yet, as he saw, the fingers that were going to dip into the food with him were oozing with pus.

There were moments, however, when the natural inclinations that seemed so thoroughly conquered welled up in him. Upon the coming of one such "temptation" he rushed out into the open, stripped off his habit, and made seven images of snow. Then, with his teeth chattering with the cold, he admonished himself, "See, Francis, this large one is your wife; these four are your sons and daughters, and the other two are your manservant and maid. Hurry and put some clothes on them, for they are freezing to death!" But here was no such visions as tormented St. Anthony of the Desert. Well might Chesterton comment on that incident, "Evil itself could not come to him save in the form of a forbidden good; and he could only be tempted by a sacrament." Perhaps Francis was thinking of one of the Brothers who had appeared to possess every virtue and who yet left the Brotherhood. He murmured to himself the name of all the virtues in turn, and he had to admit that the Brother had had every one of them. At last he whispered, "Fear"; then he added, "Ah yes, fear; that is what was lacking. It is useless for a man to seek all the virtues and to leave out fear. It was because he had no fear that that good Brother fell."

It was now that Francis received a strange gift, one that he accepted because, though it was a large one, it was of no practical use except for the purpose to which he meant to put it. Even so, he would permit no written deed of the donation to be drawn up at the time, though we know its date to have been May, 1213. The gift was a mountain, La Verna, northwest of Assisi, near the point where the Tiber and the Arno rise.

Francis had been preaching at the castle of the Count of Monte-feltro on the occasion of the knighting of its young lord. He had taken as his text the lines of a popular song:

> So great the joys I have in sight,
> That every sorrow brings delight.

He made the application in his own sense, as he stood on the parapet for a pulpit. It was afterward that the Count Orlando dei Cattani of Chiusi offered to give him this mountain as "lonely and most suitable for contemplation," adding: "If you are pleased to dwell there, I will most willingly make you a free gift of it for the love of God and I will also see that you are furnished with all things necessary for the body." On such terms it could hardly be refused. There the Brothers in their periods of retirement would be completely cut off from the world and yet have their simple needs, unobtainable in any other way in such a remote spot, supplied by this good friend.

Francis loved such retreats and there were several places of this sort frequented by him. They were not so withdrawn that, when there, he could be unobserved; and that he did not relish. There was, for instance, a young novice who was so curious about him that he tied his cord at night to that worn by Francis, so that he might know when Francis got up to pray. Though Francis was too clever for him and quietly untied the cord when he got up, very gently so as not to waken the boy friar, the Brother, upon waking a little later, followed him and saw him kneeling in a great light, and with him Christ and the Virgin Mary and St. John the Baptist and St. John the Evangelist and a number of angels speaking with him. At La Verna he could escape such inquisition.

Count Orlando's mountain, which was to be the scene of Francis's reception of the stigmata eleven years later, was a kind of tempta-tion. Or rather, when Francis withdrew to any such place "to wipe off any dust that may have stuck to me in my intercourse with men," as he put it, there would come over him a wondering question whether he should not do as others of the Brothers did and give him-self up entirely to the contemplation of divine things. This finally became so strong that he laid his doubt before his companions. "What do you counsel, Brothers?" he asked. "Shall I devote myself to prayer, or shall I go about preaching? Of a truth, I that am small and simple and rude in speech have more grace in prayer than in speaking. In prayer there seems to be the gain and heaping up of graces, in preaching a certain giving out of the gifts received from heaven." He went on, setting against one another the advantages of each manner of life, concluding that there was only one weighty consideration that might outweigh the life in which "we speak with God and hear him, and live as it were the life of angels, while we converse with angels," and this was that "the only begotten Son of God, who is the highest wisdom, left His Father's bosom for the salvation of souls." As he could get no answer that satisfied him from the Brothers after several days of discussion, he sent Brother Masseo to place his doubt before Sylvester, one of the great Franciscan contemplatives, and the Lady Clare. He had made up his mind to abide by whatever they told him.

When Masseo returned Francis received him with great honor, washing his feet and serving his meal as though he were an ambassador, as indeed he was. Then Francis took Masseo out into the depths of a wood and, kneeling down, stretched out his arms in the form of a cross, saying, "What has My Lord commanded that I should do?"

Brother Masseo answered, "To Brother Sylvester, and also to Sister Clare and her Sisters, Christ has answered and revealed that it is His will that you go throughout the world to preach, for He has not chosen you for yourself alone, but also for the salvation of others."

At once Francis sprang to his feet, glowing with fervor, with all his doubts resolved.

"Let us go in the name of God," was all that he said.

So relieved was his mind that in his lightheartedness, sure now that God had sent him to preach, he preached to the first creatures he encountered, men being lacking in that lonely spot. This was as he came toward Bevagna with Masseo and Angelo. There he saw by the side of the road a countless flock of birds. He announced, "I will go and preach to my little sisters."

He walked among them, and his habit touched them, but none moved or was in the least afraid. Instead, those that were in the trees flew down to join that congregation.

"My little sisters, the birds," his sermon ran, "you are much bounden to God your Creator, and always and in every place you ought to praise Him. He has given you liberty to fly everywhere, and He had given you double and triple raiment. He preserved your seed in the ark of Noah, so that your race might not perish. Still more are you bounden to Him for the element of air He has appointed for you. Besides all this, you do not sow, neither do you reap; yet God feeds you and gives you streams and fountains for your drink, the mountains and valleys for your refuge and high trees on which to build your nests. And because you do not know how to spin or sew, God clothes you and your young. Your Creator greatly loves you, as may be seen from the benefits He has bestowed upon you. Therefore, my little sisters, beware of the sin of ingratitude, and study always to give praise to God."

It seemed to the two friars who stood on the road wondering at this scene that the "little sisters" listened most attentively and with the utmost reverence. When Francis had finished, he made the sign of the cross over the birds. At once they flew away, knowing themselves dismissed. And they too made the sign of the cross as they went, dividing into four companies, each going in a different direction. As they flew they sang such songs as birds had never sung before.

P REACHER TO THE BIRDS

When Francis rejoined the two friars on the road he told them, "I reproach myself that I have not done that before." From this time forth his life was to be full of similar incidents.

It was not merely in exuberance that he did these things, though a mood of exuberance had started him doing them. He wished to give the most marked expression possible to his sense of kinship with all created things, his personal kinship with every star in the skies and every flower in the field. Yet in him there is not the faintest trace of pantheism, even if there might be some substance to a thesis (not so far produced) that he was a sun worshiper. His great poem embraces all creation but centers in the sun. Nature was to him not a mother but a child of God, and therefore his sister. So as not to envelop it in an abstraction that might permit it to escape by amorphously dissolving, he thought of each object, even those that were inanimate, as having its own individuality. For him it was Brother Fire and Sister Water; as they were, like himself, creatures of God, he extended to them courtesy, almost deference.

A new power now seemed to descend upon Francis. He now had a firmer certainty as to his apostolic mission. He was not in the world merely for his own soul's good but for the salvation of others. And now his more intense love for his fellow men, made in the image of God and redeemed by Christ, made him reach out still more eagerly toward all creatures, as they were all in varying degrees mirrors of His goodness and beauty.

There had been open-air saints before. St. Patrick was one. He had to be to convert the sport-loving Irish. And there was St. Mamertinus of Gaul, whose story is told in the *Golden Legend*. He was like Francis of Assisi not only in his love for animals and his power over the birds, which flew down to his hands, but in his running after the robbers who had taken everything he had, to offer them a penny they had overlooked. Kindness to animals is not necessarily, or even often, a sign of holiness, though it always indicates something good. We should miss the main truth about Francis if we make too much of this single charming characteristic.

At the same time, it cannot be overlooked, and it is important that its real significance should not be missed. As Bonaventure, his biographer and a saint himself, puts it, "He beheld in fair things Him who is most fair, and through the traces of Himself imprinted on His creatures, followed to reach the Beloved." The whole world shone and twinkled with the glory of God, and the keener Francis's sense of that glory became, the more he loved the visible world which was the home God has made for man before taking him to his eternal home in heaven. Francis discerned earth's loveliness with the eyes of the heart, reaching through this to the essential Reality which is the true goal of all philosophy and all art.

In this matter, without preaching against Manichaean ideas, perhaps without being very conscious of their existence, he did more than any other man—more even than his theological friend, St. Dominic—to rid the world of their devastating horrors. And to a world that had become Christian—if the world has ever become that—he brought the beginnings of a poetry of a kind that it had hitherto lacked. It was the poetry of innocent wonder, a beauty seen through the wide, candid eyes of a child. As Chesterton finely expresses it, water itself was now washed, fire itself purified as by fire.

The light hearts of birds were to Francis the closest to his own. Their songs, their wings, their glad liberty—these always brought him a tender delight. It was noticed that his special affection among birds was given to the larks. He used to say, "Sister Lark has a cowl like a religious and she is a humble bird, going willingly by the road for her food. If she comes upon it in its foulness, she draws it out and eats it. But flying she praises God very sweetly like a good religious, despising earthly things. Her conversation is in the heavens and her intent is always to the praise of God. Her raiment is earth-colored, in which she gives an example to religious, for earth is the vilest of elements." Equally he would murmur, "I am a worm and no man," when picking a worm off a path where a foot might squash it, as he trod on rocks with reverential care because Christ was the Rock of Salvation.

He was simple by grace but not by nature, says Thomas of Celano. But our good Thomas was a very self-conscious person, at least when he took pen in hand, and one is inclined to question some of his judgments upon a man whom he did not know very well. This judgment, however, would seem to be sound, even though it calls for some amplification. Francis was a temperamental being with contradictory strains in his make-up. Had he lacked his focus, he would almost certainly have dissipated his gifts and come to nothing. This focus he obtained in his love of God, but the complexity of his personality remained, as a problem to himself and as a problem to everybody who wishes to study him, except to those who would reduce his activities to the picking of flowers and the petting of animals. That he was a genius is obvious; what is not so obvious was that he was also an extremely clever man; and, as so often happens, these two qualities clashed at times. They were reconciled in the only way possible; that is, by the surrender of all his talents to the Giver of all talents.

Francis's love for creatures was of a practical sort, for he was a practical man, even, one might almost say, when suggesting impractical ideas. When he said that he wished that the Emperor—fancy Frederick II doing this!—would order that food be thrown at Christmas for the birds and that all who had beasts in the stable should give them extra fodder that day in honor of Christ that was born in a stable, he could not have seriously expected that such a thing would happen. The point is that he wished that this practical kindness could be done. He was not merely suggesting something that might be taken up by the Society for the Prevention of Cruelty to Animals. All true love, without ignoring the useful, manifests itself most fully in what has no use at all except to express love. Fortunately, he was not merely a practical man, otherwise there would have been no sermon to the birds at Bevagna. It was so also with what happened the same day apparently—from the *Fioretti* one would gather that it had even happened before the sermon to the birds—when he told some twittering swallows to keep silence until he had finished what he was saying to a group in the square at Alviano. Something of the same kind happened in 1220 when, passing through some marshes near Venice, he suggested to his companion that they say their office among the birds they saw in the thickets. "Our sisters the birds," he said, "are praising their Creator; let us go among them and say our office in His praise." As they could not hear themselves speak in that tuneful din, Francis told the birds to be quiet until he had done. Like the birds at Alviano, they obeyed, until he courteously gave them a sign that they might renew their song.

As for singing, we hear of his once entering—surely rather rashly! —into a contest with a nightingale. At the time he was with Brother Leo, his secretary and confessor, and poor Leo pleaded that he had no voice, leaving Francis to engage the bird alone. He continued from Vespers to Lauds—that is, from the set of sun until after midnight—but in the end he had to admit that he was vanquished. After this he called the nightingale to him, and it perched on his hand while he fed it. Then, having had his blessing, it flew away.

As might be expected, song birds were dearest of all to him. But there was a waterfowl—not the kind of creature most people would wish to fondle—who came to him while he was in a boat on the lake at Rieti. It settled down into his hands as in a nest while he said his prayers and would not go away until he gave it permission. And there were the turtledoves he bought from a young man and carried home in his bosom, where they settled under his eye and raised their family. There was a rabbit with whom he made friends during his Lent on Lake Trasimeno and a leveret caught in a trap at Greccio which he rescued and which refused to leave him. And strangest pet of all was the tench with which he was presented by a fisherman at Rieti. He at once put it back in the water, but it kept following his boat and he kept calling it Brother Tench. Really, if a man can make friends with a fish . . . ! Hardly less strange was his friendship with a cicada that perched on a fig tree at the Portiuncula and whom he used to call to him and set singing the praises of God.

His taste was so catholic as almost to embrace the ants. Almost, but not quite. Though he commended their industry (for which quality the charitable old lady had a good word to say for the devil), they were not Franciscan enough to please him much, as they stored up grain so providentially. Yet he did, after all, recognize that they were performing the will of Their Creator; and he himself acted as special providence to a hive of bees when their honey ran short by giving them sugar and honey to keep them alive in a hard winter.

Francis was, of course, under no sentimental misapprehension about his sermons to the birds and the flowers being understood. Such sermons were not really addressed to them but to himself and any human hearers who happened to be standing by, though, of course, they did also express his love for the creatures addressed. By telling them to praise God—they who could do no other than praise Him by fulfilling the law of their nature—he was urging immortal souls and rational minds to give God the praise they owed but which they, unlike beings of a lower order, might and often did withhold. It was so when he preached to the fields, the rivers, the vineyards, and even the winds. In this he was only doing what the Three Boys in the canticle sung every day at Lauds had done, but where most Christians are content to leave these things embalmed in the liturgy, Francis gave them a piercingly personal application. A thousand times with his whole heart he summoned snow and dew, fire and heat, cold and hoarfrost to bless the Lord.

This much is understandable, for it appeals to the poetry in all of us. What is astonishing is the way that Francis treated things like fire and water as though they had personality. When he washed his hands and some drops fell to the ground he would not walk there lest, one supposes, he would hurt his sister. Nor did he like to extinguish Brother Fire, even in a candle. One day when the hem of his habit began to smolder as he was sitting by the hearth, he tried to stop the friar who wanted to smother it, crying gently, "Nay, dearest Brother, harm not Brother Fire!" Let us surmise that he was in no danger on that occasion, as there must have been limits to even his delicate consideration.

He would not permit trees to be cut down so low as to leave no chance for future growth. He trod lightly on grass and even (perhaps especially) on stones. These were brothers and sisters of his. It was this tenderness that gave him his power over animals. That was but another side of the power he exercised over men—that of a humble and affectionate gentleness.

As he was a Christian, he saw in every lamb the Lamb of God. It pained and grieved him when he saw a man going along the road with a couple of these little bleating creatures slung over his shoulders.

"Why are you tormenting my brothers?" Francis asked. "Where are you taking them?"

The man stared. Then he answered, "To the market."

"And then?"

"Then I will sell them."

"And then?"

"The buyers will kill and eat them, of course."

"God forbid! This must not be. Take the cloak I am wearing and give me the lambs."

After he had bought them Francis found that he did not know what to do with them, so he gave them back to the man, on condition that he was never to sell them or do them any harm—a promise no doubt faithfully kept.

Another lamb rescued by him in this way he gave to a convent of Sisters, where he could be more sure of its fate. Still another he gave to the Countess Settesoli (about whom we shall hear more later). Its wool provided the shroud in which he was buried.

The most famous of all such stories is that of the wolf of Gubbio. Before telling it, I offer a few preliminary remarks. One is that some people in our own time have had pets quite as fierce. Another is that the tale receives some corroboration in the fact that not many years ago a wolf's skull was found embedded beneath the walls of the church of St. Francis at Gubbio. And finally, even those who find it hard to believe that Francis did actually tame a wolf must have a good deal of credulity of another sort if—in face of all the other animal stories—they can accept the suggestion that by "wolf" was meant a robber baron converted by Francis! Both common sense and imagination recoil from that.

Here is the story. Gubbio was terrified by a wolf that was prowling in the neighborhood, so Francis went out to find it despite all warnings. The wild thing ran at him with bared fangs and Francis, making the sign of the cross, said, "Come here, Brother Wolf. I command you in the name of Christ not to do any more harm, either to me or anyone."

At that conjuration the wolf ran up and lay at the feet of Francis and got a gentle scolding for his misdeeds. It ended with a promise: "Brother Wolf, if it pleases you to make peace, the people of this place will give you food as long as you live, and I know that it is only because of hunger that you have done evil. Do you promise me that you will do no more harm to man or beast?"

To this the wolf gave his assent by bowing his head meekly. So Francis was able to say, "Brother Wolf, I bid you in the name of Jesus Christ to come with me, nothing doubting, to establish peace in God's name."

The wolf lived afterward for two years there, going in and out of the houses, so tame that not a dog barked at him. At length Brother Wolf died of old age and was mourned by all Gubbio, where he had come to be loved and where the sanctity of Francis seemed to shine in him.

FIRE IN DRY GRASS

Almost as astonishing as the fact of Francis himself is that he obtained so many disciples. This can only be because the time was ripe for him and what he offered men answered something deep in their needs, of which they were not conscious at all until he appeared. He was a providential man. Without him the history of the world would have been very different. Forces were at work in the early thirteenth century that might have resulted in a disaster as great as the religious revolt of the sixteenth century. These could easily have had the success they very nearly did attain had not Francis awakened a force of a different kind.

Francis and his movement were part of a still larger movement. He and Dominic appeared simultaneously, and their Orders, as much by instinct as by design, divided the field between them. The Dominicans were a learned body engaged in a mission that concentrated on speculative heresies, while the Franciscans went out to the simple and ignorant. This explains, in part, Francis's reluctance to enter the scholastic field, though by the pressure of events the Friars Minor were obliged to do this and soon became as prominent as the Preaching Friars in the schools. It was impossible for Francis to limit the scope of the work he had initiated, for the movement grew so rapidly that he was all but swamped by it and became rather bewildered. His success was so vast that he could not control it.

In this situation it eventually came about that the authorities of the Church, acting with a party that made itself dominant in the Order, to some extent took the management of affairs out of his hands. Such a development was inevitable. Francis was not of the executive or administrative type, his function being to inspire and then stand aside. What happened was, upon the whole, desirable, even though something charming was, if not quite lost, somewhat diminished in freshness. It is easy enough to understand that some of the first disciples, and even Francis himself, tended to look upon this process as a decline.

All those who have anything of the poet in them must regret that things could not go on forever as in the first idyllic days of the movement. We are apt to become disgusted when the poetry turns into prose and the dream fades in the light of day. Yet all such regrets are idle. It is like wishing that we could be young forever. What matters is that those who grow up do not forget the dream of their youth. It is that dream that we see now, the flowers of April before the fruit comes to ripeness.

The process that began during Francis's lifetime went much further after his death. Yet the core of the Franciscan message remains unaltered and is as powerful as ever. In all except the stoniest of hearts there is a sense, if only at fleeting moments, that pleasure and money, so far from being everything, may really be nothing. Nor does it need any mystical insight to realize this, for it is affirmed by all except the hedonistic philosophies. It was, however, to the religious instinct that Francis made, and still makes, his astonishing appeal. He offered to the world, not a set of abstract propositions, but the spectacle of a man inflamed with love of Christ and concerned only with the imitation of His life.

A word, sometimes only a look, sufficed to win a soul. We hear of villages converted in a body, of whole religious communities wishing to become Franciscan to aim at a higher perfection, of husbands going to the friars and of their wives joining Clare. All over the country little houses of the fraternity suddenly appeared like birds' nests in the spring, houses usually hardly more substantial than those nests.

Most of those who entered the Order were quite simple and often unlettered men, but nobles also joined and were among the humblest of the Brothers. Scholars and dignitaries followed. The Pope's secretary took the habit and only with difficulty was recalled to what were considered more important duties. Cardinal Ugolino, himself to be Pope before he died, thought of becoming a Franciscan friar.

Some of the stories about such cases have a good deal of charm. There is, for instance, one about a well-to-do gentleman who had often received Francis with great kindness and courtesy into his house. He told Francis, "I offer you myself and all my goods, so that if at any time you have need of anything come to me and I will buy it for you. For the love of God I will do all that I can for His poor."

After they left his house that day Francis said to his companion, "This courteous gentleman would be good for our Order, for know, dear Brother, that courtesy is one of the qualities of God himself. And because I have seen so much divine goodness in this man, I would like to have him as one of us. Pray that it may be so."

A few days later Francis said to his companion, "Let us go again, Brother, to the house of that courteous gentleman, for I have sure hope in God that with the same courtesy as he gives us temporal goods he will give himself to us." Before entering, Francis went a little way apart by himself and prayed with such fervor that he was surrounded by light and was raised from the ground in the phenomenon known as levitation. Looking out of his house, the courteous gentleman saw what was happening and ran toward Francis, crying, "What would you bid me to do, my Father? Lo! I am ready to do your bidding and give to the poor whatever I possess and, thus free from all material goods, to follow you."

Another story has a touch of humor. It concerns a learned man who arrived at Assisi mounted on a fine horse and with a quantity of baggage. He announced that he had come to join the friars. Francis wondered whether a descent of this kind indicated a real vocation, and the other Brothers had their doubts too. Finally one of them suggested, "Father, would you like to know what I think? I think that if this man is prepared to be our cook we should receive him, otherwise not." So Francis turned to the learned clerk and said, "Well, Brother, you have heard what has been said. What will you do?"

The man was speechless with consternation. When he recovered himself he answered, "Yes, I am willing to be your cook or anything else that you tell me." Then Francis recognized the true Franciscan metal. A cook he was for about a month, and then, having proved himself by his humility, he was appointed a preacher by Francis and made the guardian of a house of friars.

The spirit of the Order, which is the explanation of its success, was perhaps best described by Francis himself in the account he gave of what the perfect or "ideal" friar should be. He would have, Francis used to say, the faith of Bernard, the simplicity and purity

and love of poverty of Leo, the courtesy of Angelo, the good sense
and eloquence of Masseo, the contemplative mind of Giles, the
constancy in prayer of Rufino, who, even when sleeping, had his
mind always with the Lord, the patience and selflessness of Juniper,
the bodily and spiritual strength of John (presumably the "Florentine Bruiser" of whom we shall get a glimpse later), the charity of
Roger, and the lack of attachment to place of Lucido.

Such a catalogue of virtues tells us little about the individuals
mentioned, about some of whom we know nothing except that they
were held up to admiration by Francis. But we do have very vivid
stories about others in Francis's list. They were all typically "Franciscan", in spite of their striking differences in character from one
another. In this Order there was nothing of that regimentation
that tends to mold everybody into the same pattern.

Thus, Masseo was a handsome, portly man of impressive presence,
a strong contrast to Francis in this respect. By way of training him
Francis told him, "Brother, your companions have the grace for
contemplation and you the gift for preaching. Therefore to allow
them to give themselves more fully to prayer, I am going to make
you the doorkeeper." This order was hard, but Masseo received
it so humbly and carried it out so faithfully that everybody saw that
he must be a man of great perfection.

For this reason Francis liked to have him as his companion on his
journeys. On these he managed to find means of subjecting Masseo
to further tests, some of which seemed very puzzling. On one
occasion, when they came to a place where the roads branched in
three directions—to Siena, to Florence, and to Arezzo—Masseo
asked, "Father, by which way are we to go?"

Francis answered, "By the way that God wills."

Surprised by that, Masseo inquired further, "And how are we to
know the will of God?"

"By the sign that I shall show you. Turn round and round as
little children do and do not stop until I tell you to stop."

This Masseo did until he was giddy and fell down. But Francis
made him get up and go on, he himself keeping his hands over his
eyes. At last he said, "Now stop and tell me in which direction your
face is turned."

It was to Siena, and there Masseo discovered why Francis had
chosen this queer method for learning the will of God. The city was

in an uproar, one of the common factional fights being in progress. Then Masseo, who had been complaining in his heart at the ridiculous way Francis had made him act, saw that a divine purpose had brought them there. "You are too proud," he told himself, "for what he did proceeded from God's own working. Father Francis has brought peace to this city, where two men have been stabbed and where others, except for his coming, would have been killed and gone to hell. You are foolish to murmur against what is so manifestly proved to be the will of God."

Another lesson was given to Masseo one day when they went out begging. Francis brought little back, but the tall and affable Masseo did better, though even his contribution was only a few pieces of dry bread. These Francis laid out on a stone by a fountain, and said, "O Brother Masseo, we are not worthy of such a treasure!"

Treasure! Masseo could see none in the poor little repast, and he said so. To which came Francis's "And this is what I count vast treasure, when there is nothing prepared by human hands, but all is given by God's providence, in the bread we have and this fine table of stone and that clear fountain. So I will that we pray God to make us love with all our hearts the treasure of holy poverty He has given us, a treasure so rich that Our Lord himself accepted it."

It was not the least of Masseo's good qualities in the eyes of Francis that he was rather plain-spoken. Masseo thought it only fair to make a trial of the humility of the man who had so often subjected him to tests, so one day he said to Francis mockingly, "Why after *you*? Why after *you*?"

Francis asked, "What are you trying to say?"

"What I want to know is why does all the world run after you, and why is it that all men long to see you and hear you and obey you. For you are not comely of form, or of much wisdom or of noble birth. How is it that the whole world runs after you?"

False modesty was the last thing to be found in a soul so simple as that of Francis. He answered at once, "So you would like to know why men run after me? The holy eyes of God have seen among sinners none more vile, or more lacking in all gifts, or a greater sinner than I am. He could not have found anybody lower or viler than me. Therefore He has chosen me to confound the nobleness and strength and beauty and wisdom of the world, so that men may know that all goodness comes from Him and not from the creature, and that no man may glory in himself but give all to the glory of the Lord, in whom is honor and glory for ever and ever."

In the end Masseo found the humility he sought for. It came as a gift direct from God. Praying one day for this virtue, he heard a Voice from heaven, "What would you give for the grace you are asking for?"

Masseo answered, "Lord, I would give the eyes out of my head!"

To this Christ returned, "It is my will that you have this grace and your eyes too."

From that time Masseo was so humble that his life was flooded with joy. The eloquent preacher could find no words to express what was in his heart but little dovelike sounds, "Oo-oo-oo," a kind of song he went humming all day long. When one of the Brothers asked him why he never changed his note, Masseo turned on him with a shining face and said, "When one thing brings us full content, there is no need to change the note."

Giles was a peasant with a witty tongue, which he did not hesitate to use on extremely exalted personages. Thus, to a couple of cardinals who had called on him and who, on leaving, asked him to pray for them, he made the unexpected answer, "It is not necessary that I do that, my lords, for you have more faith and hope than I have."

When they asked him how he knew that, he returned, "Because you with all your power and place and honor hope to be saved, whereas I, who live in such poverty fear that in spite of all I shall be damned."

Personages even greater than cardinals went to see a man so renowned for sanctity. Among these visitors, according to a story in the *Fioretti*, was the King of France, St. Louis, who belonged to the Franciscan third order. Not a word was spoken. Each man knelt down and embraced the other as though they were intimate friends. There was no need to speak. After the king had departed Brother Giles was reproached for having given him this kind of reception, and he merely said, "Dear Brothers, do not marvel. Neither of us *could* speak a word. But as soon as we embraced the light of heavenly wisdom showed me his heart, and my heart to him. We knew what we would say far better than if we had spoken with our lips."

He was something of a privileged character and once interrupted an English Franciscan who was a Doctor of Divinity when he was preaching before Clare and her nuns at St. Damian's. "Be quiet, Master," Giles called out, "and let me preach!" Most meekly the startled foreign visitor came down from the pulpit and let the unlettered Giles say what he wished. After Giles had spoken under the inspiration of the Holy Ghost, he allowed the learned Englishman to continue. All this rejoiced the heart of Clare, for she saw in it what Francis would have most wished, a Doctor of Divinity so humble that he would silence himself and permit a lay brother to speak in his stead.

To a friar who complained to him that the guardian had sent for him to go out begging while he was deep in prayer, Giles said, "My son, you have not yet come to understand what prayer is. True prayer is to do the will of one's superior. It is a sign of pride in one who has entered religion, and taken upon himself the yoke of obedience, if he avoids it on the plea that he would do something even better. I tell you that if a man were so devout and uplifted in soul as to speak with angels, and while thus speaking he was called by his superior, he ought instantly to leave the converse of the angels to obey the one set over him."

The *Fioretti* abounds with stories about Giles and his wise and salty sayings. One is of a time when he was staying with the Cardinal Nicholas of Tusculum at Rome. In that palace he would never eat of any of the good things set before him but insisted on going out every day to beg his own bread, and this he would bring to the cardinal's table. Then there came a day of heavy rain and the cardinal gleefully told Giles, "This day at least you will not be able to go out and so will have to eat the food I give." But Giles was equal even to that occasion. He went to the kitchen and arranged with the cook that he would scrub the floor for a couple of small loaves. These he produced in triumph when the cardinal's guests went to table.

Though he could not have had much education, being a peasant, he managed to acquire some, and there are some sonnets that he is supposed to have written. Of his many apothegms that have been preserved, here are a few: "If you love, you will be loved. Yet blessed is the man who truly loves and does not seek love in return." "If a man possessed perfect faith, he would soon come to a state of perfection in which he would have full certainty of his salvation."

"No man can come into any knowledge and understanding of God except by the virtue of holy humility." "He who does not fear shows that he has nothing to lose. If a man possesses any grace or divine virtue, it is holy fear that keeps it safe. Yet this gift of fear is not given save to the perfect, for the more perfect a man is, the more he fears, the more he humbles himself." "The heritage of the saints is always to do good and always to receive evil." "When a man wishes to do evil, he never needs much counsel as to how to do it; but for doing good, many men seek counsel and make long delay."

Often his wisdom was cast in parabolic form. Thus, he once asked a judge, "Do you believe that the gifts of God are great?" and the judge answered, "I do believe that." Giles pressed further, "I will prove to you that you do not really believe this. What is the value of your possessions?" "Perhaps they are worth a thousand pounds." "Would you not exchange these possessions for ten thousand pounds?" The judge laughed and said, "I would and very willingly." Then Giles made his unanswerable point, "Verily all the possessions of this world are as naught in respect to the things of heaven. Why then do you not give your possessions to Christ and so gain those that are celestial and eternal?"

Giles wore the Franciscan habit for fifty-three years, dying in 1262 on the anniversary of his admission to the Order. Some of the new men looked on him as an oddity, but he also found starry-eyed enthusiasts who loved to hear him talk of Francis and the early days. He was one of those who helped to keep the pure flame undimmed. But naturally enough he disapproved of the friars becoming learned men. "Paris! Paris! You have destroyed the Order of St. Francis!" was his comment on this. There is a story of how he once asked the learned Brother Bonaventure whether an ignorant man could be saved.

"Of course," said Bonaventure, "if he loves God."

"Can an ignorant man love God as much as one who is a scholar?"

"Many an old woman loves God better than a Doctor of Divinity," was the answer.

Giles had extracted what he wanted. He had a sense of mischief, so he hastened out and cried to a group of people who were waiting to see the learned Bonaventure. "Listen all of you," cried Giles. "Any old woman who is not able to read and write can love God better than Brother Bonaventure!"

Juniper has been represented to us in the legends of the *Fioretti* as almost to appear a clown. Actually he was a highly intelligent man and a very effective preacher. Clare had a special affection for him, which itself would prove that he was a good deal more than quaint, or a dear old, old fool. One can well believe that Francis said after one of his escapades, "Would that I had a forest of Junipers!"

Some of the stories told of him are manifestly pure fiction, especially that revolting tale of his cutting a foot off a live pig because a sick Brother had expressed a fancy for that delicacy. So also is the story of his having once cooked a fortnight's food at one time for the community, throwing into the pots together fresh meat, unplucked chickens, eggs in their shells, and unprepared vegetables. According to the legend, he then went to the Brothers and said, "Now you can eat well and we need not think about preparing dinner for a long time but give ourselves to prayer undisturbed!" Not even a Franciscan could swallow a mouthful of that gruesome stew; there was no pig in the land that would have touched it. One can easily understand how such anecdotes came to be related. "Why, Brother Juniper," someone would say, "He would cut off a pig's trotter if anybody said he wanted it!" It was a good way of enlivening recreation periods to invent Juniperisms.

Yet we can believe that a party of dignitaries going out to welcome him found him playing seesaw with some children. So also with his cutting off the silver fringe of the altar cloths when he had nothing else to give the poor, and his saying to a beggar, "The guardian has ordered me not to give away my tunic. But of course if you like to *take* it from me . . ." And the following story rings true. One of the successors of Francis had scolded Juniper so long and so vigorously for one of his absurdities that his voice grew hoarse. Noticing this and pitying the poor minister-general, Juniper prepared a pottage of flour and butter that he thought would do his throat good. This he took to the general's cell late at night, only to be greeted with a cross: "What hour is this that you come disturbing people!" Juniper, not in the least abashed, said, "It would do you good, but if you will not eat it, then please hold the candle for me and I will, so that it may not go to waste." At this the general, won over by Juniper's benign simplicity, said, "Come, as you will have it so, we will eat it together." This they did, and found themselves more refreshed by the brotherly kindness than by the food.

We have to take some of the *Fioretti* stories with a grain of salt. The book is largely a collection of anecdotes gathered from various sources, some far from reliable. So one suspects the tale of the simple-minded Brother John (he to whose poor family Francis returned the oxen) who is said to have carried his imitation of Francis to such lengths that he copied all his gestures, coughed when Francis coughed, and spat when Francis spat. As with the Juniper legends, this appears to be a humorous exaggeration that nobody was intended to take seriously. On the other hand, much in this book, as in the *Mirror of Perfection* and the *Legend of the Three Companions*, obviously derives from Brother Leo, the last survivor of the early Franciscans. This guarantees their authenticity, though, if it comes to that, they usually authenticate themselves by touches that could have been given only by an eyewitness of events. Of these, two may be given here. They contain all the perfume of primitive Franciscanism.

Francis and Leo could not say their office because they had no breviary with them, so Francis said, "Brother Leo, Little Lamb of God, so that we may spend our time in praising God, you must say what I tell you to say without changing a word. Repeat now, 'Brother Francis, you have done so much evil and have committed so many sins that you are deserving of the lowest hell.'"

Leo had agreed with dovelike simplicity to say whatever he was told to say, but the words that emerged from him were, "God will work so much good through you that you will go to paradise."

Francis was disgusted. "No, no, no!" he cried. "Say instead, 'Brother Francis, you have done so many iniquities that you deserve to be accursed of God.'"

Leo replied, "I will say that right willingly, Brother Francis. God has done so much for you, that among the blessed you shall be blessed."

Francis again cried in dismay, "Why do you not answer as I have ordered you? I command you by holy obedience to say what I tell you to say: 'Brother Francis, vile wretch, seeing that you have committed so many sins, you are not worthy to find mercy.' Now repeat that."

And Leo repeated, "God, whose mercy is infinitely greater than your sins, will show you mercy and pour many graces upon you."

Francis was now angry. He said, "Why are you so bold as to act contrary to obedience and say the opposite of what I have told you to say?"

Then Leo said most humbly and reverently, "God knows, my Father, that each time I meant to answer in the way you wished, but God makes me to speak according to what he wills and not according to what you will. But try me again; this time I will answer as you wish."

So Francis said, "Say, 'Oh Brother Francis, vile wretch, do you think God will have mercy upon you?'"

And Leo replied, "Nay rather, great grace shall you receive from God and he shall exalt you and glorify you for ever. And I can say nothing else, for God is speaking through my mouth."

In this way they kept watch from the hour of Matins until break of day.

There was another time when Leo and Francis were on their way home to the Portiuncula from Perugia on a cold, snowy day, Leo going ahead and Francis following. They had just left behind them the bridge of San Giovanni where Francis long years before had been taken prisoner in the only battle in which he had ever fought. Now Francis called to Leo, "Brother Leo, though the Friars Minor through all the world were great exemplars of sanctity, nevertheless write it down that not in this is perfect joy."

A little further on Francis called again, "Brother Leo, though the Brothers should give sight to the blind, make the crooked straight, cast out devils, make the deaf to hear and the lame to walk, the dumb to speak and even raise the dead, write that not in this would be perfect joy."

He went on: to speak with the tongues of angels, to know the courses of the stars and all the properties of natural things, to preach so as to convert all the world—not even in this would be perfect joy.

At last Leo turned round and asked, "Then tell me in the name of God whence comes perfect joy."

Then Francis told him, "When we come to Saint Mary of the Angels, all soaked as we are with rain and numb with cold and covered with mud, and hungry, and knock at the door and are answered by the porter in anger: 'Who are you?' and we reply, 'We are two of your Brothers,' and get from him only, 'No, you are two rogues who go about deceiving the world and robbing the poor. Get you gone!'; and if he should slam the door in our faces and leave us outside in the snow and cold, if we endure such wrongs patiently, then Brother Leo, write that in this is perfect joy. And if we knocked again only to be turned away again, there would be in this perfect joy. And if we knocked a third time begging him for the love of God to let us in, and he came out in a rage shouting, 'These are importunate rascals; I will give them what they deserve!' And if he should use his cudgel on us and knock us down, and we endured it all, thinking of the sufferings of Christ, oh Brother Leo, write that in this is perfect joy. Here is the whole matter: above all the graces and gifts of the Holy Spirit granted by Our Lord to his beloved, is the overcoming of oneself, and being willing for Christ to bear pains and insults and shame and want. For in all other gifts of God we may not glory, as they are not ours but God's. But in the cross of tribulation and affliction we may boast, for this is ours. Therefore let us say with the Apostle, 'I would not that I should glory save in the cross of Our Lord Jesus Christ.' "

Brother Leo did write it down. It must have been from the *rotuli,* those rolls of parchment on which Brother Little Lamb of God put down his reminiscences of Francis, that this and many other Franciscan flowers have come down to us.

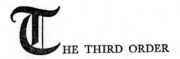

HE THIRD ORDER

It is no detraction from the originality of Francis to point out that he had forerunners. Even with regard to absolute poverty, the distinguishing mark of his life, he would have been the first to declare that it was simply a return to the manner of life of Our Lord and His Mother and the Apostles. So also with one of the most striking features of the organization he effected, the creation of the third order.

This was not quite the first time such a group had existed. The Benedictines had, as they still have, an extension of the monastic family in a number of lay men and women affiliated to this or that abbey and living according to the spirit of St. Benedict's Rule. And the Premonstratensians, whose preaching might have anticipated the work done by Francis and Dominic better than it actually did, had their tertiaries associated with the main order, in whose spiritual merits they shared and in whose habit they had the right to be buried, in which respect they resembled the Benedictine Oblates.

Moreover, at the start of the thirteenth century there was formed in Lombardy a group of lay people, into whose hands the woolen trade of Milan largely came, who constituted something very similar, except that they were a body unattached to a clerical order. They had a religious rule, though (like the Oblates before them and the tertiaries that followed) they were not bound by monastic vows but lived, except for their distinguishing dress and the devoutness of their lives, like ordinary Christians. This rule of theirs did, in fact, provide Cardinal Ugolino with a model when he persuaded Francis to organize his third order.

Of the many such groups that now exist—for the Dominicans soon copied the Franciscans, with the Carmelites and Servites and others later—the Franciscan third order is beyond all comparison the most numerous and, indeed, exceeds all the others put together, amounting to about two million members. These are today the main instrument of Franciscan influence.

The third order was not part of Francis's original designs and came into organized being relatively late in his life. At first the friars and the Poor Ladies of Clare and the immense fringe of their disciples and friends seem to have been thought of as constituting a single society. This was natural enough, for at the outset the Brothers themselves were looked upon as a movement rather than an order in the usual sense. Their rule had received only verbal and tentative approbation from the Holy See and developed (as the Order did) under the pressure of necessity. Still more was this true of the third order. What was in the beginning quite informal received form, as it was inevitable that it would, but apparently not until 1221. Though a rule was drawn up then, the earliest version of it that we have dates from 1228, by which time Francis was dead.

Francis thought of himself as having the conversion of sinners as his mission, but he converted so many of them and so thoroughly as to bring about what might almost be called an embarrassing situation. Many of his converts wished to enter religion, but, though large numbers were admitted, it was altogether impossible to handle such a multitude. Francis was therefore called upon to exercise a good deal of tact. He saw that he must not discourage their fervor and piety, and yet it was inadvisable to allow anybody who did not have an unmistakable vocation to lay upon himself the burden of the three vows. He would therefore tell them, "Do not be in a hurry, neither leave your homes. I will order what you are to do for the salvation of your souls." It is worth remarking that the third Franciscan to be canonized—only shortly after Francis himself and St. Anthony of Padua—was the tertiary, St. Elizabeth of Hungary. Over a hundred members of the third order now have been either canonized or beatified, a signal proof of its capacity to develop sanctity of the highest degree among men and women living in the world.

A fairly frequent practice among those of the penitents who were married and had domestic obligations, often including children to support, was that of husband and wife living as brother and sister. But though this sometimes caused the members of the third order to be referred to as the "continents," an absolute continence was never part of their obligations, even though it may have been encouraged. The instance cited by Thomas of Celano was, no doubt, common. It was that of a young married woman who went to Francis and told him, "Father, I have a very cruel husband who is an adversary to me in serving Jesus Christ, and my greatest grief is that I cannot perform the good wherewith the Lord has inspired me, because my husband hinders me. Wherefore I beseech you, holy man, to pray that God will soften his heart."

Francis blessed her and said, "Go, my daughter, and know that you shall soon have consolation of your husband." What that "consolation" was comes out from the rest of the story, for when the woman's husband was touched by the Holy Ghost, he said, "Lady, let us serve God and save our souls in our own house." To which she quickly answered, "It seems to me that continence should be laid in the soul like a foundation and that the other virtues should be built on it." He agreed, and they lived in this way for the rest of their days together.

Obviously, that was altogether too much to expect of all who entered the third order, nor would it have been desirable on any widespread scale. Those who were able to adopt this very difficult mode of life—all the more difficult, it need hardly be said, because of the fact that they *were* married—served to elevate the ideals of the other tertiaries, in much the same way as the presence among them of priests and nuns vowed to celibacy demonstrates to the ordinary mass of men that the chastity enjoined by the Commandments is not beyond the attainment of everybody.

Other regulations, these of a definite and formal kind, had a considerable effect on society. The point enjoined in the Rule about making a will was very much to the good. It was designed to avoid family disputes. Furthermore, it made it impossible for a feudal lord to seize the possessions of his serf, if he was a tertiary, as the lord could do in the case of one who died intestate.

The prohibition against the bearing of arms was also most salutary. Under the claims of feudalism, at a time when all sorts of small wars were fought between rival barons, tenants could be summoned to march under a feudal lord's banner. Now members of the third order could plead exemption. It made the holders of feudal lands very angry to lose so large a source of military strength, but the Church upheld the tertiaries. So many men became tertiaries—often, no doubt, with a view to escaping military service—that Pierre de Vigne, the Chancellor of Frederick II, complained most bitterly that almost all the people of Italy belonged to one or another of the third orders. Though this was, like most such statements, an exaggeration, there were enough tertiaries seriously to disrupt the belligerent schemes of the nobility and even to contribute to the undoing of the imperial party in its conflict with the papacy. We have here one of the causes of the breakdown of a feudal system that had long ceased to have any good social purpose.

Another effect of far-reaching importance was the recognition of the third order as a religious corporation, subject to the ecclesiastical and not the secular courts. They formed a society within society and as such brought about a good many changes, all to the good, in the social framework. That such changes were not designed by

Francis—nor, still less, foreseen by him—does not alter the fact that the Franciscans and Dominicans created a means of protecting the common people from injustice that served to preserve peace in the turbulent Italian communes.

It was, however, inevitable that some abuses should occur and that in an enthusiasm of this sort eccentrics should sometimes cut strange capers. An instance of this was when a friar named John of Compello—sometimes identified, though it would seem wrongly, with John da Capella, one of the first twelve—gathered around him a band of lepers, both men and women, and went wandering with them around the country. He even tried to get them formed into a religious order, and some have seen in this escapade (which occurred in 1219 while Francis was abroad) the beginnings of the tertiaries as an organized group. That it certainly was not; but it may have been that an incident of this sort brought Francis to a realization that the old free and easy methods with the Franciscan fringe would no longer serve. It was, at all events, two years afterward that the forming of this large, amorphous, Franciscan following into a definite society with definite rules and duties and privileges occurred.

Yet it must be remembered that John of Compello's plans, though strongly disapproved of by Francis, could, after all, be represented as being in line with Franciscan work. Francis had begun by tending the lepers in their little hospital near Assisi and he continued to regard such activities as a feature of his work. As lodgings in the lazar houses were of the most cheerless sort, he frequently stayed there, even when other quarters were available.

Not only is this true but the tertiaries commonly made the care of lepers their charge. They did so, however, not so much under formal rule but as a means of imitating Francis, or because they were inspired by a motive of compassion similar to his own. St. Louis of France emulated Francis in this matter and used to dress leprous ulcers with his own hands, and when dying he ordered that a large part of his personal fortune be used to erect two thousand badly needed lazar houses in his realm. The same deep compassion for lepers was shown by another royal tertiary, St. Elizabeth of Hungary. She frequently horrified her long-suffering but devoted husband with this form of her charity. We can sympathize with his feeling that, when she had laid a leper in her own bed, she had gone altogether too far. It was then that he angrily pulled aside the curtains and saw in the bed not a leper but Christ.

A miracle of that sort might happen where a saint was concerned, but it was obvious that common sense had to be shown by ordinary persons on ordinary occasions. And as such a scheme as that of John of Compello was only one way in which zeal could degenerate into fanaticism and undo all real good, Francis, who, in spite of all his poetic fervor, had a well-balanced head on his shoulders, perceived that system and regulation were necessary if enthusiasm were to be properly employed. The organization of the third order was for a number of reasons a practical necessity.

If the names of only a few of the Brothers and still fewer of Clare's nuns appear in the chronicles, it is no more than to be expected that we find specific mention of only a handful of this vast crowd of tertiaries. One was the Count Orlando dei Cattani, who gave Francis the retreat of the mountain of La Verna. He and the Countess Settesoli, of whom we shall hear more in a while, were unable, because their possessions were the feudal holdings of their families and not under their unrestricted personal control, to qualify for admission to the first or second orders, for that would have necessitated distributing everything to the poor. Moreover, the countess, when she was left a widow, had to act as the administrator of the Frangipani estates of her husband for the benefit of their young sons. But there was no woman, Clare alone excepted, who was a more intimate friend of Francis's than the one whom he used playfully to call "Brother Jacoba," a way of indicating the very special relationship she had to the Franciscan movement. In Rome her house was always his, and when he lay dying it was to her alone that he sent a message that she should come to him at once.

Many people of noble blood were attracted by the Franciscan idea to the extent of becoming members of the third order, and since the time of Francis we have among his tertiaries a line of poets from Dante to Coventry Patmore and Francis Thompson, artists like Michelangelo, men of action like Christopher Columbus, and scientists like Galvani. But, of course, the overwhelming mass of the tertiaries were, as is true of the friars themselves, people of humble station. The rich and the famous were not excluded, but the Franciscan mission was primarily for the laboring classes.

The story of two of these—Luchesio and his wife Buona Donna, is typical. They were, according to tradition, the first two tertiaries by actual enrollment, though we hear as early as 1210 of Cardinal John of St. Paul asking to be counted as one of the Brothers. It is certain that the association with the Franciscan Order of Count Orlando and the Countess Settesoli—to go no further—long antedated the formal organization of the first tertiary group near Florence in 1221. Luchesio and Buona Donna were living in that neighborhood and may well have taken the lead in this.

But their story is what matters.

Luchesio had not always been very pious. In fact, he seems to have had good reason for scruples over the means he had used to acquire his fortune, made by cornering grain in a bad harvest. Upon his conversion he gave away all that he owned, except a small farm which he worked with his own hands, helped by his beautiful young wife. The Franciscans encouraged those under their influence to give up mercantile pursuits, as these often involved practices of doubtful honesty and were conducive to avarice, and to take to farming instead.

They received the Franciscan habit from Francis and, so far as this was feasible in their station, they practiced the Franciscan virtues, living "according to the Gospel." Their cottage became a kind of hostelry at which any poor person was welcome; it was also a hospital in which the poor were received. Luchesio would even go into the malarial marshes of the Maremma and bring a sick man home, holding him up on a mule or even carrying him on his own back. These Buona Donna would nurse.

In the beginning she was sometimes irritated by her husband's excessive generosity. One day she upbraided him, saying, "Where am I to find food for them? Oh brainless head made weak by too much fasting!"

He answered serenely, "In the bin." And there, sure enough, the bread was, miraculously provided! After that she never complained again, though the produce of their little farm so often proved insufficient for their charities that they had to go out to beg for themselves as well as for their poor.

They lived together in this way nearly forty years, wearing the

Franciscan habit and engaged in their good works. Then Buona Donna fell ill and Luchesio saw that she was about to die. "You know, dear one," he said to her, "that we have loved one another all our lives, and served God together. Why should we be parted by death? Wait for me. I will call back the priest."

Gazing at his dying wife, Luchesio felt death coming upon him. So he received the last sacraments and, as soon as she was gone, stretched himself beside her and with her went to paradise. It was April 28, 1260.

UGOLINO'S GUIDING HANDS

Francis himself did not write the Rule for his third order, though in some of the early and uncritical editions of his works, all of which can be contained in one small volume, it is offered as his. But Archbishop Robinson's translation of the *opuscula,* in which he follows the Quaracchi editors, though not slavishly, omits this altogether. It is certainly the work of Cardinal Ugolino.

The cardinal doubtless consulted Francis. We get the spirit that Francis inculcated in his "Letter to All the Faithful", a document designed primarily for circulation among the tertiaries, if not exclusively for them. Here specific regulations such as appeared in the Rule are absent. But the guiding principles are evident, as in such a passage as the following: "We ought to fast and to abstain from vices and sins and from superfluity of food and drink, and to be Catholics. We ought also to visit churches frequently and to reverence clerics not only for themselves, if they are sinners, but on account of their office and administration of the most holy Body and Blood of Our Lord Jesus Christ, which they sacrifice on the altar and receive and administer to others. And let us know for certain that no one can be saved except by the Blood of our Lord Jesus Christ and by the holy words of the Lord which clerics say and announce and distribute and they alone administer and not others."

Here we find once again Francis's affirmation of his Catholicism. He was at the same moment submissive to the authorities of the Church and free. Though the direction that Francis received from those authorities may not always have been just the kind he himself would have preferred, far deeper than his personal preferences was his desire to be under the direction of the Church. Without that direction his work would have seemed to him to have no meaning. In it was his security, even when his own ideas were not entirely accepted. Finally it should be said that there was far less modification of his purposes than has sometimes been suggested. And even that, seen in the light of the history of his Order, was the kind of modification in regard to details that saved the general plan.

For Francis, as for the whole Church, a decisive date was 1215 when the Fourth Lateran Council was held. This he attended in his capacity as head of a religious order, though he was then (and remained) no more than a deacon. This was the great reform council of the Middle Ages and was presided over, in the person of Innocent III, by one of the most remarkable men ever to occupy the papal throne.

To sharpen and simplify what was accomplished by its decrees, it may be said that the council was primarily concerned with two crusades—one, the fifth attempt on the part of Christendom to wrest the Holy Places from the grip of Islam; the other, a crusade for the destruction of heresy within the body of western Europe. The doctrinal aspect of this internal crusade was entrusted to Dominic, whose order of preachers was established and approved in 1216, but the Franciscans were thought of as playing an equally important role in revivifying Christian life. To further this, strict obligations were imposed upon all bishops to preach and to provide preachers.

It was on this occasion that Innocent III delivered his famous sermon on the ninth chapter of Ezekiel, in which he declared himself as typifying "the man clothed in white linen with a writer's inkhorn at his loins." Upon nobody present was a greater impression made than upon Francis by the words, "Go through the midst of the city, through the midst of Jerusalem, and mark *thau* upon the foreheads of the men that sigh and mourn for all the abominations that are committed in the midst thereof." From that time forth he took the Hebrew *T,* the cross minus only Pilate's inscription, as his private sign manual.

It was at this time that Francis probably first met Dominic. He had established himself at Toulouse and had come to Rome to seek approbation for the founding of his order. He was restricted by a regulation of the council which forbade the drawing up of any further religious rules and so had to base his upon that of St. Augustine, whereas Francis, because his Rule had been approved (though only provisionally), was able to retain the general lines of the one he had submitted to Innocent in 1210. It made possible the retention of the distinctive Franciscan character in later years when pressure was brought to bear upon him to conform more closely to the prevailing concepts of monasticism.

What was more important than this and the subsequent meetings with Dominic was the fact that Francis soon afterward came under the direction of Cardinal Ugolino, who was to play a very decisive part in Franciscan history, and who seems to have become the official protector of the Order not long after the council.

That office had hitherto been held by Francis's first friend in the Roman Curia, the Cardinal John of St. Paul. He does not appear to have exercised much more than a benevolent interest, possibly because matters had not yet developed sufficiently to warrant direct and positive intervention on his part, but probably also because he was of a gentle and retiring nature.

With Ugolino, who was Cardinal Bishop of Ostia and also papal legate for central and northern Italy, it was different. He was a forceful character, and his position demanded that he should actively supervise all that was happening in the territories under his legatine authority. Moreover, he had a special concern in monastic reform and a statesmanlike scheme for using the two new Orders of friars to the best possible advantage. Even so, we shall do the cardinal a grave injustice if we think of him as dictating Franciscan policy or doing much more than guiding it when he was asked for his advice. The Three Companions report him as saying to Francis, "I do offer myself unto you, ready to afford you help, counsel and protection, according to your good pleasure." We shall also do an injustice if we fail to see that he did more than anybody else to give the order the form and stability without which it might have come to little.

He became protector of the Order at Francis's express request. Francis saw that the Brotherhood was growing so very rapidly that the control of this vast multitude of Brothers, nearly all new to the religious life, was getting beyond his unaided power. "It therefore behooves me," he said, "to commend them unto Holy Church."

Accordingly he went to Honorius III, the new Pope, and said, "My lord, I have pity for you, by reason of the anxiety and perpetual toil wherewith you must needs keep watch on behalf of the Church of God, and sore ashamed am I that you should have so much care and anxiety for us, Brothers Minor. For while many nobles, and rich men, and very many religious cannot enter into your presence, great awe and shamefastness there ought to be in us, that be poorer and more despised than the other religious, not only in entering your presence, but even in standing before your threshold and daring to knock on the Tabernacle of Christendom. Wherefore I do humbly and devoutly beseech Your Holiness that you will deign to grant this Lord Bishop of Ostia to be our Father, that in time of need the Brethren may resort to him, saving always the dignity of your presence."

Francis treated the cardinal with such reverence that he made it his custom to address him in letters not as Bishop of Ostia but as Bishop of the Whole World. This may have been, in part, a prophecy that Ugolino would eventually become Pope, but its main point was that, so far as the Franciscan Order was concerned, Ugolino was this, in effect, already.

As for the cardinal, Celano relates that he "conformed himself to the behavior of the Brethren, and in his longing for holiness was simple with the simple, humble with the humble and a poor man with the poor. He was a Brother among the Brethren, among the lesser least, and strove as far as might be to bear himself in life and conduct just like one of the rest." He goes on to say that he would often put off his costly garments and, arrayed in the Franciscan habit, walk barefoot among the friars. Ugolino did, in fact, seriously think of joining them, and must be counted among the tertiaries, who were organized at his suggestion and along the lines he proposed.

One may surmise that this request for Ugolino as protector followed a sermon preached by Francis before the Pope and the assembled cardinals during the winter of 1218–19. Ugolino, to make sure that Francis acquitted himself well before so august an audience, made his protégé learn a sermon by heart—according to one account, even writing this sermon for him. When the time came for its delivery Francis could not remember a word of it. Therefore he fell back upon his usual method of preaching by direct inspiration. The cardinal must have been in an agony of suspense, and this increased when, his prepared sermon forgotten, Francis nevertheless proceeded in his own way and was so carried out of himself that, while he spoke, his feet seemed to dance. There was a serious danger that the Pope and the cardinals would have thought the performance ridiculous. Instead they were deeply impressed. So much so that Francis shrewdly recognized that this was an excellent opportunity for approaching the Pope with his request that Ugolino be appointed to a supervisory jurisdiction.

If there was any conflict between the ideas of Francis and the cardinal, it is obvious that Francis must bear at least some share of responsibility for this because of having asked for his appointment. However, there does not seem to have been any of that thwarting and even betrayal of which the protector of the friars has sometimes been accused. This is not to say, of course, that Francis, had he been left to himself, would always have acted as Ugolino did. But Francis did not wish to be left to himself. He had sought the cardinal out for his personal qualities and because he felt the need of a person in authority to guide him in the name of the Church. Ugolino was the best choice he could have made. As Gregory IX he became the first codifier of canon law and has sometimes been called the Justinian of the Church. Though he was not the very great statesman that Innocent III was, he had a good deal of the statesman in his composition. He was the sort of practical man who gave substance and direction to ideals that might, without him, have soon evaporated. As Dr. Burkitt truly remarks, "It would have been more picturesque if the Friars had remained in their primitive poverty and simplicity—only we should never have heard of them at all." Something had to be sacrificed to save the Franciscan idea or, rather, to make it workable among a large and rapidly increasing number of men, few of whom could have had much personal contact with

Francis himself. If there is any element of tragedy in what follows, it is that of the tragedy inherent in the imperfection of human nature.

In view of all the suggestions that have been made about shrewd ecclesiastical politicians diverting idealism to their own ends, the remarkable fact is how much sympathy Francis received from the very highest officials of the Church even from the start, when he was quite unknown and might have been subject to suspicion. The favor of the Church toward Francis—one is inclined to say its favoritism —was constantly shown but, perhaps, never more than in the giving of the Portiuncula Indulgence, something that occurred before Ugolino had officially taken Francis under his wing though, per- haps, not before he was showing (unofficially) some interest in his work.

First perhaps one should briefly explain in a book of this sort what is meant by an indulgence and how unprecedented at the time such an indulgence was.

An indulgence is not a pardon for sins that have been committed. In fact, it is obtainable only if the soul is free from sins of the graver sort and is in a state of grace. In the giving of an indulgence the temporal penalties that God imposes upon the sinner are re- mitted, either in part or entirely.

An indulgence was therefore one of the greatest incentives to the making of such a pilgrimage and accounts for the opposition that arose to the granting of Francis's request.

Only Francis could have carried such a thing off successfully. Coming from anybody else the request would have been regarded as preposterous and would have been rejected at once, with a severe reprimand for being presumptuous. Only Francis's humility and reputation for sanctity and, perhaps, his disarmingly naïve air gave him any chance of success.

Honorius was at Perugia when Francis, accompanied by Brother Masseo, went before him and said, "My lord and Holy Father, of late I have repaired a church in honor of the glorious Virgin. I beseech Your Holiness to bestow on it an indulgence which is to be granted without any oblations."

Such a request made the Pope gasp, but he answered mildly, "This cannot conveniently be done, for whoever seeks an indulgence should stretch forth a helping hand to deserve it. But tell me for how many years you want it and how great an indulgence I am to bestow."

To this the Pope got the answer, "Holy Father, may it please Your Holiness to grant not years but souls?"

"What do you mean by souls?"

"Holy Father, I desire that all who shall come into that church contrite and confessed and absolved by the priest, shall be freed from all punishment from the day of their baptism until the hour of their entrance into that church."

The Pope said, "This is a very extraordinary thing that you seek, Francis. The Roman Curia has never been accustomed to grant such an indulgence."

To which Francis answered, "My Lord, what I am seeking is not on my own behalf but on behalf of Him who sent me, Our Lord Jesus Christ."

Moved by that, for Honorius was convinced of Francis's sincerity, he said, "It is our will that you should have it." He repeated these words thrice.

Now the cardinals present intervened. They protested that such an indulgence would be to the prejudice of the Holy Places and that nobody would make the arduous and dangerous journey there if a plenary indulgence could be obtained by a pilgrimage to the Portiuncula. Under this pressure the Pope, though he would not go back upon his word, restricted the indulgence to one day a year.

Even that was something unheard of. For this reason Francis was careful not to trumpet too loudly what he had obtained, lest further pressure be brought to bear on the Pope to withdraw his favor. It was possibly shrewdness as much as simplicity that led Francis to accept what he had been given without having it put down in writing. When Honorius called to him as he was leaving, "Simpleton, what have you got to show that this indulgence has been given you?" Francis returned blithely, "Holy Father, I have your word and that is sufficient. The Blessed Virgin Mary shall be my charter."

The account of this appears in the *Legend of the Three Companions* but is clearly an appendix that wears the look of having been added later. The lack of official documentary attestation and, still more, the secrecy with which the Franciscans prudently surrounded the matter have led some people to question whether this indulgence was given at all. It is to be noted, however, that though Paul Sabatier and Johannes Jörgensen were among those who disputed the historicity of the fact, they both later announced themselves convinced by the evidence, as this includes a number of statements sworn to before a notary later in the thirteenth century. There is no need to argue the question here.

The essence of the matter is that Francis, in his love for souls, was longing for some means whereby, short of going on a crusade or making a pilgrimage to the Holy Land, the poor and simple might benefit. It was with radiant joy that he went into the pulpit when the restored St. Mary of the Angels was reconsecrated and announced, "I want to send you all to paradise!" That the indulgence had been conferred is another instance of the idealism of the Church and the furtherance that was given in the very highest quarters to what Francis was attempting to do.

We find indications in the chronicles that Francis's previous friend in the Curia, the Cardinal John of St. Paul, had done a good deal of quiet spadework for him and so had prepared the way for his later success. He interested several of the other cardinals in the Brotherhood, so much so that some of these tried to attach friars to their entourage, not so much for any service the friars might render as because they liked to have holy men near them. It was a state of affairs that was somewhat embarrassing. Not always was it possible to refuse such well-intentioned invitations, and yet a protracted stay out of their environment was detrimental to those called to such an absolute poverty. Their sanctity made them esteemed, and then the esteem was liable to destroy their sanctity.

Perhaps an even greater danger arose from the plan Cardinal Ugolino devised of drawing upon the two Orders of friars for bishops. Between 1215 and 1218 Francis and Dominic met several times and formed a close friendship, dissimilar though they were in character, based upon the enthusiasm they shared for the Catholic cause. A word had better be said about this friendship before proceeding to Ugolino's scheme for their co-operation with him.

The story is that just before they met at Rome (presumably for the first time at the Fourth Lateran Council in 1215) Dominic had a dream in which he saw himself and a man unknown to him presented by the Blessed Virgin to Christ as those who were chosen to further His gospel in the world. The very next day Dominic encountered Francis and recognized him as the stranger of his dream. He at once went up to him and embraced him.

Then or later—more probably later—Dominic is said to have proposed to Francis that they join forces and form one Order; though Francis would not consent to this, Dominic did successfully beg his friend to give him the cord that girdled his waist. This he ever afterward wore under his own habit. It is also reasonably sure, however slight approval such a suggestion gets from Dominicans, that Dominic, though he had previously lived in poverty, made the practice of it among his Brothers much stricter and closer under the influence of Francis. The two Orders did, in fact, act and react upon one another in various ways. Because of this Francis was probably sound in his instinctive feeling that much would be lost and little gained by their amalgamation. At the same time one can see that the history of the Franciscans might have been much less turbulent had they had engrafted upon their fervor and enthusiasm the Dominican genius for organization.

The two friends were at one in the way they met Cardinal Ugolino's proposal that he draw upon their Orders for bishops. "In the primitive Church," he reminded them, "the pastors of the Church were poor, and men who glowed with charity and not greed. Why do we not make bishops and prelates of your Brethren, as they excel other men in teaching and example?"

The words created consternation. It was not a question merely of wishing to avoid high office out of humility. Had this plan been carried out then, as it was to a considerable extent later, it would have meant a heavy drain upon the best men of the two Brotherhoods and so have much diminished their effectiveness in their special work. A century or so afterward the orders could more easily afford to give men to the general use of the Church; at the time that Ugolino approached the two saints, to have surrendered any of their disciples to bishoprics would have been a serious loss.

Dominic looked at Francis and Francis looked at Dominic, and each saw what the other thought, and each urged the other to reply for them both. At last Dominic spoke. "My lord," he said, "my Brethren, if they only recognize it, have already been raised to a high position. Therefore, so far as I am able, I will not allow them to accept any other mark of dignity."

Then Francis answered the cardinal, "My lord, my Brethren have been styled Lesser so that they may not presume to become greater. Their calling teaches them to be in lowliness, and to follow the footsteps of Christ's humility, and thereby at last they may be exalted above the rest in the eyes of the saints. If you would have them bear fruit in the Church of God, hold them to the state to which they have been called, and bring them back to lowliness should they wish to stray from it. Therefore, Father, I pray you by no means to allow them to rise to high office, lest their pride should be disproportionate to their poverty and they should wax arrogant against the rest."

There was much to be said on both sides of the question, but in the main there can be no doubt that Francis and Dominic were right. They were perfectly willing to be used in the service of the Church, and they were also willing to submit their own judgment as to what was advisable to the proper authorities; but to have allowed their Orders to become a kind of nursery for bishops would have been to abandon their distinctive character and to diminish greatly their usefulness to the Church. This could be most surely attained by their remaining unattached, not only for the good of the individual friar or the good of the Order but even for the good of the Church as a whole.

Even so, their phenomenal success had put them in a position in which all refusal of ecclesiastical office was not going to be possible much longer. Already their prestige was creating a problem.

T HE CROSS AND THE SULTAN

There might be some plausibility in the suggestion that the Roman authorities, while lacking idealism themselves, shrewdly understood how to utilize the idealism of others, were it not that they would have been imbecile in their policy had they failed to see that enthusiasm, to be useful at all, must be maintained. This means that it must be constantly renewed. Therefore it is absurd to suppose that they would have wished to modify the Franciscan idealism in such a way as to destroy or even diminish it. Theirs was the extremely delicate task of directing it so as to preserve it from dissipating its energies and to help it to keep the enthusiasm bright and fresh. To do this it was necessary for them to show not merely statesmanship but a sympathy with idealism. To show such sympathy it was necessary that they should themselves be idealists, at least to some extent. The position demanded, indeed, that they be sagacious, yet sagacity would have defeated its own object had it been nothing else. The temper of the authorities was one of hopefulness and helpfulness toward the new movement that promised so much.

This is all the more remarkable because the temper of the official mind in any department of human activity is not usually very supple. One would have expected Francis to have met, almost at every turn, with some degree of opposition. Instead he found encouragement. Although this does not mean that those in charge always considered his plans advisable, it does, at least, indicate that they recognized that he was a spiritual genius and one of those men who must be allowed to do their work in their own way if they are to do it at all. It would be hard to know where to look for an enterprise entangled with less red tape.

It may have been because Francis feared that he would involve himself in hampering conditions by asking for special privileges from the Holy See that he made it a strict rule that the Brothers were never to seek them. For with his engaging simplicity went a good deal of shrewdness. Yet deeper than such a consideration was his conviction that he was called upon to go forth depending solely on God and not asking any help from the authorities other than the approval already given to his life lived according to Gospel perfection. This was to bring his first missions beyond the borders of Italy into considerable trouble, and yet, though they ended in a fiasco, he retained the principle of freedom of action and in the end found it of great advantage to him.

Very early in his career he had tried to go to Syria to preach to the infidels, and upon the failure of that attempt he had managed to get to Spain to preach to the Moors, again to be baffled, but only by the accident of illness. Yet so far from being discouraged, he brought his plans forward again at the Whitsun general chapter of 1217.

This general assembly of the Brothers marks a new phase in the development of the Order, not merely because of the initiation of missionary enterprises but because a new machinery of administration was set up. The Brothers had been accustomed before this to meet Francis at the Portiuncula from time to time, but in an informal way. Now their vastly increased numbers necessitated a division and delegation of authority. This must have existed before, at least to some extent, but now it was regularized. Accordingly, several provinces were established, each under the direction of a minister-provincial who would supervise the various houses of his jurisdiction, of which each was under the charge of a friar known as the guardian. Francis permitted no titles that would indicate superiority, not even that of "prior." The titles of the superiors—for these had to be—indicated that they were the servants of those committed to them. Rather than "fathers," they were "mothers," a term that came to be used in Franciscan circles and which was peculiar to them.

It was at this chapter that missionaries were sent out to other European countries and also, either at this time or the following year, to Syria under the charge of Brother Elias. For the moment he need not concern us, as the interest centers upon what happened to the missionaries assigned elsewhere.

In his address to these missionaries, Francis said in part, "Dearest Brethren, it behooves us to be the pattern and example of all friars. If therefore I have sent some of you to distant parts to bear labors and shame, hunger and thirst and other privations, it is just—and holy humility requires it—that I should likewise go to some distant country so that the Brothers may the more patiently sustain adversity by knowing that I am bearing the same. In the name of the Lord go two by two on the way humbly and decently, and especially with strict silence from the dawn till past the hour of Tierce, praying the Lord in your hearts. And while you walk let your conversation be as seemly as if you were in a hermitage or in a cell. For wherever we are we may always have our cell with us. For Brother Body is our cell, and our soul is the hermit."

Francis chose France for himself, partly because he had always had a personal affection for that country as the home of poetry—was he not named "the Frenchman"?—but also because, as he announced, "Therein is a Catholic people who more than all other Catholics manifest a special reverence for the Body of Christ." As his companion he selected the brother poet Pacifico.

He never got to France, but only because he encountered Cardinal Ugolino at Florence and the cardinal dropped a hint that it would be inadvisable for Francis to leave Italy just then "because there are many prelates who would willingly hinder the good of your Brotherhood in the Roman Curia." This is the only hint we get of such a thing, but Ugolino must have known what he was talking about. He urged that the other cardinals favorable to Francis could do more for him if he stayed at home in control of affairs. It must be remembered that, as Ugolino was not yet the official protector of the order, his powers were limited. Moreover, Francis did not preach that sermon before the Pope and the cardinals until the following winter. He therefore still had to consolidate his position among them.

Francis was not convinced at first and argued, "It would be a great shame to me to send my other Brothers to remote provinces and not be a sharer with them of their tribulations."

The cardinal countered, "Then why send them out to die of hunger?"

To this Francis replied, "Think you, my lord, that my Lord has sent the friars to serve only in the provinces here? God chose them for the profit of the whole world. They shall go even to the lands of the infidels."

In the end Ugolino managed to persuade Francis to remain in

Italy. So Pacifico went to France in charge of the mission to that country.

As a man familiar with the soft language of Provence Pacifico ran into no special difficulties, except being suspected of Albigensianism. Those sent to Spain were received well enough, perhaps because they were under the command of Bernard da Quintavalle, who had already been there. It was otherwise with those who trudged through the Brenner Pass to Germany and Hungary.

They knew nothing of the German language, and as soon as they had learned the word "Ja" they let it suffice for everything. This was all very well when they were asked if they would like some food. Then "Yes" was the proper answer. But it was disastrous when they were asked if they were heretics and beamingly answered "Ja" to that question too. Then they were beaten and put in the stocks. The Germans had never been popular in Italy. Now the Brothers were convinced that they were all barbarians.

In Hungary the linguistic achievements of the friars did not stretch even so far as "Ja" and "Nein." The rude peasants descended upon them and demanded with unmistakable gestures that they surrender their cloaks. These with Franciscan courtesy and grace they bestowed. But after being stripped of everything else, they had to divest themselves even of their breeches. They found that these were safe only when smeared with cow dung. It was humiliating to be reduced to such a disgusting expedient to keep even one rag about themselves. They got back to Italy so thoroughly disheartened by their experiences that they introduced into their prayers the formula, "May the Lord preserve us from the heresy of the Lombards and the ferocity of the Germans!"

But Francis was not discouraged. At the general chapter, after their return, plans for missionary work were again brought forward. This time, however, Cardinal Ugolino insisted that they take commendatory letters to the bishops of the countries they were to visit. These letters had to be phrased very tactfully to avoid offending Francis's scruples about accepting such things, but Ugolino was equal to drawing up a papal bull (dated June 11, 1219) in such a form as not to appear too official and yet be official enough to serve the desired purpose. It ran: "Our dear son Francis, and his companions of the Order of Friars Minor, having renounced the vani-

ties of the world to choose a mode of life which has merited the
approval of the Roman Church, and to go forth after the example
of the Apostles to cast in various regions the seed of the word of
God, we pray and exhort you by these apostolic letters to receive as
good Catholics the friars of the above-mentioned society, bearers
of these presents, warning you to be favorable to them and to treat
them with kindness for the honor of God and out of consideration
for Us." Without such an attestation they could have accomplished
nothing.

The chapter at which the discomfited missionaries made their
reports and at which further missionary enterprises were discussed
is the one perhaps best entitled to be called the Chapter of the
Mats, though that title has been bestowed on other chapters. The
truth would seem to be that all of the chapters of these years could
be described in this way, for all were on a huge scale, with from three
to five thousand of the Brothers attending, and with no way of
housing them except in hastily constructed huts of rushes or branches
or, at best, mats stretched over poles.

The problem of providing food for so large an assembly seemed
altogether too great to St. Dominic when he attended one of them
in company with several of his friars. It horrified his sense of system
that nobody was in charge of the commissariat, and he was startled
to learn that this was at the direct order of Francis, who had said,
"I command you, by the merit of holy obedience, that none of you
take care or thought about anything to eat or the needs of the body,
but turn all your thoughts to prayer and the praise of God. Cast all
your care upon him, for he careth tenderly for you." He was even
more astonished when he saw that this trust in Providence was
justified, when the people of the cities and country districts nearby
brought in so much food—laden on sumpter beasts and carts, along
with pitchers and tableware and even napkins, and with knights
themselves not disdaining to wait upon the Brothers—that they had
far more than even so large a number actually needed. It was then
that he apologized to Francis for having thought him indiscreet;
so, kneeling before his friend, he said, "Of a truth God has special
care of these holy poor little ones, and I did not know it. From
henceforth I promise to observe Gospel poverty." It was after
what he had witnessed that he made an absolute poverty binding
on Dominicans.

Cardinal Ugolino was also present. He was so impressed that he was moved to tears when he saw how the friars lived, sleeping on the bare ground and having nothing but the bare ground for their tables. He moved among them barefoot and clad in the Franciscan habit, greatly edified but also greatly edifying the Brothers by his own humility and piety.

Nevertheless, Ugolino saw that a little prudence would not come amiss. He may have had this impressed upon him by a party already arising among the Brothers. Quietly and steadily he brought pressure to bear in favor of changes that would make the Franciscan idea more workable. The first step in that direction was his inducing Francis to accept the bull certifying the orthodoxy of the friars to foreign bishops. This was a sensible provision in no way in conflict with Franciscan life. It did, however, presage other adjustments to new conditions. As such it had an importance not immediately apparent.

This time the concentration of effort was on Islam, though European countries were not ignored. To Tunis went Brother Giles in charge of a band of friars, but they were at once forcibly put on a ship by the Christians living there, who feared strife with their Mohammedan neighbors if there were any Christian preaching. The one man who was left behind, Brother Electus, was speedily put to death, being decapitated kneeling, holding the Rule in his hands.

As for the missionaries to the Miramolin of Morocco, they were all martyred. Yet the miramolin, Abu Jacob, was disposed to be friendly, if for no other reason than that he employed Dom Pedro, the Infante of Portugal, as commander of his army. When the Christians began to preach after having learned a little Arabic, he merely ordered that they be sent home.

They promptly returned and began preaching again. This time the miramolin was so angry that, after he had had the friars rolled on broken glass, he cut off their heads with his own hand.

Though Francis did not know of their deaths until 1221, he himself certainly went out in 1219 to Egypt in the hope of receiving martyrdom or, at least, in the expectation that he would, in all likelihood, receive it. Partly to provide for this, but also to ensure some effective government of the Order during his absence, he appointed two vicars to act for him. One of these, Matthew of Narni, was to stay at the Portiuncula and the other, Gregory of Naples, was to travel through the provinces.

This time Cardinal Ugolino made no attempt, or none that we hear of, to persuade Francis to remain at home. Sabatier suggests that this was because the cardinal thought it would be as well to have him out of the way so that the remodeling of the Order could proceed without his interference. Such an inference goes too far. The situation had greatly changed. Ugolino was in the position of being able effectively to exercise any protection that was needed, and Francis was now far more securely in the favor of the Curia. Moreover, the cardinal probably perceived that it was no longer possible to restrain Francis and that his missionary ardor should be allowed free rein. Overjoyed with this fulfillment of his old ambitions, Francis set sail from Ancona in June 1219.

There were so many volunteers for this expedition that the ship could not carry them all. Francis explained that if he chose which of the Brothers should go with him, he might appear to be showing favoritism. "Therefore," he said, "let us try to find out the will of God."

His method, very typical of him, was to call a small boy who was standing by and to say to him, "As I cannot take all these with me, we shall let you choose, and that we will take to be God's will. Which then shall I take?"

"This one," answered the boy, touching one of the friars at random. "And this, and this, and this." He kept on until he had picked out eleven Brothers in all. With that method even the disappointed ones were satisfied.

After a stop at Cyprus, Acre was reached in mid-July and Damietta, which was being besieged by the crusaders, by the end of the month. A victory over the Saracens had been won a couple of days before Francis's arrival, but on the last day of July an attack on Damietta was beaten back with considerable loss to the Christian army.

What Francis saw depressed him. He was full of idealism about the sacredness of the crusade, therefore the conduct of many of the crusaders seemed to him quite scandalous. When a new storming of the city was planned in August he said to one of the Brothers, "The Lord has revealed to me that if they fight they will be defeated.

Yet if I tell them this I shall be considered a fool, while if I keep silence I shall go against my conscience. What do you advise me to do?"

His companion answered, "Make no account of being judged by men. This is not the first time that you have been called a fool! So discharge your conscience."

Francis followed this advice, though it is evident that even without it he would have felt obliged to give his warning. But, of course, he was merely ridiculed, until on August 29 the crusaders suffered a setback in which they lost six thousand men killed or captured. Yet this did not get him much credit, for people have a way of holding the prophet responsible in some way for the disaster he foretells. Francis felt compassion for the discomfited besiegers, especially for the Spaniards, as these, having shown more bravery than all the other contingents, were almost wiped out.

Now Francis found an opportunity for doing what he had come there to do, to preach to the Sultan Malek el Kamil. He was warned against attempting so foolhardy a mission and told that the sultan had offered a gold ducat for every Christian head. Francis was not to be frightened, so accompanied by Brother Illuminato he went toward the Saracen lines.

They were, of course, seized at once by men brandishing scimitars over their heads. But Francis called out, "Soldan! Soldan!" so convincingly that the soldiers, supposing he might be an emissary, perhaps come to sue for peace, took him into Malek's presence.

A kind of lingua franca existed in which conversation could be carried on after a fashion; and by this means, and perhaps with the help of interpreters, Francis succeeded in making himself understood. The sultan was a courteous man, with something of the grace of his famous kinsman, Saladin. He listened willingly enough, at first because he hoped to find a little diversion and afterward because, in spite of himself, he was impressed. Though of a rather skeptical cast of mind, he recognized in the burning-eyed little tatterdemalion a remarkable person. A Christian saint was something new in his experience.

Just what happened during the friar's stay in the Saracen camp is not very clear. Obviously, the *Fioretti* embellished the story in making Malek tell Francis, "Brother, I would gladly turn me to the faith of Christ. But I fear to do so now, for if my subjects were aware of it, they would kill me and you too." He also, according to this account, asked that a priest might be sent him later to baptize him, something which happened when the sultan was on his deathbed. All that is pure fiction. Celano says merely that Malek received Francis honorably; and Bonaventure, that he offered Francis a sum of money to bestow on the poor or on Christian churches, money which, of course, Francis refused to take.

We must also doubt very much the tale of Francis offering to throw himself into a fire, on condition that the Mohammedan priests did the same, as a means of proving which religion was true. Yet it may be that Malek el Kamil did spread a carpet before Francis in which there were crisscross designs. "If he treads on the crosses," the subtle Oriental said, "I will accuse him of insulting his God; if he refuses to walk upon it, I will accuse him of insulting me." Francis met the ingenuity with ingenuity of his own. He explained that the particular crosses upon which he was treading were those of the thieves between whom Our Lord had been crucified. "And these I am not ashamed to tread upon!"

Francis returned to the crusaders' army having at last preached Christ to the infidel. Nobody had expected to see him again. But when, after the arrival of large reinforcements, the crusaders attacked again and this time, on November 5, took Damietta, Francis was unable to rejoice in the Christian triumph. For the city was sacked, and the army gave itself over to the wildest debauchery.

The worst excesses occurred only after Francis had left, but he had seen enough to disgust him. As he had met, according to one story, the Sultan of Damascus when in his brother Malek's camp and had received from him a free pass to all the Holy Places, he went there some time in December, perhaps to spend Christmas in Bethlehem. As he also would have been sure to have spent Good Friday in Jerusalem had this been at all possible, he may be supposed to have done so. Though we have no definite records as to his movements during the winter and spring of 1220–21, we find him by the summer at Acre, where he had already established a mission under Brother Elias.

There there reached him a Brother Stephen with bad news. The two vicars appointed by Francis had been introducing regulations quite contrary to the Franciscan Rule. Though these seem to have had nothing to do with any relaxation of poverty but rather tended in the direction of a more formal strictness, what Francis heard about the imposition of special fasts for the Brothers was disturbing. Francis had gone on the principle that, except for the fast days enjoined by the Church, the Brothers were to eat whatever was set before them. He recognized in all this a tendency to exchange Franciscan freedom for the rigidity of conventional monasticism.

Stephen found Francis in the refectory eating a simple meal with Peter Cathanii. According to the new regulation of the vicars, this, as it contained meat, was at variance with the vicars' regulations. With a humorous twinkle in his eye Francis turned to Peter and asked, "What are we to do now?"

To this Peter returned, "Whatever you say, for it is you who have the authority."

"In that case," said Francis, "let us eat what is set before us, in accordance with the holy Gospel."

Francis saw that his presence was needed in Italy, and he was never one to delay action. He was aware that a revision of the Rule was being talked of, and it would not do to allow precedents to be established that could be written into that Rule when it was drawn up. Gentle though Francis was and little inclined to assert himself, he had to act at once, lest what was not *his* Order but the Gospel life he had been commissioned to restore to the world should get smothered under a mass of constitutions that might destroy its distinctive character.

He took with him when he sailed three of the ablest men in the Order, Elias and Peter Cathanii and Caesar of Spires. He had more intimate friends among the Brothers, but none whose judgment he trusted more. These would be at his side to uphold him when he encountered the vicars at the next general chapter.

FRANCIS RESIGNS

They sailed for Italy probably in June, though the date has been put as both earlier and later by recent biographers. Their destination, instead of the more convenient Ancona, was Venice, far to the northwest. From there they had a long overland journey to Assisi.

It was too long for Francis, who was now ill and was to remain ill for the rest of his life, to make it all the way on foot. They had to find him an ass to ride, and this unwonted consideration of the needs of Brother Body made one of the friars accompanying him, a man named Brother Leonard, feel some unspoken dissatisfaction. He was thinking, "This man's family was not of equal standing with my own. And now forsooth he rides, and I go on foot leading his ass!"

Leonard was greatly abashed when Francis read his thoughts and dismounted, saying, "It is true, Brother. It is not fitting that I should ride and you walk, for you were in the world of much better birth than myself." Leonard blushed for shame and fell at Francis's feet, admitting his fault. It was with difficulty that they could persuade him to remount.

Their road led through Bologna, and at this place there occurred another incident equally Franciscan, though not one for which all modern readers will feel an equal sympathy. Francis heard that in that city Peter Stacia, the Provincial of Lombardy, had established a house of studies for the friars, it may be with the idea of opening a school of theology at the university there similar to that conducted by the Dominicans. Francis was very angry, so angry that he would not so much as cross the threshold of this fine building, one very different from the simple dwellings of the friars—at best like peasants' cottages on a slightly larger scale, and at worst (though this was what Francis considered best) huts of mud and wattles, or even caves. He at once ordered the friars to leave; nor would he even permit a sick man—who seems to have been young Thomas of Celano—to remain. Leave they must, and instantly.

His objection was on two grounds (about which we shall hear more later) : the possession of property and the pursuit of learning within the order, which he did not consider in accord with the humble vocation of his friars. It was his first brush with this particular dragon, and he was victorious for the moment. Later he did permit the occupation of this house when Cardinal Ugolino showed him that he and not the friars owned it. Even so, it went against the grain for Francis to tolerate such a substantial dwelling for any of the Brothers, and he continued to fear the seductions of study.

It was with heavy forebodings that he went on to Assisi.

Another shock awaited him when he reached the Portiuncula. He found that a house of stone had just been erected there, nothing very grand but too grand for the poverty of the Brethren. At once he went up on the roof and started throwing down the tiles by way of beginning the demolishing of the whole structure. He was stopped only by the arrival of a party of officials from Assisi, headed by his brother Angelo.

They called up to him: "Stop! You are destroying our property."

"But I thought this was for the Brothers."

"It *is* for them. But it belongs to us. We built it and we own it."

Upon that Francis desisted and came down. The city council was quick to pass an ordinance that the podesta should always keep that house in repair. Against such ill-advised kindness, as he considered it, Francis could do nothing. The principle of poverty here as at Bologna had been preserved under the legal fiction that the friars were merely permitted to use the building. Though it was under a similar fiction that Francis merely "rented" the Portiuncula from the Abbot of Mount Subasio, there was a difference. He held with a loose hand and was always ready to let go, and what he put up as shelters were hardly more than huts. Now the principle was being stretched, and Francis did not like it at all.

There was, however, a great joy in being home again, and he was gladdened by the way the Brothers, as soon as they heard of his return, streamed toward Assisi to see him. Yet at the Michaelmas chapter that year there was not a little secret consternation mingled with the joy. The vicars and their supporters were well aware that Francis would disapprove of the changes they had made.

Nevertheless, changes there had to be and this was made very clear to Francis by Cardinal Ugolino. It was high time that a new Rule be drawn up, one better fitted to conditions vastly different from those ten years earlier. Without waiting for that, the Holy See issued a bull decreeing that for all those entering the Order there should be a full year's novitiate, during which their fitness might be tested. Up to that time Francis had given men the habit and had taken their vows on the day of their admission. It had too frequently happened that men had joined him who were moved by a sudden enthusiasm that quickly evaporated or who were, whether consciously or not, looking for what they thought would be an easy life. Francis had several times had to deal with a "Brother Fly" who ate well and slept well but who never did a stroke of work. It was obviously much better not to admit such people at all than to eject them later as undesirable.

The Pope's bull indicates another abuse that had come up, that of men wearing the Franciscan habit but wandering wherever they pleased and so escaping all effectual control. This was now strictly forbidden. The bull indicates that during Francis's absence discipline had to a large extent broken down, despite the rather fussy new regulations that the vicars had introduced regarding fasting. But it must be supposed that Francis himself did not quite escape all implications of criticism. Clearly, the Pope (or his agent Cardinal Ugolino) wanted the Order rebuilt on a firmer foundation. This had to be done before formal approbation could be given, and without that the Order could not be allowed to continue.

Francis, of course, promptly removed his vicars from office, which, for that matter, terminated at the moment of his return. Yet he felt too ill to cope with administrative details and wished to be free to devote himself to the important matter of drawing up a Rule to be presented to Honorius. He therefore resigned, except for retaining the title of general, and handed over the day-to-day responsibilities to a new vicar, Peter Cathanii.

His speech of resignation, made on St. Michael's Day, 1220, ran, "From henceforth I am dead to you. But behold Peter Cathanii, whom both I and all of us will obey." Throwing himself to the ground, he was the first to promise Peter obedience. While the other Brothers wept, he rose to his feet and continued, "Lord, I commend to thee thy family which hitherto thou hast committed to me. And now on account of the infirmities which thou knowest, O Most Sweet Lord, being unable to care for it, I commend it to its ministers, who shall be held in the day of judgment to show cause before thee, O Lord, if any Brother should perish through their negligence, or evil example, or too harsh correction."

One catches here that Francis had no very glowing hope in the outcome or, at any rate, no great confidence in the qualifications of either Brother Peter or the provincials. Yet these were the best men that Francis could think of for their offices, and if they never proved to be all that he wished, this was because nobody could have been that. Francis was a perfectionist, and, however sincerely he might declare himself to be the worst of sinners, he must have seen that nobody could measure up to the standard he set in his own manner of life. Perhaps he had a notion that by dropping all responsibility for the humdrum details of discipline he would be able to exercise more influence in the shaping of the eventual Rule of the Order, the one that would crystallize for all time the Franciscan idea. It was to that task that he now meant to address himself.

As he was still a relatively young man—only thirty-eight—he might have expected that many fruitful years remained to him, in spite of poor health. There seems to have been a hypochondriacal streak in him under his gaiety, and this may have led him to believe that his time would be short. There was to come a period of mental depression, though from this he emerged in the end. At the moment he felt that he could do no more than frame the definitive Rule. And he meant to set himself to give with greater emphasis than ever an example to the Brethren.

Wadding, the Franciscan annalist, says that just before the Michaelmas chapter of 1220 Cardinal Ugolino persuaded Francis to go with him to the Camaldolese monastery of the Cassentine forest, and it was there that Sabatier supposes that Francis was talked into compliance with the cardinal's plan. Father Cuthbert objects that we have no positive proof that Francis—or the cardinal —was there at all. But while Sabatier's idea of the nature of the talks—"with an excess of condescension they had let him go his own way, and the result was the saddest of lessons"—is no more than surmise, it probably hits rather near the center of truth. That there was some official intervention is proved by the fact that a papal bull was issued just before the assembling of the friars. Yet, surely, it is very unfair to say of Ugolino that he was "the very soul of the group who were compromising the Franciscan ideal." So far from that, he was trying to save it. A crisis had come about, and it was one that Francis could not deal with unaided.

One therefore cannot but believe that the plans for the new government of the order were made only after consultation with Cardinal Ugolino. Indeed, some have supposed that it was not until this date that Francis asked the Pope to appoint the cardinal as protector. Even if that be so, it is certain that time after time Francis had acted according to the cardinal's advice and that Ugolino had been in effect, even if not officially, the protector since shortly after the death in 1216 of the Cardinal John of St. Paul. In everything that follows the guiding hand of Ugolino may be seen, though this is not to throw all the responsibility upon him. Throughout Francis must bear his share of this—Francis and other men in the Order.

It was a curious relationship that existed between the great dignitary of the Church (who was its future Pope) and the humble friar. On the one side there was deference to authority, freely and eagerly given; on the other there was admiration for genius and sanctity. The affection was equal and undisturbed. Francis, free though his spirit was, did not have a trace of the kind of independence that is based on self-assertiveness. Indeed, he may perhaps be criticized sometimes for not asserting himself enough. To command was not much in his nature, and he governed by love and, therefore, all the more effectively when he could be in personal contact with those over whom he ruled. But while ruling, he still felt a need to be subject to somebody within the Order. Even as general at the head of everything, for his personal concerns he sought somebody who would give him orders, under whom he might practice the virtue of obedience. Nor did he care who his own "mother" was; the most callow novice would do as well as anybody else. In addition, he was always willing to have a director in weighty general concerns, somebody to whom he could subject his personal ideas about the government of the Order. Having chosen in Ugolino the wisest man available, he did not demand that Ugolino should always see eye to eye with him. And it was so also with regard to his choice of Peter Cathanii as his vicar. To him was entrusted the management of affairs; to himself he reserved only the right to reaffirm when necessary what it was he felt that he had directly received from heaven.

The freedom with which he treated the cardinal is shown in a story of how, when Francis was staying in his palace, he came in at dinnertime with a shining countenance and some scraps of black bread he had just begged. These he passed round to all the guests. They were all edified, some eating their bread and others keeping it as a memento of the occasion. When afterward Ugolino expostulated with him, saying, "My Brother, why did you put me to shame in my own house by going out for alms?" Francis replied, "I have rather shown you honor, as I have honored a still greater Lord. Mine is a royal dignity and a pre-eminent nobility—that of following Christ, who for our sakes became poor." Ugolino deeply reverenced him for such things, but he did, after all, have somehow to solve the problem of preserving this humble spirit among a large body of men. It was for him to seek means of imposing a degree of organization that was foreign to Francis's special talents.

Francis was well aware that he was not by nature an administrator, and he was now glad to find in his failing health a valid excuse for putting the direction of affairs in the hands of another man. In Peter Cathanii he thought he had found the man most capable of taking charge. The history of the Order might have been rather different had Peter lived. But he died the following year, necessitating the appointment of another vicar. This time the choice of Francis (and again the cardinal's) fell upon Brother Elias.

Elias has received a good deal of blame, though most of his high-handed arrogance did not appear until after Francis's death. We do get some hints that even under the less forceful Peter changes were often being suggested, though he did not insist upon them. Thus one day he proposed that the Rule be relaxed to the extent of permitting future novices to reserve some portion of what they possessed instead of giving it all to the poor. Francis would not hear of this, and poor Peter pleaded, "Then what shall we do? I cannot provide for all our Brothers in their necessities!" To this Francis returned, "Then strip the Virgin's altar. Believe me she would be better pleased to have her altar destitute of ornaments than to see it shining with precious things and her Son despised. The Lord will send someone to restore to His Mother what He has lent us!"

In the same spirit, when the mother of two of the friars came to Francis asking for help that she urgently needed, he turned to Peter to find her some alms.

"There is nothing in the house of any value," Peter said, "except the breviary out of which we read the lessons at Matins."

"Then give her that," Francis told him. "I believe that this gift will be more pleasing to God than that we read out of it."

Peter Cathanii seems to have been willing to defer to Francis not only in such matters but in others of greater importance. Yet we can see that he was not always firm enough in his rule to keep things under control. We find Francis on one occasion complaining to him that he had heard a Brother blackening the reputation of another. He declared, "This must be stopped! There is danger to the whole order unless slanderers are put down. If you find the Brother innocent of what he has been accused, hand his accuser over to the Florentine Bruiser if you are unable to punish him yourself." Francis himself never resorted to corporal punishment, though he freely imposed humiliating penances upon offenders. Yet he wished Peter, if he was unable to deal with the situation in any other way, to use this Brother John, known as the Florentine Bruiser, to administer a few lashes on the bare back of any friar who needed them.

We hear of these things only casually and accidentally, as it were, but they make it plain that the order did need a strong hand and that Peter did not possess this. In the matter of poverty he was ready to make concessions. Though there Francis checked him at once, it must be evident that it was partly because Francis himself felt personal repugnance to governing with the assistance of the Florentine Bruiser that he was only too glad to be relieved of the cares of office. It may also be safely surmised that, though he mourned Peter's death, he was glad he could replace him with a stronger and abler man, Brother Elias.

THE REVISED RULE

Francis spent the six years of life left to him living for the most part in one or another of the hermitages. He, like most of the other friars, had been accustomed to withdraw there for spiritual refreshment after his preaching tours. From now on this life was to be almost as permanent for him as it was for such Brothers as Bernard and Sylvester, who were virtually hermits. He did from time to time remember the word sent him through Clare and Sylvester that he was not called merely for his own salvation but for the salvation of others, and so he did still go out occasionally to preach. This was relatively rare until, immediately following the stigmata, there was an outburst of energy which everybody saw to be the last flaring-up of the dying candle.

For the first year, he withdrew to seek heavenly guidance for the Rule he had to draw up. The actual writing of this, especially as it was done with the help of a secretary, could not have been a particularly onerous undertaking; but he did need much time to think and to pray. For Francis a task of this sort was far more complex than it would have been for a legal-minded man, who could have produced the desired article with decisive dispatch in a few days, everything in apple-pie order. To Francis the Rule meant the minimum of definite regulations and the maximum of exhortations; therefore, the pinning of himself down to something explicit that would satisfy the various parties in the Order, now more clearly emerging, called for qualities that were not native to him. It was for this reason a labor of considerable difficulty.

The primitive Rule, the one shown to Innocent III in 1210 and given tentative approval, is no longer in existence. In one sense it was never in existence, for it was hardly a religious Rule as that term is usually understood but little more than a short anthology of texts from the Gospel. To this, additions and amplifications had been made from time to time as necessity arose, but the result was far from a well-rounded scheme of life and had long needed reduction into symmetrical order. Francis at the same time had to satisfy the Brothers—including the "progressives" among them and those of the "old school"—and the Pope, and his own conscience. That, he knew, was not going to be easy.

Already there had been a number of departures from the kind of spontaneity, controlled only by a few prohibitions, that Francis aimed at. For instance, though Francis was opposed to accepting any kind of special priviliges from the Holy See, Cardinal Ugolino had persuaded him to accept commendatory letters for the Brothers. Before this happened we hear some of the Brethren pleading with Francis, "Father, do you not see that sometimes the bishops will not allow us to preach, so that we have to stand idle many days in a place before we can announce the word of the Lord. It would be better if you should obtain a privilege from the lord Pope in this matter, as it would be for the salvation of souls." To this Francis would only retort, "You Friars Minor do not know the will of God, and do not allow me to convert the whole world in the way that God wills. For I wish by perfect humility and reverence first to convert the prelates. They, when they shall see our holy life and reverence toward them, will beseech us to preach and convert the people, and that will help your preaching more than the privileges that would lead you into pride. For my part I desire this privilege from the Lord, never to have privilege from man, except to do reverence to all, and to convert the world by obedience to the holy Rule rather by example than by word." Here, though there was much to be said for Francis's position, common sense weighed against it. The Church is an organization as well as an organism, and the purely idealistic thing, though charmingly attractive, is not always feasible. Francis on this point had to yield, though he did not change his views.

If in one sense there was no real Rule at all, in another sense there were too many Rules. What, of course, applied to all the Brothers was the practice of poverty, chastity, and obedience. The mode of life could hardly be uniform for the itinerant preachers and for those living in hermitages. Therefore we find a special Rule for the withdrawn men, those who periodically sought a retreat as well as those who lived more or less permanently as hermits. This enjoined that those in a hermitage were to be only three or, at most, four Brothers. Of these, two were to be the "mothers" and the other two the "sons," the mothers leading the life of Martha so as to leave the sons free for the life of Mary. Those giving themselves completely to contemplation were to live and sleep in an enclosure apart, breaking their silence only for the saying of the office. But after Tierce they might break their silence and go to their mothers to "beg an alms of them like other poor people for God's sake." Except for this, they were to talk to nobody, unless their superior happened to visit the hermitage. This was to continue until such time as the positions were reversed and the "sons" became the "mothers" and the "mothers" the "sons." Under such a Rule even the Marthas were more withdrawn from the world, and more like Marys, than was possible outside such retreats.

Along much the same lines were the regulations for the Portiuncula, though there the community was somewhat larger and there was a constant coming and going of Brothers to consult the minister-general. But those stationed there were to be a select group, chosen for their holy lives and for their ability to chant the office with fitting solemnity. The lay brothers, too, were to be distinguished for their piety. None of them were to indulge in any idle speech, in which Francis included "this world's news." Nobody was to be admitted inside the enclosure, though it was merely protected by a hedge, "but the place was to be preserved pure and holy in hymns and the praise of the Lord." Francis declared his object, "I will that this place be blessed, and that it remain forever a mirror and a good example of the whole Order, and like a candlestick before the throne of God and the Blessed Virgin, always burning and shining. On account of this the Lord will have mercy on the defects and faults of all the friars, and always preserve and protect this Order and this His tender plant."

These regulations for select groups would suggest that Francis was troubled in mind about those that did not belong to them, which of course included the vast majority of the Brothers. The real problem was how to deal with the men who went wandering about—always, they could claim, in the spirit of liberty that had been attained by the first disciples, though actually, as is apparent from the Pope's edict against these unattached friars, in some instances making that an excuse for avoiding all discipline.

We hear that at the Chapter of the Mats some of the Brothers approached Cardinal Ugolino and said, "We wish you would persuade Brother Francis to follow the counsel of the wise Brethren, and to allow himself to be led by them." To show more clearly what was in their minds, they quoted to him from the Rule of St. Augustine and that of St. Benedict and also that of St. Bernard, the implication being that the Franciscans would be well advised to base themselves upon the older monastic traditions that were well tested instead of following what some of them were inclined to consider Francis's private fantasies.

When the cardinal told Francis of what the Brothers had said and indicated that he agreed with it, Francis, in a high state of excitement, took him by the hand and led him at once to the assembly of friars and in his resonant voice called out, "My Brethren, my Brethren, the Lord called me by the way of simplicity and humility, and this way He has shown me as the way for me and those who follow me. Therefore I do not wish you to mention any other Rule, neither that of St. Augustine, nor of St. Benedict, nor of St. Bernard, for the Lord wished me to be a new convenant in the world, and He leads me another way. I say that God will confound your wisdom and punish you unless you return to your first state."

At this outburst the cardinal and all those present were astounded. Francis did have a good deal of support among the Brothers, even though there may have been more for the proposals of the "progressive" men. Although the demand for making Franciscanism approximate more closely ordinary monasticism was dropped, never to be revived, what did not end was a demand for a new Rule, or rather a thorough revision of the old one.

Some time during the summer of 1221 Francis did produce this Rule. It was to be presented to the Michaelmas general chapter for the approval of the Brothers, but in the meanwhile it was entrusted to Brother Elias, the vicar appointed by Francis at the previous Whitsuntide, following upon the death of Peter Cathanii on March 20. Brother Elias, when the time came for its production, explained that he had lost it. There is a note of incredulity in the accounts that mention this circumstance, and it is probably no great breach of charity to believe that the loss was deliberate.

Yet we may also extend Elias some charity. He may well have seen after studying the new Rule that it had little chance of acceptance and so wished to avoid the embarrassment for Francis that would have come from its rejection. Also he may have surmised that, even had it been accepted, it would not really meet the situation, and therefore had scant chance of being carried out. By this method of calculated delay he could give Francis a chance to reverse some of his more uncompromising positions. While it was being rewritten Elias counted upon being backed by the cardinal to persuade Francis to frame something that would serve the new conditions better. After all, it did have to be presented to the Pope and be approved by him before it could have any legal force. Honorius would be sure to reject anything which a considerable part of the Brothers, perhaps a majority, thought unsuitable. Also, of course, Honorius would consult the Protector of the Friars Minor before accepting anything, and it was well known that Cardinal Ugolino was in favor of moderation and practicability.

To make a third and last attempt, Francis retired with his secretary, Brother Leo, to the fastness of Fonte Colomba. It was one of many such retreats to the south of Assisi frequented by Francis during his last years, almost as withdrawn as La Verna but less inaccessible. There is an almost Alpine air there, with skies bluer and brighter than the tender haze that hangs over the valley of the Spoleto. Francis loved contemplation in places whose beauty seemed a mirror of the divine.

Somehow it got out that what he intended this time was only a repetition of the lost Rule. It may even have been rumored that he was making the Rule still more stringent and, therefore, all the more impossible of observance. At any rate, a delegation of the ministers, headed by Elias, the vicar, sought Francis out there. It seems clear from the account given in the *Mirror of Perfection* that in this Elias was not the moving spirit. Practical man though he was, he wished to be loyal to Francis and felt that he might be able to serve him best by standing between him and the alarmed superiors of the Order. For the *Mirror* reports that they said to Elias, "We have heard that Brother Francis is making a new Rule, but we fear that he will make it so harsh that we cannot carry it out. We want you to go to him and say that we will not be bound by this new Rule of his; so let him make it for himself and not for us." To which Elias answered that he would not go unless they went with him. He did not wish to appear as the leader of the opposition.

They arrived, and Elias called up to where Francis was, on a rocky ledge on the side of the mountain. Francis called down to him, distinctly annoyed, "Who are these men and what do they want?"

Brother Elias, carefully disassociating himself from those with him, said in return, "These are the ministers, and they say that the Rule you are making is too strict, so they wish to tell you that they will not consider themselves bound by it."

At this Francis turned his face toward heaven and cried out, "Lord, did I not say well when I declared that they would not believe me?"

To this there came an answer from the sky audible to all, "So do it. There is nothing of your own in the Rule, but whatever is there is Mine, and I will that the Rule be observed to the letter, without gloss, without gloss. Let those who will not obey it leave the Order."

Then Francis turned to the trembling ministers and said, "Do you wish that I have that said to you again?"

So runs the story. In an attempt to explain it sufficiently to allow it to be accepted, Dr. Burkitt remarks that at Fonte Colomba there is an echo to any shout, of which "at least two syllables are repeated." Therefore, he says that he can quite understand that Brother Leo, whose report we presumably have, really believed that he had heard an answer to Francis's dramatic appeal to heaven. Such explanations, as is so often the case, explain too much. At least *two* syllables of an echo came back, says Dr. Burkitt. But what came back on this occasion, if we are to accept the story, were several sentences. The echo theory has to be ruled out as absurd.

As for this story coming from Brother Leo, there is no proof of that, for though I believe that a good deal of the *Mirror of Perfection* derives directly from him, this story appears as a kind of preface to that book and appears to have been written after its main contents had been compiled. The most that can be safely affirmed is that all this may have been based upon a story that Leo related, but one which has become garbled. And, alas, its propaganda purpose points to an authorship of the fourteenth century.

What, then, are we to believe? That God's voice was actually heard? That creates a psychological difficulty in my mind much greater than the one Dr. Burkitt has tried to circumvent. Can the ministers be imagined as continuing in their opposition after having heard with their own ears so emphatic a corroboration of Francis straight out of heaven? We do know that they and their successors actually did interpret some of the provisions of the Rule in a sense of their own. Would they have dared to do so if this Voice had really spoken?

Francis completed the making of the new Rule in 1223, and this is still taken as the basis of their life by all branches of the Franciscan family. Yet what finally emerged was a compromise, though as much as possible of the primitive rule of 1210 was retained. Over the protest of Francis, "I have announced and do announce those things which the Lord for their salvation and mine placed in my mouth," the party of the ministers managed to have removed from the Rule the provision, "Take nothing with you in the way." And though Francis understood by poverty that "the Friar Minor should have nothing except a tunic with a cord and breeches, and to those who are forced by manifest necessity, sandals," under one pretext or another the Franciscans came, in fact, though not in theory, to have more possessions than he could countenance.

On the other hand, Francis won his point in twice writing into this Rule the principle of the liberty of the Gospel: the Brothers might eat of all foods placed before them. While they were free to practice private asceticism in this matter, it was not imposed upon them by specific regulations. The conclusion reached by an eminent Capuchin of our own time, Father Cuthbert, is, "All through it is the same rule . . . set forth in a more chastened mood. Yet, wrought in the crucible of sorrow and heart-pain, the Rule had gained perhaps a certain strength and durability even if it had lost something of its inspiring idealism." And as Archbishop Robinson points out in his translation, *The Writings of St. Francis,* Honorius, when confirming the Rule of 1223 made no distinction between it and the Rule of 1210. "We confirm," he said, "the Rule of your Order approved by Pope Innocent, our predecessor of happy memory." Though it was not precisely that, it was not precisely a new Rule either. Under the circumstances, it was the best that Francis could have hoped for.

That the difficulties were solved by compromise was due to the guidance of Cardinal Ugolino. Without his assistance there would probably have been no Rule upon which the various parties could have agreed. What seems to have happened was that Francis gave his ideas which Ugolino then wrote down in legal form. The cardinal promised to arrange matters in such a way that "the intent of the Order shall not be changed but only the form of expression." And though one may think that on several points he modified to such an extent as to make what were really changes, he saw these to be unavoidable. If there is a somewhat cold and subdued tone about the final result in place of the former eager enthusiasm, he did make possible the keeping of enthusiasts in tolerably comfortable harness with somewhat less enthusiastic but more sensible men. It was a great triumph of tact that he contrived a compromise of this sort.

The Rule was ratified by Pope Honorius III on November 23, 1223. Many crises for the Order still lay ahead and even many bitter quarrels, but the threat of total collapse had been averted.

BROTHER ELIAS

The strange and enigmatic figure of Elias Bombarone, better known as Elias of Cortona, has already been mentioned several times. But at this point an attempt will be made to depict him a little more clearly. He was a man far too complicated to permit any black-and-white treatment of his character, though, if it comes to that, even the few defenders he has had do not try to maintain that the main element should be white.

The picture usually drawn of him is that of the Judas of the Franciscan Order. Nor can it be denied that he showed extraordinary ambition, love of power, considerable arrogance, and sometimes lack of scrupulosity in achieving his ends. These qualities seem to have grown upon him by degrees when he came to hold office and were not suspected until then. It is only fair to remark that he was not out to obtain office at all costs; rather, he took the generalship reluctantly and only after laying down certain conditions. That he must have had a large element of idealism in his make-up is proved by the fact that he became a Franciscan at all. If further proof is needed, it is to be found in the fact that Francis trusted him.

Moreover, in any disagreements that came to exist between Francis and the ministers of the Order, Elias, though undoubtedly in favor of change, was so only moderately. He was affectionately attached to Francis and in the main acted as a kind of buffer between him and the more radical party. In view of his subsequent career, we must ascribe to Elias a personal loyalty that was sometimes at variance with his personal opinions. In one sense, he may almost be said to have loved Francis too much. While his friend was alive he tried to serve his ideals. Afterward he forgot the ideals, which perhaps he had never really understood, and thought only of the glory of his friend and of the Order his friend had founded.

One thing must always be borne in mind. In the literature of the Franciscan "Spirituals" Elias is taken as a convenient whipping boy to whom all that the Spirituals consider deplorable developments in the order may be attributed. They pursue him with a rancor so manifest that it is naïve, so that it is unsafe to believe all that they relate of him. One may think of him as a hotheaded and misguided man (though nobody can think him other than an extremely able one), but one can hold that he was a rascal only if one holds that Francis was a fool.

His standing offence in the eyes of the old friars who had been Francis's companions—and this struck them in the face the moment they came within sight of Assisi—was the great basilica he had built as a shrine to Francis. But if one is going to say that that is too magnificent to be appropriate for Francis, one must also say that there are hundreds of Christian churches too magnificent to be appropriate for the Son of Man. One can understand Brother Giles's gibe when he was shown through it, "Wonderful! Now all that you need is wives!" But though Giles was undoubtedly a better Franciscan than Elias, he never could resist a witticism. We need not take him too seriously. In any event, the basilica was a papal possession and included a papal palace. It was only under the care of Franciscans.

The truth about Brother Elias is that he was unfortunate. He was, of course, primarily unfortunate in being the kind of man he was, with the overbearing temper that inevitably made enemies and without anything of the graciousness and affability that attracts other men. He may have shirked carrying other crosses; this cross he could not shirk, and it must have been heavy to one who had spiritual insight and who might, in other circumstances, have been a great saint. He was unfortunate, too, in his thankless task of trying to govern a very unruly and individualistic mob, many of whom felt themselves able to plead independence of him on the ground of their adhesion to the primitive Franciscan idea. Though some of these men used that argument sincerely and perhaps justifiably, it was also used by men who merely wished to evade discipline. The orderly mind and the masterful will of Elias could not tolerate such people, and they heartily hated him.

Yet under the opposition of the noblest of those who disagreed with him was a grudging admiration. When the news came of his deposition from the office of general in 1239, Brother Giles stretched himself on the ground, saying, "I want to get as low as I can, seeing that so great a man has fallen by striving to reach too high." That remark has sometimes been taken as sarcastic; but this was a time when the sharp-tongued Giles felt awe and sympathy for one whose policies he did not approve.

It should be noted that Elias, who was vicar at the time of Francis's death, could have had the generalship for the asking had he wanted it. He preferred to devote himself instead to the building of the shrine of Francis at Assisi, and, if he was not the actual architect of that stupendous structure, it was assuredly he who inspired the general design of the fortress-church. When in 1232 the Brothers wanted to make him general in place of a well-meaning incompetent, he pleaded ill-health. So eager were they to secure a man of his proved talents that they told him that he could dispense himself from all the rules and have his own cook and a horse to ride, if his infirmities needed them. (The cook, in the stories of his enemies, was exaggerated into a provider of Lucullan banquets—had Elias not been told that he might eat gold if he wanted to?—and the horse into a whole stable of costly palfreys.) His enemies had no justifiable complaint on this score.

The real ground of their objection was that in his determination to impose order he was ruthless and highhanded. It should be noted, however, that the attack against him was led not by men like Giles and Leo but by the new generation of learned Franciscans, especially by the Englishmen from Oxford. They wished to have only priests as superiors in the Order, whereas Elias, at least in this respect, stood for the primitive Franciscanism in which there was no distinction between priests and laymen in the government of the Order.

It culminated in 1239 in a scene far from edifying, in which charges of "Liar!" were bandied about, until the Pope, Gregory IX, our old friend the former Cardinal Ugolino, stood up and said sternly, "These are not the manners of religion!" Yet he deposed Elias, which was perhaps the only thing he could do, on the ground that it was apparent that he was no longer acceptable to the Brethren.

The career of Elias was by no means over. Disgruntled and disgusted, he went over to the party of the excommunicated Emperor Frederick II, thereby himself incurring excommunication. By the Emperor he was employed as an ambassador. He then developed talents—hardly surprising in the builder of the basilica of St. Francis —as a military engineer, as such constructing a chain of castles for the Emperor. This ex-mattress maker was also something of a scientist, and his enemies accused him of dabbling in alchemy. It was all astonishing in a man of his humble antecedents and slenderness of formal education. We may not be able to call him a great man, but he was at least one of the most remarkable men of his age.

The story that Francis prophesied his apostasy and damnation must be regarded as a malicious invention. Had Francis held this opinion of Elias, he obviously would not have appointed him his vicar in 1221 or, having appointed him, failed to remove him from office. Instead, the will of Francis, made during his last days, was largely aimed at those who were rebellious against the authority of Elias. On his deathbed the saint laid his hand on Elias's head and blessed him "as much as I can—and more than I can."

We have at no time a very clear picture of Elias, and perhaps he was one of those "abstract" men who are remembered for what they accomplished rather than for what they were. Yet we do get glimpses of the affection that existed between him and Francis, how-

ever little affection Elias may have had to spare for anybody else.
At the general chapter at which he was appointed vicar, we see
Francis sitting at his feet and pulling his habit whenever he had any
suggestion to make. (He was by then too ill to feel equal to making
a speech himself, especially to so large an audience.) So Elias would
bend down to him and Francis would whisper in his ear, and Elias
would straighten himself up and say, "The Brother wishes me to
say. . . ." It is clear that Francis, ill as he was, was continuing to
exercise unofficially an authority to which Brother Elias, like Brother
Peter before him, was very deferential.

Two views can be taken of Elias. One is that he was, if not precisely a bad man, at least one who tried to beat the devil at his
own game. And we all know that he who sups with the devil needs
a long spoon. This view represents Elias as being so worldly-wise as
to defeat—it is usually implied that this was of set purpose—the
whole purpose of Francis.

To this it may be answered that Francis himself did not think so.
It must have been his opinion that if anybody could cope with the
situation, that man was Elias. Nobody can deny that he did address
himself manfully to his task, whatever may have been his errors of
judgment. Even here one must be cautious in judgment. Other men
might have been more amiable than Elias and also have accomplished less than he did.

The second view of Elias is that, though his defects of character
ruined him, he did save the Franciscan Order; it may even be urged
that the defects in his character that were his personal undoing were
those of the masterful man who was needed if the Order was to be
saved. Whether or not Elias developed the Friars Minor along the
right lines, he brought them to a very high point of prestige, a
prestige which is the measure of the success of Elias in a very difficult set of circumstances. In his own way he was a kind of providential man. And if that be considered too much to be said, at least
one might reflect on the comment of Mrs. Oliphant, who certainly
was anything but pro-Elias, "It is difficult to make out how this
Brother should have been so much to blame and yet so persistently
supported and forgiven." Whether or not he was loyal to Francis,
Francis backed him up to the end.

It is true that Francis came to be depressed by conditions in the

Order, but he did not attribute these to Elias but rather to a general decline, though even that has probably been greatly exaggerated. He saw that Elias was doing his best and better than any other man could do. At all events, that was Francis's opinion, and if he was mistaken he must bear some share of the blame.

This does not mean that Francis considered Elias perfect. Toward the end of his life, one of the Brothers came to him and asked if he would indicate one of the Brothers, if he knew one, "on whom the burden of the minister-general might be worthily imposed." It was a moment when Francis could have designated his successor, as was expected of him. He might have named Elias, or he might have named somebody else. He refused to bind the order by his dead hand, but, instead of simply evading the question, he drew a picture of the "ideal" general and then admitted that he could think of nobody who corresponded to this ideal. What he did say was that the general ought to be of serious life, of discretion, of good report, without private affections, of a zeal for prayer, yet not so absorbed by prayer as to have no time to spare for his other duties. Especially should he be devoted to the Mass, and in the presence of Christ on the altar he should put himself and his flock under the divine direction. Afterward he should be available to all and be ready to deal with everybody in charity and patience and gentleness. He should be no acceptor of persons, but should have as much regard for the simple as for the learned. "Let a habit and a book be sufficient for him, and for others he should have an ink-case and a reed." He should not be a collector of books—a point about which we shall hear more in a moment—nor should he be too much of a student, as that would take time that should be given to his office. He should console the afflicted and be solicitous of the sick, and, in order to bend the unruly to obedience, he should be gentle. "To the runaways of the Order, as to sheep that have perished, let him be merciful, knowing that the temptations have been great that have caused any fall, and remembering that he might himself fall from a still greater precipice." He was not to smile on honors but, rather, to rejoice in injuries. If he should need more pleasant and better food than that given to the other friars, he should take it in private. And he should not pay much attention to the censorious. "Let him always think and feel the office of his prelacy rather a burden than an honor to him." So the list of qualifications runs on, and though, as it is found in the *Mirror of Perfection,* one suspects that it has been touched up in such a way as to be pointed at some of the defects of Elias, probably Francis did say something like this.

The main point stands firmly. If Elias did not correspond very completely to this picture of the ideal minister-general, nobody, as Francis explicitly said, did correspond. Elias was the best man available, and nobody knew this better than Francis himself.

GROWTH AND CHANGE

There had been a development, one that occurred within ten years, of a kind of which Francis had never dreamed when he gathered his first disciples and lived with them. The primitive mode of life of its nature could not last; beautiful youth had to pass into robust maturity, and the speed with which maturity was gained should be taken as a measure of the Franciscan vigor. If there was any loss in this, there was also compensating gain. Had the Order continued on its primitive lines, it would have consisted of a number of enthusiasts but of a larger number of crackpots, with the lazy tramps predominating over both. To prevent this, the Order was obliged to extend the scope of its activities and to assign to each of its members a definite job.

Francis probably did sometimes have misgivings about the new efficiency that was being introduced and sighed over the days of sweet spontaneity. Yet had he moaned and groaned over them he would have shown himself a sentimentalist. He did not merely acquiesce in the need for change, he deliberately promoted it by appointing Elias to act as his vicar. He could have appointed Giles or Leo or Bernard instead, any one of whom would have upheld the old traditions. Instead, he chose Elias. Franciscanism had to consent to be organized. It had to come down to earth. It had to be practical and prosaic. Either that, or it would have floated away and dissolved. Its subsequent history showed that there was even a danger of its drifting into heresy. It was because that danger was dealt with by the creation of an organization that imposed discipline, that the later danger, when it arose, could be successfully dealt with.

Basically the problem was one of the practice of poverty. Here there was in Francis a literalness of view that might seem to have made poverty almost the whole object of the Christian life. But though the Franciscan emphasis may sometimes have been exaggerated—the worst exaggerations did not come from Francis but from some of the rigorists of the next century—it served a useful purpose. Sensible people are those who keep the world going, but they are rarely those who give the world a decisive push. Though ideals are perhaps by their very nature unattainable, they serve a practical purpose. Life cannot be wholly a dream and yet is of no value without the dream.

How to maintain the spirit of poverty was a difficult question. Begging had never been regarded as more than an expedient to be fallen back upon when the friars were unable to support themselves by the work of their own hands. But where were such large numbers of men to find day labor? This had been readily obtainable when two or three Brothers wandered from village to village, helping the peasants in return for a few vegetables. It was not possible to large communities when they had so greatly multiplied.

So it was also with regard to the household service that the Brothers had sometimes undertaken. They were permitted to do this on condition that they accepted only menial tasks. Now people were too respectful to the Brothers to ask or permit that. Now they were pressed to enter the service of the well-to-do as secretaries or tutors or even to reside as honored guests, with merely nominal functions to perform. Great ecclesiastics especially were glad to attach friars to themselves in this capacity. It was almost always demoralizing to the Franciscan.

Yet unless work were found for the Brothers their demoralization would have been even greater. It was found by shifting the main centers of Franciscan activity from the little hermitages scattered through the countryside to large convents in populous towns. It was to these that people were steadily moving, as the feudal system crumbled and commerce grew. To go after souls, the whole purpose of the Franciscan apostolic life, meant that the Brothers had to follow the people.

This meant several other things besides the erection of substantial convents that were not much in keeping with the huts and caves of the primitive Franciscans. It meant organized social work for the poor, and it meant the training of men to preach in large city churches. This involved the transformation of the Friars Minor from an essentially lay movement to a society of priests with lay brothers as their auxiliaries.

In the end this change in character of the Order, though it was made possible largely through the support Elias gave to what he saw to be a necessary process, destroyed him. Though the bitterness of the opposition to him was occasioned by the severity of his rule, the principle at stake was that only priests should be eligible for office. That change, too, was necessary and inevitable. Having done his work, Elias was ruthlessly discarded.

Francis distrusted some of these changes, though he lived to see only their beginnings. In particular, this was so with regard to the emergence of learned men. It was not so much that he disapproved of learning as such; what he feared was the pride so often engendered by learning. He had been called to the way of simplicity and humility and poverty. And the new way was not his.

One can see his point. The gifted man may reflect that his gifts come from God and are therefore no occasion for self-complacency, but the scholar's accomplishments are his own, and for this reason scholars are commonly pervaded with a subtle pride. This need not happen, of course; the greatest of scholars are often very simple and modest men. They know so much that they know how little they know. The trouble is that few great men are found in any department of human activity. In the process of producing one ripe scholar, a hundred pedants are manufactured as by-products.

Trained men, however, had to be produced for the pulpit. The scope of Franciscan preaching had to be broadened from the moral exhortation to the consideration of doctrine. From the start only those commissioned by Francis were permitted to go into the pulpit, but soon after his death his friend Cardinal Ugolino, as Pope Gregory IX, insisted upon examinations and licenses for preachers.

Earnestness and goodness of heart were no longer the only qualifications, though this does not mean that Franciscan preaching lost its popular and colloquial character. Nor did the Friars Minor neglect the preaching of penance just because they were empowered to treat of dogmatic or biblical themes. Here, as elsewhere, their development did not so much consist of leaving one thing for another as of taking in a new field while continuing to till the old. When Roger Bacon, one of the many learned Franciscans on the point of appearing, praised the greatest Franciscan preacher of his day, Berthold of Regensberg, it was not on account of Berthold's learning (though he had it) but because of the simple, direct, unaffected manner of his sermons.

Simplicity might be retained, but poverty could hardly be practiced in just the same fashion as formerly. The reckless lack of all provision which startled St. Dominic when he attended the Chapter of the Mats, though amply justified on that occasion, had about it an almost miraculous element upon which it would have been presumptuous to count for everyday uses. Therefore, St. Bonaventure stated the more mature and settled Franciscan view when he said, "If we consider the Gospel closely, it is clear that it forbids us to be *solicitous* but not *provident* for the morrow. Solicitude denotes anxious care, as well as the illicit procuring and greedy storing up of superfluous things. For just as we should put our hope in the Lord in matters of salvation, so should we also leave the care of our bodily sustenance to Him; yet we should provide needful things; in so far as this can be done without injury to our spiritual welfare, and not tempt God to provide our food in a miraculous manner. Therefore, although the first friars out of zeal for higher perfection were wont to gather less alms than what is done now, it was nevertheless not forbidden them, nor is it now, to think of the future and to provide at a given time those things which we shall not be able to beg later." This was not an abandonment of the principle of poverty but merely a more reasonable application of it.

So it was also with the question of the friars making themselves into a learned body. That this had some drawbacks must be admitted, but so does everything have its drawbacks. What matters is the attainment of some preponderant good. Though the rivalry between the Franciscans and the Dominicans was the cause of jealousy, nobody is likely to say that rivalry is not an incentive to one's best efforts just because it can bring about some unfriendly feelings. It was beneficial even to the Dominicans, that great Franciscan scholars rose to challenge their eminence in the schools. From their triumphs at Paris the Franciscans passed to Oxford, arriving there in the very month of Francis's stigmata. Grossteste and Alexander of Hales and Duns Scotus and Roger Bacon, these all came out of England during the first Franciscan century, with William of Occam just a little later. Even did Junipers grow in forests, one would be willing to give them all for one man of this type.

Why, then, was Francis antagonistic to learning? The answer is that he was not antagonistic to learning except in so far as it might be detrimental to what he valued still more, simplicity and humility and poverty. He wished to conserve the scattered energies of the heart. He conceived his mission as one of love, and he saw that love might wither away in a too intellectual atmosphere. Could he have been reassured regarding this, his objection, such as it was, would have at once disappeared.

Francis was no great reader of books, not even of the Scriptures. But this, so Thomas of Celano explains, was because "Memory supplied the place of books; for if he heard a thing once it was not in vain, because his affection ruminated it with continual devotion." This he used to declare was a more fruitful way to read than to wander through a thousand treatises. Once when he was ill and one of the Brothers suggested that he read aloud to him from the Old Testament prophets Francis replied, "It is good to read the testimonies of Scripture and good to seek Our Lord in them; but for myself, I have already mastered so much of the Scriptures that I have an ample store for meditation and reflection. I need to know no more, my son; I know Christ the poor Man crucified." What we have there is simply a preference of culture, obtainable only by thoroughly digesting a few books, to the kind of information whose chief book is the encyclopedia, of profound over superficial reading, little of which is remembered and still less really understood.

Francis had slight curiosity about things unrelated to the spiritual life. He had no wish to burden his mind with what was useless to him. Yet he had a reverence for the written word so great that it will strike many people as extravagant and even superstitious. If he found any kind of writing lying on the floor or the road, he would pick it up and place it where it would not be in danger of being trodden upon. When one of the Brothers asked him why he was so respectful even to a scrap of pagan or secular writing he answered, "My son, it is because the letters there are those of which the glorious name of God is composed. Therefore the writing does not belong to pagans but to God the All Good." Similarly, he would not allow any word that he had written or dictated to be erased, even though he saw it to be redundant or badly placed. This accounts for his somewhat diffuse style, for he had to repeat a good deal in the hope of phrasing it better at the second attempt, yet permitting the first unsatisfactory attempt to stand.

Francis had an objection to the friars becoming learned because he feared that this would be detrimental to Franciscan poverty. Books in his day were very expensive, as all of them had to be written out by hand; and, though there were excellent copyists in the Order whose work cost nothing as it could be produced in their spare time —among these copyists we know that Brother Leo, some of whose books are still in existence, was a most beautiful penman—once produced, books were valuable. And even a small collection of books in a Franciscan house had to have a room in which they could be kept.

As was always his way, Francis could put what he wanted to say most forcibly not in an exordium but in a dramatic incident. The incident that remained in everybody's mind was that of a young Brother who had obtained permission from the vicar to have a book but wished, for the satisfaction of his conscience, to have Francis's permission as well. At first Francis would give neither a definite yes or no. He answered obliquely, "The heroes Charlemagne and Roland and Oliver fought for the faith, and so gained their renown. Now people try to gain it by *reading* of great deeds, and bring themselves almost to believe that they have done these by reading about them. So also with the lives of the saints; men read them more than they imitate them."

As the novice was not content with this, he spoke to Francis a day or two later, seeking a more explicit answer. He got it. Francis said, "After you have a psalter, you will want a breviary of your own. Then you will sit in your chair like a great prelate and say to your Brother, 'Bring me my breviary!'" To emphasize the lesson, Francis bent down to the hearth by which he was sitting and threw ashes over his own head, crying, "I, a breviary; I, a breviary!" He repeated this many times and then said, "Brother, I also was tempted to have books, but not after I had sought the will of the Lord by opening a copy of the Gospels. And in this I read: 'Unto you it is given to know the mysteries of the kingdom of God, but unto others in parables.' "

Even after that the novice persisted with his request and kept this up for several months. So at last Francis told him wearily, "You can do what the vicar tells you." He said this while he and the novice were walking along a road together, and a few moments later he was conscience-stricken at the consent he had given. So he said, "Let us go back to the place where I said that." Then, kneeling at the precise spot, Francis said, *"Mea culpa!* Brother, *mea culpa!"* By quoting a passage from the Rule he gave his answer: "The Friar Minor should have nothing except a tunic with a cord and breeches, and to those who are forced by manifest necessity, sandals."

When Francis referred to himself as an ignorant man, that was, of course, only a fashion of speaking. He had all the learning he required for his purpose and overflowed with genius and what does not always go with genius, a really brilliant cleverness. Yet his power did not lie in any of these qualities or even in his quite extraordinary charm, however useful all these assets were. He could, in fact, more than hold his own with scholars, and we hear of a Doctor of Divinity of the Dominicans who, after talking with Francis, exclaimed, "Brothers, the theology of this man soars aloft to heaven on the wings of truth and contemplation like an eagle, while our science laboriously creeps on the earth." One of the most detailed accounts of his preaching comes from Thomas of Spalatro, a man who attained some distinction, of a sermon he heard Francis deliver at Bologna on the Feast of the Assumption, 1222, at which time Thomas was a student at the university there.

Francis preached in the largest square of the city before a thickly packed audience, many of whom were university students and who probably did not have much respect for the unlettered friar. Their respect could hardly have been increased by Francis's appearance, which Thomas described as unimposing. They saw a little man of rather plain features who was wearing a stained and patched habit. His fervor soon caught the crowd, and they were astonished at the masterly way he handled his announced theme: "Angels, Men, Demons," the kind of a discourse suited for that learned audience and yet far removed from the usual academic manner. It was delivered, Thomas noted, not in the style of a preacher but conversationally. Here was a man of the people talking to the people. Though the subject was more abstract than was customary with Francis, "God gave such efficacy to his words that he brought back to peace and harmony many nobles whose savage fury had not stopped short from the shedding of blood." Even there it was, in its effect, the typical Franciscan discourse that stressed peace and penance.

Whenever the true spirit was preserved, Francis did not show himself opposed to the development of learning in the Order. This is clearly shown in his attitude toward St. Anthony of Padua. He had been an Augustinian in Portugal, but he was so deeply moved when the bodies of the five Franciscans martyred by the Moors were brought to Coimbra that he left his Order to join the friars. Among his new associates he was for some time not specially regarded because, out of humility, he kept his eloquence and learning hidden. They were discovered only by accident, but once discovered, Anthony leaped into fame as a preacher.

Not only that; he became a lecturer in theology at Bologna in 1223, and so much with Francis's approval that the letters of Francis to him were addressed to "Brother Anthony, my bishop." Though Francis remained uneasy about Franciscans founding schools of theology, he saw that, if it had to be done, a man like Anthony was the one to do it. If he was of the new type of Franciscans in his scholarship—this has recently brought him the title of Doctor of the Church, which was also obtained by his near-contemporary St. Bonaventure—he was, like Bonaventure, thoroughly Franciscan in his simplicity and emotional warmth.

Yet more remarkable than Anthony's famous sermon to the fishes —which may be only a fastening on to him of the kind of animal stories told of Francis himself—is the other story of how, while he was poring over his reading, he saw the Child Jesus standing on his book. That was how it should be: learning should increase piety, from the book should come Christ, from the word the Word.

T HE DARKNESS GATHERS

Though it is at least questionable whether the modern biographers are right who suggest that everything that happened after 1221 was done against the will of Francis, there is no doubt that the years 1221–23 were for him dark and troubled. Things had turned out somewhat differently from what he had expected, and he was so pure an idealist that anything in the nature of compromise was painful. But it should be remembered that he was always in very poor health after his return from Egypt and the Holy Land, and that the source of his depression was, at least in part, due to this fact. There is also the mystical explanation that the darkness through which he passed was the preparation for further illumination of spirit. In any event, he had far too much humility (not to mention humor and good sense) even to approach anything like disillusionment.

He no longer had any official standing in the Order except the nominal title of minister-general. The actual authority was in the hands of Brother Elias, and, though he seems to have acted loyally toward Francis, he could not but recognize that new conditions made new methods necessary. The tightening up of discipline put Elias in the anomalous position of a Franciscan bureaucrat, restrained for the moment mainly by Francis's dislike of rigidity and dictatorial methods.

As to just what his own position was Francis was, perhaps, not very clear in his own mind. As he had resigned all office, he had no more than a moral ascendancy, and he was too gentle and humble to assert himself. Yet his ascendancy may have been all the greater for this very reason, and he continued to be regarded as the real head of the order, as he was certainly its soul.

If things were at times rather difficult for him, we may surmise that he sometimes made things a little difficult for those in authority, for an appeal could always be made from their instructions to primitive practice. There were occasions when some of his first companions urged him to back them up and to make his weight more decisively felt. There were even moments when, without any such urging, he was almost on the point of doing this. Then he would exclaim, "If I come to the chapter, I will show them what my will is!" His more normal mood was found in his saying (possibly to Leo), "It seems to me that I would not be a true Friar Minor if I acted except in this way: when the Brothers invite me to the chapter and, moved by their devotion, I go and preach the word of God to them, and when, at the end of my sermon, they cry out, 'We will not have you to rule over us, for you are not eloquent but are simple and ignorant.' I would not be a true Friar Minor if I did not rejoice to the same extent when they reproached me and cast me off as when they venerated and honored me. For when they honor me there may be danger to my soul, so I ought to rejoice over the profit to my soul when they blame me."

On another occasion a Brother said to him, "Father, forgive me, but I must call to your mind how formerly through the grace of God the whole Order flourished in purity of perfection. Then all the friars were fervent and carefully observed poverty in all things, having only small buildings poorly furnished and few books and clothes, and were of one mind in their love of God and their neighbor, as men truly apostolical and evangelical. But of late this purity and affection have begun to change, and some of the Brothers have such blindness that they think that people will be edified by the new rather than the former way, and they live more comfortably, counting for naught the holy simplicity and humility and poverty which were the foundation of our Order. Now some of us, considering these matters, believing that they are displeasing to you, wonder why you permit them and do not correct them."

To this Francis answered, "May the Lord have mercy on you, Brother, for you go contrary to my thought and would mix me up in things that do not pertain to my office. For so long as I held office over the friars and they remained true to their profession and vocation, though from the beginning of my conversion I was always infirm, yet with my small solicitude I satisfied them by example and preaching. But later, after the Lord had multiplied the number of the friars, they, on account of their lukewarmness began to depart from the right and secure way in which they had formerly walked. Therefore I handed over the rule of the Order to the Lord and to the ministers. But though in the general chapter I excused myself from holding office because of my infirmities, nevertheless, if even now the friars would be willing to walk according to my will, I would wish that they had no other minister except myself to the day of my death. Indeed, so much would I rejoice at the profit of the Brethren that if I were lying in bed, I would be willing to serve in office, as that is only spiritual. But since I am not able to correct and amend them by preaching and example, I will not become an executioner, punishing and flogging them like a magistrate in the world. So until the day of my death I shall teach the Brethren only by good example, teaching them what I have been taught, so that they will be inexcusable before God. Otherwise I am not obliged to give any account of them to God."

Had Francis taken any other attitude, he would probably have brought about a schism in the Order, and this might have resulted in its collapse. Had he been more of a "strong man," as that term is generally understood, he would have yielded to this temptation. That he did not do so is the real measure of his strength. Nevertheless, to a German friar who came to him and said, "I ask one favor: it is that if the Brothers ever come to live no longer after the Rule, you will permit me to separate myself from them, either alone or with a few others, and to observe the Rule in its completeness," Francis answered "with great joy": "Know that Christ as well as I authorize what you have just been asking." Then, placing his hand upon that Brother's head, he blessed him, saying, "Thou art a priest forever after the order of Melchisedech." Similarly, he wrote to Brother Leo, "I say to you: Yes, my son, and as a mother. For in this word and counsel I sum up briefly all the words we said on the way, and if afterward you have need to come to me for advice, thus I advise you: In whatever way it seems best to you to please God and to follow His footsteps and poverty, do so with the blessing of God and in my obedience. And if it be necessary for you on account of your soul or other consolation and you wish, Leo, to come to me, come."

From this it is evident that, though Francis refused to make any public pronouncement, he privately issued permission that those who wished to follow the Rule according to the primitive practice might do so and that, should a contingency arise which made them feel it was necessary to separate from the main body to live a true Franciscan life, they were free even to do that. Though he could have withdrawn with a large body of followers, he never thought of doing so. Nor did he seem to believe that things had as yet come to such a pass as to make this advisable for anybody.

In his difficulties it was his custom to betake himself at once to prayer. Afterward he seemed not only to be at peace but to have no recollection of whatever it was that had distressed him. Never did he comment, "So and so did not please me by what he did," or "That Brother said something that I did not like." For the sake of peace he put up with what was going on, contenting himself with doing what he wished others to do but avoiding all contention and complaint. It was a kind of surrender: he washed his hands of all responsibility except that of observing the Rule himself, so keeping the torch of the spirit of the Order alight. Being less than the least was his way of being most completely the minister-general.

Yet he must not be considered as having failed. Actually, he was one of the most successful men who ever lived, the only man who could conceivably have done what he did. Imperfectly Franciscan though some of the friars were—the Order had grown too large and had had too rapid a growth, and only a small percentage of its members could be expected to have thoroughly assimilated the founder's ideas—even the imperfect were affected by his influence. Francis had given the world an inspiration that has never ceased to operate upon it.

He eventually reached a deep serenity of mind. One day when he was praying, "Lord, I give thee back the family which thou hast given me," he heard Christ's answer: "Tell me, simple and feeble-minded manikin, why you are so sad when the friars do not walk in the way I have shown you? Also tell me, who has planted this Order of Friars? Who has made them to be converted to penitence? Who gives the virtue of perseverance? Is it not I? I chose you not because you were learned or eloquent, but in order that the works I work in you, may work in themselves. I will watch over my flock. Wherefore I say to you, be not so sad, since I have planted in eternal charity the Order of Friars. Even should there remain only three, yet even then it shall be my Order and I will not give it back forever."

One catches now and then during the years of his gloom an insistence upon obedience which, in its rigidity, strikes one as Ignatian rather than Franciscan, as when he said that it lay in allowing oneself to be moved at the will of the superior as though one were a corpse. Previously obedience had not been so much demanded as spontaneously offered. Now it had to be stressed: "Dearest Brothers, fulfill a command at the first word, not waiting to have it repeated. Do not argue or judge, for you will be asked to perform no impossibilities, for even were I to ask you to do what is above your strength, strength would be given in obedience itself."

Temptations to despair now came upon him, as they had occasionally even in past years. During the Lent he made in 1211 on the island in Lake Trasimeno—as long ago as that—the devil had taunted him, "There is salvation for all men except a self-tormenter, such as you are!" So, until he was finally relieved from his depression toward the end of 1223, it had sometimes seemed to him that he heard demoniac voices telling him, "It is all in vain, Francis! Pray as much as you will to God, but it is to me that you belong!"

Perhaps he helped to set himself free from such temptations by having to save others from the kind of despair to which sensitive and introspective minds are peculiarly liable. Thus there was the case of Rufino, Clare's cousin. The devil appeared to him in the guise of the Crucified, saying, "O Brother Rufino, why do you afflict yourself in penance and prayers, seeing that you are not among those predestined to eternal life? I know those who are predestined, and do not believe the son of Peter Bernardone if he tells you the contrary, nor question him on this matter, for neither he nor others know, but I alone, Who am the Son of God."

Rufino was so overwhelmed that he did not tell Francis what had happened, thinking this useless. But Francis, divining his trouble, sent Brother Masseo to him, only to get a curt, "What have I to do with Brother Francis?" At this Masseo, seeing that Rufino must be under a delusion of the devil, begged him to go with him to Francis. When Francis saw him coming, he called out to him while he was still far off, "O miserable Brother Rufino, in whom have you believed?" When he had dragged the story out of him, Francis told him how to treat that apparition of the Crucified and insult it, being sure that it was really the devil, promising that if he did so the apparition would disappear. "You may take it," he assured Rufino, "as a sure sign that this is the devil, and not Christ, because Christ never hardens the heart to all good, while the devil always does so."

Rufino followed Francis's advice, and the devil fled in such a rage, says the *Fioretti*, that there was a tremendous fall of rocks from Mount Subasio, and the valley was lit up with horrible flashes of fire. So completely was Rufino set free from his despair that Francis afterward, noting his holiness, used to say that God had revealed to him that Rufino was one of the three holiest souls in the world. Therefore, while he was still living, Francis used to call him "Saint Rufino."

To another Brother who asked Francis to pray for him that he might be delivered from temptations that were beyond his strength, Francis said, "Believe me, my son, that I believe you to be all the more a servant of God because of this very thing. Therefore know that the more you are tempted, the dearer you are to me. Temptation conquered is a kind of ring whereby God espouses the soul. Nobody should count himself a servant of God until he has passed through temptations and tribulations."

Francis himself had prayed that the Lord would set him free from his tribulations. Then one day in the church of St. Mary of the Angels he heard the words of the Gospel spoken by an interior Voice, "If you have faith as a grain of mustard seed you shall say to that mountain, 'Remove hence to another place,' and it shall remove." And Francis asked, "Lord, what is this mountain?" Again the Voice spoke, "This mountain is your temptation." And Francis answered, "Lord, it is done to me as Thou hast said." Immediately he felt completely delivered, so that it seemed to him that he had never so much as had any temptations. The mountain had, indeed, been cast into the sea.

In all this, as Francis used to say, the sovereign cure was spiritual joy. "The devil," he declared, "exults most when he can filch joy from one of God's servants. He carries dust with him and casts it into the conscience by the smallest chink; but when joy is there he can do nothing. The devil cannot hurt Christ's servants when he sees them filled with holy mirth. Therefore when we are troubled about anything we should pray, and remain in Our Heavenly Father's presence until He restores the joy of our salvation. For if we tarry in gloom, that Babylonian stuff will increase, and unless it is purged out will produce rust in the heart."

Apparently he had already passed out of the clouds of his melancholy before the approval of the Rule by Honorius III in November, 1223. That event increased his joy, for, though the Rule was not quite all that Francis had hoped for, it did embody his ideas, even while moderating them somewhat. Now there could be no justification for those who wanted a different kind of life. Whether or not they were faithful in observance, the Rule stood and would stand. With that the heart of Francis sang.

On the occasion of his visit to Rome to present the Rule to the Pope, there occurred an incident that reveals that, ill though Francis was and prematurely aged, he had become once more the gay and cheerful Francis of his youth. He gave Brother Jacoba, the Countess Settesoli, a lamb that he had rescued, as he had rescued so many others, when it was on its way to the butcher's. This the countess kept in her own room, and when she went to church it kept closely by her side going and returning. If the countess was a little late in rising for Mass, the lamb would gently nudge her with its head and bleat until she got up.

She kept it until it was full grown. From its wool three years later she wove the shroud for Francis's burial.

That Christmas was to be for Francis the happiest of his whole life, and for him Christmas had always been the feast of feasts. Once when it had fallen on a Friday and the friars had intended to keep the usual Friday fast, Francis declared, "I would that the very walls eat flesh on such a day, or, as they cannot, that they should at any rate be greased outside!" He had been given to saying that he wished that he knew the Emperor and could ask for an edict that corn be scattered on the ground for the birds that day. Now he sent word to a man named John Vellita, who had given the Brothers a woody cliff at Greccio, that he wished to celebrate Christmas at a cave there. "And so make haste," the message added, "if this pleases you, to go before and prepare what I tell you. For I would make memorial of the Child who was born in Bethlehem, so that in some sort we may behold with our bodily eyes how He lay in a manger on the hay with the ox and ass standing by."

The Brothers in all the places nearby were asked to attend, and the country people flocked there with exulting hearts, carrying torches. The woods rang with their voices, and the echoes of their jubilation came from the rocks. There they all saw the manger straw in the cave and the ox and the ass. It seemed to some that they saw even more, for they declared afterward that they had seen a Child asleep in the manger, Who, when Francis went near, stretched out His little arms to him. And when Francis, as the deacon at the midnight Mass, preached, whenever he uttered the word "Bethlehem" he did so as though he were a sheep bleating, and when he named the Christ Child, he licked his lips as though his whole mouth were filled and dripping with sweetness.

It was this crib of Greccio that seems to have originated the custom, now universal, of a crib in all Catholic churches at Christmas. But these have only plaster images as representations. At Greccio there was Mass in a cave and a real ox and a real ass and, most wonderful of all, the Child Jesus himself asleep on the hay!

Even so, Francis made his dramatic protest in favor of poverty. When later that day in the refectory at Rieti one of the Brothers read of the penury with which the Blessed Virgin was surrounded when she gave birth to Her Son, Francis rose from the table in tears and ate the rest of his Christmas dinner sitting on the bare ground.

Again at Greccio on Easter Sunday, when the tables had been laid with special care for a feast, with table linen and glassware—furnishings that Franciscans rarely used and had probably borrowed for the occasion—Francis came in, but, says Celano, "on the smiling table he by no means smiled." He quietly went outside and begged the use for a little while of the battered hat and the ragged cloak of a poor man he found there. Then after the meal had started Francis came in—muffled up and with the hat pulled over his eyes—crying, "For the love of God give alms to this poor sick pilgrim!"

The guardian answered, "Come in, good man, for the love of Him whom you have invoked." Then Francis took off his hat and everybody saw who it was. But he insisted upon eating the food they gave him sitting by the hearth among the ashes.

"*Now*," said he, "I am sitting as a Lesser Brother should! I saw a table spread and adorned, and I knew it was not the table of poor men who go begging from door to door."

THE FINAL SEAL

From the day when, seventeen years earlier, he had knelt in ecstasy before the Byzantine crucifix at St. Damian's and had heard Christ speak to him from the cross, Francis had borne the stigmata in his heart, though not as yet in his flesh. Now the hour was coming for that great marvel. The marks of the Lord were about to be imprinted upon him. His life was on the point of receiving what Dante called the final seal—*l'ultimo sigillo*.

He had long been a man given to prayer, but since his retirement from the active direction of his Order he had been completely given to it. Whatever he was doing, whether walking in the woods or sitting with others or eating or drinking, he never really ceased praying. Even in the hermitages where he now lived nearly all the time, at Greccio or Fonte Colomba or the Carceri, he was withdrawn into a more remote retirement, rarely seeing any of the Brothers and emerging from his cell only when food became absolutely necessary. Usually he ate his poor meals alone; he always did so when he felt a great craving for contemplation. Wherever he happened to be he yielded to the Spirit of God when he felt it descending upon him. If he was at that moment with the Brothers, he found means of giving them a signal they understood that they were not to talk to him, and either he went off alone or they left him, or, if that was not possible, he pulled his cowl or drew his sleeve across his face. A silence then fell, or if the Brothers still had to talk, it was in awed whispers. Yet he was most careful when he was with others to give no outward indications in the form of gestures or even a deep breathing of being absorbed in God.

Already he was a fellow citizen of the angels. Already he possessed some share of the beatific life. His resignation of office had made possible at last what he had always longed for, an undistracted contemplation. Though he had experienced a period when he had felt depression and pain, this had passed and he had reached a perfect serenity that was never again to be disturbed.

It was the preparation for what was about to be experienced.

Even when he had felt grief over the shortcomings of some of the Brothers, the conduct of others had gladdened him and filled him with hope for the future of the Order. When word came as to how admirably the friars in a Spanish hermitage were living—one of those groups of four that interchanged the roles of Mary and Martha—he turned toward the west, where Spain was, and made the sign of the cross in blessing over them. What had specially moved him was a story of how when the bell rang for the meal and one of the Brothers was late, because he was absorbed in prayer, he nevertheless, when at last he was brought to the refectory, knelt down in *culpa* as though he had committed a fault.

The Pope had now approved his Rule. And Honorius had gladdened him still further by a special privilege given the following month. It was that from henceforth the Brothers living at the hermitages might have Mass said there at a portable altar. Until then they had been obliged to come down from their eyries to the nearest church. As this was in no case very near and in some weather inaccessible, Mass had not always been possible. Moreover, there was a temporary loss of the sense of solitude and therefore some distraction in their prayers when they entered a town. Now the stillness could be unbroken and Mass said as well. So, though priests were not available for all the hermitages, as the Friars Minor as yet consisted of those who were, in an overwhelming majority, laymen, Francis had a priest in Brother Leo, his secretary, and therefore he could always be sure of having Mass.

The solitude of the hermitages in the Rietine valley to the south of Assisi was great, but there came a time when Francis felt the desire for a still more perfect seclusion. So in the summer of 1224 he decided that he would spend the private Lent he usually kept—one of four such Lents—from the Feast of the Assumption on August 15 to the Feast of St. Michael on September 29, at La Verna, the mountain given him eleven years before by Count Orlando dei Cattani. He had been there several times already, and this was the last time he was to go there. He seems to have had a secret intuition that something extraordinary was to happen.

When Francis had sent a couple of Brothers to take possession of it in 1213, they had gone under an escort of fifty armed men supplied by the count. This was because of the bandits that infested those trails through the woods. Since then the bandits had discovered that the tattered friars had nothing upon them worth stealing, and perhaps also their reputation for sanctity protected them. This time Francis dispensed with a guard and took with him only a chosen body of Brothers—Leo, Masseo, Angelo, and Illuminato.

They trudged along the valley of the Tiber to where it had its source and then began their steep ascent along a winding path through the pines and beeches. Though all that country was rugged, La Verna overtopped the other mountains and stood apart, almost a column of solid stone, pointing straight and solemn into the sky. Under their feet were precipices, and along the slit chasms strong winds roared, threatening at any moment to hurl on their heads enormous lichen-covered boulders that seemed to hang by a thread or even to be poised in empty air. From the summit one can look out for miles toward range on range of mountains. Francis could not have found a place more completely desolate or more grandly beautiful.

On the last stage of the ascent they asked a peasant if he could lend his ass to carry Francis, who was weary and ill, up to the difficult crest. When he found that this was the Brother Francis of whom he had heard so much, he turned to him and said, "Try then to be as good as people think you are!" At this Francis got off the ass and kissed the man's feet in thanks for this admonition.

The day was hot, and after a while the peasant began to moan, "I shall die of thirst unless I can find some water to drink!" As there was no sign of water there, and the peasant knew of no spring, Francis again got off his ass. This time he knelt in prayer. Then he said, "Hasten to yonder rock and there you will find a spring." So it proved to be, though water had never flowed there before, nor was it ever found again, though it was often looked for afterward.

When they reached the summit they rested a short time under an oak, and at once a flock of birds flew towards them. Some perched on Francis's shoulders or on his outstretched hands. Smiling happily he said to the other Brothers, "It must be God's will that we should come here. See how much our sisters the birds rejoice at our coming."

The count had built a little chapel there—dedicated like that of the Portiuncula to St. Mary of the Angels—and the day after their arrival he came over with supplies of provisions, saying, "I want you to send a messenger to me for anything you may need; I shall be very angry if you fail to do this." Although Francis promised that they would do so, after Count Orlando had gone back to his castle at Chiusi Francis told the Brothers, "Do not pay too much attention to what Lord Orlando has said. We must remember holy poverty."

There seem to have been a few days of pleasant rest before the Lent began. On his bed on the bare rock Francis, before he at last sank into the little sleep he permitted himself, had a vision of an angel. "I will play for you," said this shining one, "as we play before the throne of God." With that, the angel drew his bow across the string. But he made only one stroke. Had he made another, Francis told the Brothers next morning, he could not have endured so ineffable a beauty and his soul and body must have parted.

At morning he had waked to a different kind of music. A falcon awakened him with its cries. Every morning after that it came to the overhanging rock where Francis lay. On such mornings as Francis was weighed down more than usual with his infirmities, he noticed that Brother Falcon, in his courtesy, came later to allow a little more sleep.

Looking back upon all this, the Brothers surmised that the birds may have been sent as precursors for the seraph who was soon to appear.

It was fitting that this angelic apparition should come at the close of Lent kept in honor of St. Michael. The devotion that Francis had to the warrior archangel, the captain of the hosts of heaven, was that shared by all knightly souls. Indeed for all angels, those who are with us in our earthly warfare, Francis had a special reverence. He taught that their presence must never be outraged and that we should not do before them what we would not do in the sight of men. In St. Michael he honored all those pure spirits.

When the time for beginning the fast arrived on August 15 Francis withdrew more completely from his companions. He made an arrangement with Brother Leo that he alone should visit him, but even Leo was to come only once a day to take him some food and once at night to say Matins with him. Moreover, those nightly visits were to be permitted only under certain conditions. Leo was to stop and say at his side of the little wooden bridge that went across the chasm, on the opposite side of which Francis had his retreat, *"Domine, labia mea aperies."* Then if Francis made the response, *"Et os meum annuntiabit laudem tuum,"* Leo was to venture to cross. If no reply came, he was to go back and leave Francis undisturbed.

Once when Leo arrived but did not get any response he nevertheless crossed the bridge and, not finding Francis in his "cell," his bed in a hollow of the rock, began searching for him on tiptoe through the wood. At last he heard Francis's voice. It was saying over and over again, "Who art Thou, O my Most Sweet God? And what am I except Thy most vile and unprofitable servant?" Leo saw descending from heaven what seemed to be a torch of fire which rested on Francis's head. A Voice spoke out of the flame, but Leo could not understand the words.

Fearing to disturb Francis, he withdrew and watched from a distance. After what seemed a long while he saw Francis, with eyes fixed on some point far off, stretch out his hands three times to the flame, after which it went back to the skies. As Leo was trying to tiptoe away, Francis heard the leaves rustling under his feet and called to him, and Leo was very afraid, lest for this disobedience he be afterward deprived of Francis's companionship.

Francis now came toward him, crying, "Who is there?"

Leo answered, "It is Leo, my Father."

Then Francis said, "Why did you come, Brother Little Sheep?" At the tender nickname Leo's heart lifted, knowing that Francis could not be very angry. Yet Francis demanded, "Have I not told you not to come watching me? Tell me by holy obedience whether you have seen or heard anything."

Kneeling down, Leo related what he had seen, what he had heard. Even so, he made bold to ask Francis what all this meant. Francis told him: "Know, Brother Little Sheep of God, that two lights were shown me. In one I saw and understood myself, and in the other I saw and understood My Creator. The flame you saw was God, and he spoke to me as of old he spoke to Moses. And He said to me, 'Search in thy bosom and give me what thou findest there.' So I searched and found there a ball of gold. That I offered to God. And I did this three times. And these three balls were holy obedience and most high poverty and glorious chastity."

They sat there talking an hour or so, and then Francis, having told Leo never again to dare cross the bridge unless he got the signal, sent him back to his cell and turned himself to prayer.

On the eve of the Feast of the Holy Cross, September 14, a month after the Lent had begun, Francis had an angel sent to him to forewarn him still more strictly to prepare himself "humbly and with all patience to receive whatever God will give thee and work in thee."

To which Francis answered, "I am ready to endure with patience all things whatsoever my Lord will do unto me."

The next morning, before the break of dawn, Francis prayed, "O My Lord Jesus Christ, I pray thee to grant me two graces before I die. The first is that I may feel in my soul and in my body, so far as this may be, the pangs thou didst bear in the hour of thy most bitter passion. The second is that I feel in my heart, so far as this may be, the exceeding love that enkindled thee, O Son of God, willingly to endure such agony for us sinners."

The climax was now approaching.

It did not delay long. Just before daybreak the stigmata were imprinted upon him.

While Francis was kneeling in prayer there came toward him from heaven a cross. Upon it was the figure of a seraph. It was not the figure of Christ, though in an attempt to explain the mystery, St. Bonaventure and others have suggested that it was Christ in the aspect of a seraph. Though this may be so, it would be best not to attempt any rationalizing of what happened. The face of the Figure crucified was beautiful beyond all imagining, though it was the face of suffering.

Two wings were stretched above the seraph's head; two were spread as though for flight; and two wings covered the luminous body. After shining there a moment it vanished.

Then Francis fell into thought. He wondered how it was possible for an immortal spirit to be subject to mortal pangs. We may be permitted to think that the very fact that the vision was so strange and that Francis was perplexed is a guarantee of its genuineness. A mind fabricating something, knowing that it was necessary to produce a story that was logically defensible, would have proceeded in another fashion.

As he stood there pondering this mystery, it was somehow revealed to him that Divine Providence had shown him the vision in this form in order that he might understand that it was not by the martyrdom of the body but by the enkindling of the mind that he must be wholly transformed into the image of Christ Crucified.

Perhaps he had stood or knelt there in a trance of wonder until the fall of night; perhaps all this happened so quickly that the morning light had not yet dawned on Holy Cross Day, for the *Fioretti,* immediately after telling of Francis's attempts to understand what had happened, relates on the same page that the whole mountain seemed to be burning and the peaks and the valleys were all flooded as with the light of day. Some muleteers who were on their way to Romagna and had slept in an inn that night, rose and saddled their beasts, thinking it was morning. Not until they were some distance on their road did they see the light die out and then the material sun rise.

It is easy to believe that Francis lost all sense of time. The vision had seemed to him to have lasted an age, though it was probably something unsustainable and had been only an instant. But his wonder-struck ruminations may have been drawn out for hours. When he came to himself he became conscious of something extraordinary having happened to him. He looked at his feet and hands; they appeared to be pierced through with nails, the heads of which were in his palms and insteps. Where the points came out on the other side, they were bent over; his finger could be slipped in as into a ring. But the nails seemed to be formed of his own blackened flesh.

He put his hand to his side. From it there came a slow trickle of blood. When he tried to walk he could not put the soles of his feet to the ground.

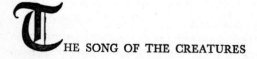

HE SONG OF THE CREATURES

It is unnecessary to attempt here any explanation as to how the stigmata could have happened. All that need be said is that nothing like it had ever occurred before, unless St. Paul was alluding to the same phenomenon when, at the end of his Epistle to the Galatians, he wrote, "From henceforth let no man trouble me: for I bear in my body the marks of the Lord Jesus." What is certain is that the stigmata have been conferred many times since that Holy Cross Day 1224, so that there are now over a hundred well-authenticated cases, including several people still living.

The evidence for the fact of Francis's stigmata is so overwhelming that it had to be accepted even by a mind as skeptical as that of Sabatier. Indeed, there are few historical happenings to which there is stronger attestation, and none that has so convincing a documentary proof as we have on a parchment which contains one of the two existing specimens of the handwriting of Francis. It is alluded to by Celano and Bonaventure and may still be seen at Assisi.

On the front of this parchment Francis has written the blessing from the Book of Numbers: "The Lord bless and keep thee. The Lord show his face to thee and have mercy upon thee. The Lord turn his countenance upon thee and give thee peace." Not content with writing this in his own hand, in a script larger and not nearly so elegant as that of Brother Leo's, Francis added, dividing what follows with his sign manual of the *thau* (this time standing upon the rough drawing of a skull): *"Dominus benedicat Leo te."* The misplacement of the words is obviously intended to indicate a special emphasis, and that the *thau* comes through the *Leo* shows that this blessing is like the liturgical blessings of the missal.

On this parchment—it is five and a half inches long and four wide—Leo has written by way of authentication, "Blessed Francis wrote with his own hand this blessing for me, Brother Leo," and "In like manner he made this sign *Thau* together with the head with his own hand." He added for good measure, "Blessed Francis two years before his death kept a Lent in the place of Mount La Verna in honor of the Blessed Virgin Mary, the Mother of the Lord, and of Blessed Michael the Archangel, from the feast of the Assumption of the holy Virgin Mary until the September feast of Michael. And the hand of the Lord was laid upon him; after the vision and speech of the Seraph and the impression of the stigmata of Christ in his body he made and wrote with his own hand the Praises written on the other side of the sheet, giving thanks to the Lord for the benefits conferred on him."

What is written on the other side is a kind of poem in Latin in Francis's script. It is in part illegible, but it has been reconstructed from copies made of it centuries ago, and is given here in the translation made of it by Archbishop Robinson:

"Thou art holy, Lord God, Who alone workest wonders. Thou art strong. Thou art great. Thou art most high. Thou art the Almighty King, Thou, holy Father, King of heaven and earth. Thou art the Lord God Triune and One; all good. Thou art good, all good, highest good, Lord God living and true. Thou art charity, love. Thou art wisdom. Thou art humility. Thou art patience. Thou art security. Thou art quietude. Thou art joy and gladness. Thou art justice and temperance. Thou art all riches to sufficiency. Thou art beauty. Thou art meekness. Thou art protector. Thou art guardian and defender. Thou art strength. Thou art refreshment. Thou art our hope. Thou art our faith. Thou art our great sweetness. Thou art our eternal life, great and admirable Lord, God Almighty, Merciful Saviour."

What Leo wrote on this parchment was added later, but what Francis wrote was writen before he left La Verna. One day he said to Leo, "Bring paper and ink and I will write down words of God and his praises, which I have pondered in my heart." Having done this, he said to Leo, who seems to have been passing through a period of depression, "Take this paper and keep it until the day of your death." And Leo did most carefully preserve this relic, dear to him but even more important to us because of what it witnesses to. And there is every reason to believe that it was mainly from Leo, though also with contributions from Masseo, that we get what is a wonderfully detailed and explicit account of the most wonderful happening in Francis's whole life. There had indeed been given to him the final seal. He could now wait in a kind of eager calm for death.

The very day after the Michaelmas Lent had ended on September 29 Francis left La Verna. About this we have a letter written by Brother Masseo which tells how early in the morning, immediately after Mass, Francis, riding upon an ass sent by Count Orlando (because now he was unable to walk), set out with his companions for the Portiuncula. To the friars left behind he made an address, knowing that he would not be there again, commending to them the care of the sacred mountain, which they were never to allow to be profaned. And they were to love one another with a special affection. To Masseo he said afterward, "Brother Masseo, my will is that here should live the best of my Order. Ah! ah! ah! Brother Masseo! I can say no more."

He gave its charge to Masseo and Sylvester and Illuminato, mystics fitted to care for so holy a place. He said adieu to them all with, "Peace be with you, my dearest sons! Adieu! I go from you in the body, but I leave my heart with you. I go away with Brother Little Sheep of God to St. Mary of the Angels and I shall not come back again. Adieu! Adieu to all! Adieu, holy mountain! Mount of the angels! Adieu, dearest Brother Falcon! I thank you for the love you bore me. Adieu, adieu, Sasso Spicco! Never again shall I come to visit you. Adieu, St. Mary of the Angels! To thee, Mother of the eternal Word, I commend my sons."

He spoke in tears in this farewell that was a benediction, extended even to the falcon and the overhanging rock under which he used to pray. All the brothers were also in tears. "He, weeping also," says Masseo, "carried away our hearts." Writing his account of that parting, the Brother ends, "I, Brother Masseo, have written this in tears. The Blessing of God be upon us."

They came down slowly from the mountain and followed the valley of the Tiber again. Everywhere people came out to meet Francis with the cry, "Behold the saint!" Stories of wonderful happenings had spread abroad, for the local shepherds had seen the bright light that shone on La Verna sixteen days before and took it to be the sign of some great miracle that had been wrought on Francis, though they could have had no definite news as to just what this was. As they wanted to kiss his hands, he bandaged them still more heavily, though they were bandaged already; and they got only his finger tips to kiss.

He was half in a trance all the time or, at least, had his mind so set upon prayer that he was hardly conscious of what was happening. People thronged around him, touching him and some of them even snipping off little bits of his habit to keep as relics; but he was scarcely more sensible of all this than if he had been a corpse. Some distance beyond the town of Borgo San Sepolcro he came back enough to mundane matters to ask, "When do we get to Borgo San

Sepolcro?" He was quite unaware that they had already passed through it. That night they rested at a lepers' hospital.

It must have been the following night that they were caught in a lonely place by an early snowfall. They huddled up for shelter under a hollowed rock, and there the muleteer lent by Count Orlando grumbled about the cold, against which they could not even make a fire of sticks. He began to rail at Francis for having brought him to this plight. Upon this Francis, having compassion for him, touched him with his wounded hand, and at that he felt warmed and fell asleep. When dawn broke, the man told Brother Leo that he had never rested more soundly in his bed.

The next day they reached the Portiuncula. And as they came toward it Brother Leo saw a cross, and on it the Crucified, that went before Francis. It was of such splendor that it lit the whole road through the dark woods. In this way they came to St. Mary of the Angels.

Francis made no secret of the fact that he had had a vision of a seraph. For he told Brother Leo to wash with water the stone upon which the apparition had rested. When he had done this, Francis told him, "Now wash it with wine." Then he had to wash it with oil and balsam. And Francis confided to him that the Lord had promised him four things: that the Order of Friars Minor should last until the Judgment Day, that nobody who persecuted the Order should prosper, that no evil liver should remain in it for long, and that all who loved the order, even though they should be sinners, would obtain mercy at the last.

But Francis was very secretive about the stigmata, though this was something difficult to conceal from those with him. Brother Illuminato, noting that something extraordinary had occurred, went to Francis and said, "Brother, we know that divine secrets are shown you, but these are not only for your own sake but for the benefit of others. You might be guilty of hiding your talent should you keep this to yourself."

Though Francis was accustomed to say, "My secret to me," this time he told Illuminato of the coming of the seraph, though he was still guarded about what had happened to him.

Perhaps it was by way of drawing something out of him that Brother Pacifico, the poet, told him that one day while he was absorbed in prayer he was rapt into heaven and saw many seats, among them one more glorious than the others, and he heard a Voice that said, "This was the seat of Lucifer, and in his place will be seated the humble Francis." He asked Francis point-blank what was his opinion of himself.

The answer he got was, "It seems to me that I am a greater sinner than anyone else in the world." And when Pacifico protested that that was not the truth, Francis said again, "If Christ had shown such mercy to a criminal, however wicked he might be, that He has shown to me, he would be tenfold more perfect than I am."

Whether Pacifico actually had such a vision—or, at least, its genuineness—may be open to doubt. But this can be taken as sure: he discovered the truth about the stigmata, and he even found a way of showing them by ruse to another Brother. "I will say at departing," he told him, " 'Dearest Mother, give me your hand to kiss.' And while I am kissing it, you may take a look at it."

Though he succeeded in this pious trick, Francis saw through it and called Pacifico back to say to him, "God pardon you, Brother; for you give me much distress sometimes."

When Pacifico asked, "What distress?" Francis made no reply and let the incident close in silence.

It was inevitable that rumors about the stigmata should circulate, try as Francis might to hide what could not be hidden. When one of the Brothers caught sight of his feet and exclaimed, "What is this?" he was told sharply, "Mind your own business!" So the Brothers found it advisable to turn their eyes away when Francis was obliged to uncover his hands or feet.

He now wore, for the first time since he had adopted the habit and the unshod mode, not only sandals but socks to cover his wounds. Even so, it was impossible to conceal the fact that he could now walk only a few steps and even these with the utmost difficulty. His hands he usually kept in the sleeves of his robe, and if any of the Brothers asked to kiss them, they got merely the finger tips.

Yet a Brother John—whether the one nicknamed "the Simple" or the Florentine Bruiser or another of the same name does not appear—once asked outright that he might see and kiss the stigmata and was permitted to do so. And Rufino by a stratagem managed on one occasion, only one, to touch the wound in Francis's side. But St. Bonaventure tells us that a few people, even of those outside the Brotherhood, saw the stigmata in the hands and feet, among them several cardinals, including the future Pope Alexander IV. He had testified to this in Bonaventure's own presence. People were so curious that Francis did not like receiving visitors, and when they were admitted he quickly dismissed them, for fear of his secret being discovered. The means for doing this was left to one of the Brothers. The moment Francis murmured the words, "I have hidden Thy words in my heart that I might not sin against Thee," the signal had been given that the visitor had on some pretext—which had to be courteous—to be led away at once.

There now came upon Francis not only a sense of liberation but also an energy so vastly increased that he began to make great plans. The effect of the stigmata was an immense compassion toward men, for this was what he had asked of God. Though he had had this among his many virtues before, he now would say, "Let us begin, Brothers, to serve Our Lord, for until now we have made but little progress!" He wished to return to the service of the lepers, and he went out preaching, sometimes visiting four or five villages in a single day. It seemed to those who heard him that he made a tongue of his whole body, not so much by gestures—for of these he was sparing now, lest he reveal the stigmata—but because he was from head to toe incandescent with love.

It would seem to have been at this time that he had an encounter with a leper who was more than usually surly, though most of these unfortunates were exacting. This man, when Francis gave the salutation, "God give you peace, my brother most dear," answered toughly, "What peace may *I* have from God, who has taken all good from me and left me stinking and rotten?"

The gentle answer came, "My little son, have patience. The infirmities of the body are sent by God for the salvation of the soul, and are of great merit when borne patiently."

But the leper complained again, "How can I bear with patience the pain that racks me day and night? Not only am I afflicted with my disease, but the Brothers who are here to do me service, do not serve me as they ought."

To this Francis returned, "Then my son, I will do the service you need, since you are not content with others."

"What can you do more than others?"

"Whatever it is you wish, that I will do."

"Then I wish you to wash me all over, for I stink so vilely that I cannot endure myself."

Upon this Francis made water hot and put into it sweet-smelling herbs and bathed the ill-tempered leper. As he did so, the leprosy departed wherever the fingers of Francis touched. The man's soul began to be healed also. His heart melted with compunction for his sins. It was so great a miracle that Francis had to hurry at once to a distant place to escape the glory that would be given him for so wonderful a thing.

Though Francis had returned to activity—the only sign of his bodily weakness being that he now rode everywhere on an ass—the Brothers, and especially the watchful Brother Elias, were not deceived as to his condition. They urged him to rest and to seek the care of a doctor. Elias had had a dream while staying at Foligno in which there appeared to him an aged priest clothed in white who said, "Go and tell Brother Francis that eighteen years have passed since he renounced the world and that only two more remain before the Lord will call him to Himself."

At last Francis yielded to these entreaties; and, indeed, he soon found that his weakness was growing to such an extent that it would not permit further work. As soon as he consented to stop, he suddenly found himself very ill. To make matters worse, he was threatened with the loss of his eyesight, as he had come back from Egypt with an eye disease. So he retired to a hut beside the convent at St. Damian's, a hut that Lady Clare had helped to build for him with her own hands. He would not yet put himself under medical treatment.

Clare had had a kind of infirmary for the Brothers, and sometimes she had even cured some of them by making the sign of the cross over them. In Francis's case she apparently attempted no miracle, divining that he was about to depart as he wished to that heavenly home for which he longed. It was enough that he should rest there under the care of her nuns.

It was little rest that Francis got. Into his rush-woven hut there came swarms of field mice, running across him at night and even climbing upon the table when he was eating. They worried him very much, and, for once, he had no endearing words for these little brothers and sisters. Therefore one night he prayed, "Lord, give me help in my infirmities, that I may be able to bear them patiently" —and received the answer, spoken in his soul, "Tell me, Brother, if anyone should give you for these tribulations so great a treasure that the whole world would be nothing, would you not rejoice?"

Francis answered, "If all the world I would be content and glad. I am not worthy of so precious a treasure."

And the Voice said, "Rejoice, Francis, for this is the treasure of eternal life which I have laid up for you, and from this hour I give it to you, and this affliction is the earnest of that treasure."

From then on Francis had his gladness again, and the nuns would hear him singing as of old the songs he had been accustomed to sing. The voice was weaker now, but it had a new sweetness. Hearing it, their hearts were filled with sweetness.

Clare was herself very often ill, but she was always at work with her needle making altar linens. Lying in bed she made Francis a pair of specially constructed sandals which would let him walk on his wounded feet without too much pain. Upon these he tottered to the convent refectory one day when she was well enough to be there, and they ate what must have been their last meal together.

All at once he was seized by something which, if not properly an ecstasy, was at least the kind of ecstasy that poets know. He began to intone what has been claimed as the first true poem in the Italian vernacular. He had turned from his faulty French and his faulty Latin to sing in the mother tongue. And what he sang was his "Song of the Creatures," sometimes called his "Canticle of the Sun." Two stanzas were subsequently added, each called forth by a special occasion, and these will be introduced in the proper place. But what came from Francis that day, which has been translated into English by many hands but is given here in the version Matthew Arnold made, was this:

"O most high, almighty, good Lord God, to Thee belong praise, glory, honor, and all blessing.

"Praised be my Lord God with all His creatures, and especially our brother the sun, who brings us the day and who brings us the night; fair is he and shines with a very great splendor: O Lord, he signifies to us Thee!

"Praised be my Lord for our sister the moon, and for the stars, the which he has set clear and lovely in heaven.

"Praised be my Lord for our brother the wind, and for air and cloud, calms and all weather by which Thou upholdest life in all creatures.

"Praised be my Lord for our sister water, who is very serviceable unto us and humble and precious and very clean.

"Praised be my Lord for our brother fire, through whom Thou givest us light in the darkness; and he is bright and pleasant and very mighty and strong.

"Praised be my Lord for our mother the earth, the which doth sustain us and keep us, and bringeth forth divers fruits and flowers of many colors, and grass.

"Praise ye and bless the Lord, and give thanks unto Him and serve Him with great humility."

Though that very obviously owes a good deal to the canticle sung by the Three Boys in the fiery furnace, the tone is Francis's own, and it seems to us the summation of his life of praise.

The tradition is that Brother Pacifico helped Francis polish these verses. This seems unlikely, for a "professional" poet like Pacifico, the King of Verses and the Laureate of the Emperor Henry VI, would have polished only to spoil them. This is something Pacifico would have been the very first person to understand. They are what they are by virtue of their naïeveté, with stanzas of varying lengths and with assonance used as often as rhyme. Even if Pacifico was ever asked to touch up Brother Francis's canticle, his literary sense even more than his personal reverence would have made him decline.

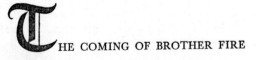

HE COMING OF BROTHER FIRE

Brother Pacifico, however, did have a special commission with regard to the canticle. Francis had made a tune for it, as he had made tunes for some *laudi* he had composed for the Sisters at St. Damian's, though these have disappeared. Pacifico had been not only a poet but (as then often went with a poet's profession) a teacher of singers, and he was a famous player on the lute. So Francis told him to select a band of friars with whom he was to go out singing. First a Brother was to preach to the people, and then all the Brothers should sing them Francis's song. And when the praises were finished, Francis wished the preacher to speak again and say, "We are the minstrels of the Lord, and like other minstrels we wish to be paid for what we do. The payment we ask from you is that you do penance for your sins."

Now at last the Brothers, and especially the ever-solicitous Brother Elias, prevailed upon Francis to travel to Rieti, where Cardinal Ugolino was staying, in order to be treated for his eyes. The decisive word came from the cardinal, who told him, "Brother, you are not doing right in not seeking a cure, for your life is very useful not only to the friars but to the whole world. If you had compassion on your Brothers you would not be so cruel to yourself. For this reason I command you to get cured." It was all very well for Francis to embrace his sufferings; that edified the cardinal and everybody else. Ugolino kept insisting upon medical treatment, and in the end Francis yielded.

On the way to Rieti Francis stopped for the night at San Fabiano with the local priest. Such a concourse of people came there to see him and they plundered the priest's vineyard to such an extent that scarcely any grapes were left. Ruefully the good man looked at the damage and exclaimed, "Though it is only a small vineyard, I used to get from it all the wine I needed, and this year there will be none!"

Francis called him and said, "Do not be disturbed any more, because nothing can be done now. But trust in the Lord, and he will make up your loss in full. Tell me, how many measures of wine did you get from your grapes?"

The priest answered, "Thirteen measures."

"Be sad no longer, and say no harsh word to anybody about what has happened. But if you do not have twenty measures this year I will make it up to you."

Those who were present were able to testify later that at the time of vintage there came from that despoiled vineyard twenty measures of the best wine it had ever yielded.

At Rieti, before finding a more settled abode, Francis stayed for a short while at the house of Theobald the Saracen. There Francis called Pacifico when night fell and said, "Brother, I wish you would borrow a lute and sing a song to bring comfort to my Brother Body, who is full of pain."

Pacifico was embarrassed by this and answered, "My Father, I fear that people would set this down to levity on my part."

Francis smiled gently and said merely, "Then Brother, let us give it up." He had little care for appearances, but he did not wish to bother Pacifico.

He got his music, however, after all. For that night, while Francis was meditating upon God, suddenly a lute sounded upon the silent air. Francis looked out of the window, wondering who it could be that made even the famous Pacifico seem an amateur. He could see nobody, though the music, as it came first from one side of the house and then from the other, marked the movements of a player passing to and fro.

Pacifico himself heard nothing, and at morning Francis told him, "The Lord who comforts the afflicted did not leave me comfortless. For though I did not hear your lute, I had a music sweeter still." This time it had not been like the single stroke of the angelic bow at La Verna. That, as Francis said, was so unbearably beautiful that he would have died at a second stroke. The lute player at Rieti was there to give him solace in his pain, and therefore continued all night, charming the sleepless Francis until he felt himself transported into another world.

When the doctors at Rieti told him that he would have to refrain from weeping so much if he hoped to keep his sight, they got the answer, "It is not meet, my brothers, that for the love of the light that we have in common with the flies, the visitation of the Eternal Light should be impaired, even though only a little. For the spirit did not receive the blessing of light for the sake of the flesh, but the flesh for the sake of the spirit." He would let the doctors do what they could, but he can not have helped them greatly by making it so clear that he preferred to become blind rather than check his tears. Otherwise he was extremely considerate of the doctors who were trying to help him. We hear of one of them being invited to dinner at the hermitage where Francis was staying. "Give him a good dinner," Francis said to the Brothers.

At this they threw up their hands in dismay. "Father, we blush to say it," they told him, "but we are ashamed to invite him, as we are so poor."

"Do you want me to tell you again?" was all that Francis would say.

The doctor, who was standing by, answered tactfully, "As for me, dear Brothers, I shall take your penury for delicacies."

The Brothers did their very best, but they could produce only a little bread and not very much wine, though the kitchen garden managed to supply a few vegetables. They were looking with shame at the poor dinner they were going to offer, when there came a knock at the door: there stood a woman with a basket full of fine bread and fish and pasties of crayfish, heaped up with honey and grapes. It was for them a feast indeed. The doctor could only exclaim in his astonishment, "Brothers, you do not know how holy that man is, nor do we of the world know it!" Good as the food turned out to be, what really satisfied them that day was the miracle rather than the banquet.

A miracle of the same sort occurred when Francis was moved, to be nearer the doctors, to the bishop's palace at Rieti. There Francis's habit was so threadbare that he asked the guardian to get him some cloth to have a new one made. While the guardian was wondering how he was going to obtain this cloth, a man arrived with a bolt of rough brown frieze, saying, "Brother, here is enough for six habits. Keep one for yourself and distribute the others at your pleasure." It proved what Francis had so often told them: "Since all earthly things are the property of God, he who belongs to God shall lack for nothing, if he does not fail God. It is therefore no hazardous venture but a safe refuge to leave all things to devote oneself entirely to God."

Into that same palace there came one day a poor woman from nearby Machilone. Seeing her, Francis said to the guardian, "Brother, you know that we must restore to others what belongs to them."

"Yes," said the guardian. "But what is it we need to restore?"

"The cloak you are wearing," Francis told him.

"But that belongs to me! If you want to borrow it, you may; but I shall want it back."

To this Francis returned, "Brother Guardian, you have always been very courteous to me. Be courteous now."

"Do whatever you like, Father," said the guardian, "whatever it is to which you are prompted by the Spirit."

So then Francis called a man and said to him, "Take this cloak and twelve loaves and give them to that poor woman yonder, and say, 'The poor man to whom you lent your cloak thanks you for the loan and now returns it.'"

The woman thought at first that she was being made game of. When she saw that there was no deception, she was afraid that somebody might take away what she had obtained so easily, so she decided to leave that night and go home, though she, like Francis, had come to Rieti to be treated for her eyes.

To this same period belongs a story as Franciscan as the others, but in a deeper way. Francis had gone to make a visit to his first disciple Bernard da Quintavalle at the retreat where he was staying. When he got there and did not find him in his cell he went to the surrounding woods and shouted, "Bernard, Bernard, come to this blind man!" But Bernard did not answer, and Francis, hurt by what he took to be coldness, betook himself to the solace of prayer. In prayer it was revealed to him that Bernard was rapt in ecstasy and that that was why he did not hear. Filled with remorse, Francis waited until Bernard's ecstasy was over and then threw himself on the ground before him. So lying, he said, "Now I am going to command you to do something by holy obedience."

Bernard promised that he would do whatever Francis commanded.

"Then," Francis told him, "to punish me for the arrogance and rashness of my heart I order you to put one foot on my neck and the other on my mouth, and in this way to pass three times from one side to the other, saying as you do it, 'Lie there, you churlish son of Peter Bernardone.'"

This Bernard did, as he had promised and as it was a command given under holy obedience. But he carried out the command with all the gentleness possible.

But Francis saw that this penance was more of a penance to Bernard than it was to himself. So he said to Bernard, "Now I promise you obedience. Command me whatever you would wish me to do."

Bernard said promptly: "Then I command you by holy obedience that whenever we are together you correct me harshly for my faults."

It was a mistake on Bernard's part to say that, for Francis held him in high reverence for his sanctity. Yet as he was not quite without faults, and as Francis had promised obedience in this matter, Francis took care not to see him again very often, so as not to be obliged to correct him.

At last a most drastic operation was advised; it was the cauterization of the brows. Thomas of Celano rightly gives his account of this in a series of chapters treating of Francis's affection for birds and other wild creatures and his courtesy even to water and the wayside stones. Now he had to face Brother Fire.

The surgeon made the irons hot in the brazier and was preparing to draw them across Francis's temples to the top of his ears. Just what this was supposed to effect is not clear, as the treatment was for the eyes, but it was hoped that it would give some relief. When Francis dimly saw the surgeon standing there with a glowing streak brandished before his face, he trembled, and the friars with him fled in horror, unable to bear the sight. Francis spoke to the fire and said: "My Brother Fire, you who outvie all other things in splendor, the Most High has created you mighty, fair, and useful. Be kind to me at this hour, be courteous, for I have loved you of old in the Lord. I pray the great Lord who created you to temper your heat so that I may be able to endure it. Be courteous to me, Brother Fire." And he signed the branding iron with the sign of the cross.

The doctor drew the iron across his face, each side of it, and when the Brothers ventured back they found Francis smiling. "Fainthearted and poor-spirited ones, why did you run away? I tell you only the truth when I say that I felt no pain." Then turning to the surgeon he said, "If the flesh is not well burnt, apply the iron again." That probably would have done no good, and the doctor might have flinched from a second application of his dreadful remedy. He had been amazed by the way Francis had seemed to feel nothing and took it as a miracle. "I tell you, Brothers," he said to the friars, "I have seen wondrous things today."

Apparently the cauterization was merely the preliminary to a further operation; for all of Francis's veins from the ears to the eyebrows were cut open and another surgeon bored through both ears with a red-hot iron. It is hardly surprising that all this did Francis little good.

Yet he had made up his mind to do all that he was told. As he was putting himself into the doctors' hands, he would do so completely, as an act of religious obedience, and when Cardinal Ugolino asked him to consult with another doctor, this time at Siena, he made the journey there.

He was accompanied by one of the eye specialists of Rieti, who may have felt that it would be unsafe for him to make the journey alone. He was a man who was intending to join the order and so was only too willing to give this service. As they were crossing the plain between Campiglio and San Quirico, three poor women stood by the wayside, so much alike in features and age and build that they seemed replicas from the selfsame mold. As Francis came to the point where they were, they bowed to him and gave him a new greeting, "Welcome, Lady Poverty!"

No greeting Francis had ever had pleased him more. Thinking that they really were poor women, he asked the doctor to give them some money. This he did, leaping from his horse and placing some coins in their hands. But when the Brothers and the doctor, having moved on, turned round to look where the women had been, they saw nobody in sight on that open plain. These they concluded could not have been women, as they had flown away more swiftly than birds.

So far from the Sienese specialist doing Francis any good, the general condition of his health rapidly grew worse. Suddenly he had a bad hemorrhage and they thought he was about to die. Francis must have thought so too, for he sent at once for Benedict di Pirato, the priest who said Mass for him daily in the room where he lay, and asked him to write a will to his dictation. It was replaced by a later and more lengthy will, but this one ran: "I bless my Brethren who are in the Order, and all who shall ever come to the end of the world. And since on account of my weakness and pain I cannot speak much, in these few words I make plain my will and intention: in token of my memory and benediction they should love one another as I have loved them and do love them, and they

should always observe our Lady Poverty and remain faithful subjects to the prelates and clergy of holy Mother Church."

It was now a question of getting Francis back to Assisi as quickly
as possible, lest he die away from home. He had three other illnesses
beside that of the eyes, being troubled with his stomach, spleen, and
liver. We also hear of dropsy. He himself wanted to be in Assisi,
but Elias and the Brethren, not to mention the civic authorities of
Assisi, wanted the body of their saint when he was dead, as they
knew he soon would be. Siena would never give it up if he died
there. Indeed, there was a real danger that even on the road he
might be kidnapped; especially there was danger of this on the
part of the rival city of Perugia. Elias hurried to him with the
utmost speed and made all the arrangements, acting with secrecy
and dispatch. He provided a strong escort of knights to protect
him from capture.

Of that journey home two incidents are recorded. One was very
similar to what happened at the bishop's palace at Rieti, though it
is not necessary to believe from this similarity that it is another
version of the same story. Francis never had any objection to re-
peating the same action or words several times. The cavalcade
passed a beggar. Francis could dimly see him, his eyesight being
not yet completely gone and perhaps even being momentarily improved by what the doctors had done. He was wearing a cloak
over his habit, one that he badly needed just then because of his
weakened condition. But he at once said, "We must restore this
cloak to that poor man, for it is his. I had it only as a loan until
I found somebody poorer than myself."

Everybody protested at this, but Francis insisted, saying, "I think
that the Great Almsgiver would account it a theft in me did I not
give it to one who needs it more than I do." So the cloak was given
away.

The other incident occurred at the little village of Satriano. The
knights tried to buy provisions there but could find none for sale
in so poor a place. Therefore they went to Francis and told him
that he would have to give them something, though what they
supposed *he* had would be hard to say. Perhaps they counted upon
his working a miracle. What he did was better than that: he taught
them a lesson. "You have been trusting more in your money than

in God," he told them. "This time go and humbly ask for alms for the love of God. And do not be ashamed, for everything we have is given us by the Great Almsgiver, bountiful alike to the worthy and the unworthy." After that they got all the food they required, for the people vied with one another in giving gladly. Francis had proved to them that opulent poverty was able to prevail.

WELCOME, SISTER DEATH

It was with a great sense of relief that the Brothers and the city of Assisi got him safely back. He was lodged in the bishop's palace, around which a guard was set day and night to prevent any raid by the Perugians. Assisi welcomed him with joy, and the people rejoiced still further in the knowledge that he could not live long, and then they would have a saint's body among them. The live saint was a good thing to have, but he did, after all, have his inconveniences. He had a way of reminding people of the need for repentance, and though he might occasionally work a miracle— Francis was rather sparing of this—he would be as likely to perform his miracles elsewhere as at Assisi. But his body, safely dead, was a permanent possession, Assisi's glory and also Assisi's guarantee of protection. No wonder the city set a guard to protect him.

Yet the Assisians had their own very definite ideas as to how a saint should die, and when Francis, who was rejoicing in the approach of death for reasons other than theirs, was heard singing nearly all the time, they were rather scandalized. So some of them went to Brother Elias and said, "Why does this man show such lightheartedness at such a time? He ought to be thinking of death." Perhaps they feared that this indecorous behavior might prevent his canonization. And Elias, profoundly convinced though he was as to

Francis's holiness, shared their fears. He did not want Francis at the last moment to ruin his chances for the aureole.

Accordingly, he went to him and said, "Dearest Brother, I am greatly consoled and edified by the gladness you are showing, but there are some people who think you should weep rather than sing, and they even look upon your singing as setting a bad example. Let them see that your mind is upon death."

With a smile Francis answered, "Brother, you remember that vision you had at Foligno that warned me I had only two years to live. Ever since then I have thought day and night of death more solicitously than ever. I have already wept for my sins; now suffer me, Brother, to rejoice in the Lord."

It was now that Francis added a new stanza to the "Canticle of the Creatures."

There had often been clashes between the ecclesiastical and civic authorities in Assisi, and just then there was one more than usually bitter. Bishop Guido excommunicated the podesta, and the podesta retaliated by ordering the merchants not to sell anything to the bishop. Francis devised a means of reconciling them. A very large part of his mission had been to bring peace between enemies, for he knew that otherwise they could have no peace with God. So now he wrote a stanza which he hoped would bring peace to Assisi:

"Praised be my Lord for all those who pardon one another for His love's sake, and who endure weakness and tribulation; blessed are they who peaceably shall endure, for Thou, O Most Highest, shalt give them a crown."

Then he said, "It is great shame to us, the servants of God, that the bishop and the podesta should hate one another, and that nobody concerns himself with making peace between them." So he told one of the friars, "Now go and ask the podesta on my behalf to go to the bishop's palace with the magnates of the city."

When the city fathers agreed to do this, Francis sent Pacifico and another good singer, telling them, "Sing my canticle about Brother Sun, and this new strophe, and ask the bishop to come and listen to it."

In the open court of the cloister of the palace—perhaps the very place where Francis stripped himself of his clothes so many years before—the song was sung. It may be that the enemies would not have consented to be there had it not been Francis who was asking it. But they could not refuse that much to their dying saint. When the song was ended, with its new stanza, the podesta, deeply moved, said, "If anybody had slain my blood-friend or my son I would forgive him." Then throwing himself at the bishop's feet, he added, "Behold I am ready to make satisfaction as it shall please you for the love of God and his servant Francis."

The bishop drew him up, answering, "My office bids me be humble. Because I am by nature prone to wrath, it is fitting that you should pardon me."

With that the two men embraced, and their foolish quarrel was over.

But the "Canticle of the Creatures" was still not quite complete. Still another stanza needed to be added. It came about in this way.

A doctor of Arezzo named Buongiovanni came to see Francis, and Francis, not wishing to address him as "good"—as only One is good, even God—used instead his private nickname for him of "Bembenignate" and asked what he really thought about his dropsy.

The doctor answered in the evasive fashion of medical men, "Brother, it will be well with you, by the grace of God."

Francis was not to be put off. "Tell me the truth," he insisted. "Do not be afraid; I am no faintheart. By the grace of God I am so much one with Our Lord, that I shall be equally content with death or with life."

Then the doctor said openly, "Then I believe you will die at the end of September or the beginning of October."

Upon hearing this, Francis lifted his hands toward heaven and cried, "Welcome, my Sister Death!"

After the doctor had left, Francis composed his verse about Death, regarding even that as one of God's creatures:

"Praised be my Lord for our sister, the death of the body, from which no man escapeth. Woe to him who dieth in mortal sin! Blessed are they who are found walking by Thy most holy will, for the second death shall have no power to do them harm."

He sent at once for Brother Angelo and Brother Leo, and he asked them to sing his canticle, with the new lines inserted. It was in tears and with broken voices that they did so. Francis listened with a radiant face.

He did not wish to die anywhere but at the Portiuncula, and his wishes were not opposed, though Assisi sent the guard to protect him there.

Under this strong escort he was carried out by the principal gate of the city, by the road that goes to the leper hospital. At the fork of the road Francis asked that his litter be set down and that he be turned so as to face Assisi, the city he could no longer see. Lying there, dying and blind, he lifted up his hands and blessed the place, saying, "Blessed be thou of God, O holy city, seeing that through thee many souls shall be saved and that in thee shall dwell many servants of the Lord!"

Then he let them carry him to St. Mary of the Angels, where he was put in the infirmary.

He had told his sons before, but he repeated it now, "Never desert this place. If you are driven out by one way, come back by another; for this place is truly holy, and the abode of God. In all places the divine grace may be given, but our Little Portion I have found to be filled with the richest of God's graces and to be frequented by the celestial spirits. Here, when we were few, the Most High increased us; here He enlightened the hearts of His poor men by His wisdom and has kindled our wills by the fire of His love. Here he who prays with devout heart shall have what he asks, but here too those who are sinful shall be more heavily punished. Therefore, my little sons, deem the place of God's habitation worthy of all honor, and there with all your heart and with the voice of exultation give thanks to God."

He was suffering so intensely that he told the Brothers that he would willingly take any kind of martyrdom in exchange. Yet he said, "It has ever been dearest and sweetest and most acceptable to me what my Lord performs in me, to Whose will I desire to be conformable in all things." Another time he exclaimed, "I give Thee thanks, O Lord God, for all these my pains!" And he called his pangs his sisters; they were dear to him.

It was probably about this time that he dictated the document known as his testament, and it is supposed to have been taken down by Brother Angelo Tancredi. About its authenticity there can be no question, for it is cited by Gregory IX in his bull *Quo elongati*, issued on September 28, 1230. It did, however, raise some controversial questions, the chief one being decided by Pope Gregory when he declared, as he was bound to declare as a canon lawyer, that it had no legal force. Even Francis explicitly said in it, "This is not another Rule; for this is a remembrance, a warning and an exhortation and my Testament which I, little Brother Francis, make for you, my blessed Brothers, in order that we may observe in a more Catholic way the Rule which we have promised to the Lord. And let the Minister General and all the other Ministers and Custodes be bound by obedience not to add to these words or to take from them. And let them always have this writing with them beside the Rule. And in all the chapters they hold, when they read the Rule let them read these words also. And I strictly enjoin on all my brothers—clerics and laics—by obedience, not to put any gloss on the Rule or on these words." The intention is perfectly clear: the Rule was to be considered as irrevocable and to be accepted in its most literal sense.

The document is too long for detailed examination here. It is sufficient to remark that it is, in part, a brief history of the primitive Franciscan life; in part, a reaffirmation of poverty and of the principle, so dear to Francis, that no special privileges be asked of the Roman Curia; and, finally, an exhortation to obedience to the superiors.

This, the strongest paragraph in the will, comes at the end and indicates that much unruliness must have existed among the friars to have called forth such stern words. The only possible inference is that we have here an attempt to uphold the hands of Brother Elias, who may have explained to Francis the difficulties that beset him. In spite of this, however, a section of the Brothers used Francis's will for their own purposes, stressing only what it said about poverty and using that as an anti-Elian weapon.

The passage about obedience runs: "Let all the Brothers be bound to obey their Guardian and to perform the Office according to the Rule. And those who may be found not performing the Office according to the Rule and wishing to change it in some way, or who are not Catholics, let all the Brothers wherever they may be, if they find one of these, be bound by obedience to present him to the Custos who is nearest to the place where they have found him. And the Custos shall be strictly bound, by obedience, to guard him strongly day and night as a prisoner so that he cannot be snatched from his hands until he shall personally place him in the hands of the Minister. And the Minister shall be firmly bound by obedience to send him by such Brothers as shall watch him day and night like a prisoner until they shall present him to the Lord of Ostia, who is master and protector and corrector of this brotherhood." If the gentle Francis on his deathbed used such unequivocally harsh language, it could only have been because the maintenance of discipline in the Order had become a grave problem.

Francis, however, did even more in the way of upholding Elias. The Brothers were summoned on one of these last days, and Bernard knelt at the right hand of the bed and Elias at the left. Francis crossed his arms and laid his right hand on the head of Elias, asking, "On whom does it rest?"

They told the blind man, "On Brother Elias."

"That is my wish," he said. "I bless you my son, in and through all things, and as the Most High has in your hands increased my brethren and sons, so also through you and in you I bless them all. God the King of all, bless you in heaven and earth. I bless you as much as I can—and more than I can."

The *Fioretti* gives a different version of the matter, one that makes Bernard receive the blessing. Indeed, we may believe that Bernard, as the first disciple, did get a special blessing that day. But Elias is pointedly ignored, and even Thomas of Celano, though he could not recall what he had written in the *Vita Prima* when writing the *Vita Secunda,* after the fall and apostasy of Elias, does not refer to him except as the "vicar" and indicates that the blessing was not indefeasible but had been forfeited. Yet the story must stand as first told. To Elias Francis said, "I bless you as much as I can—and more than I can." Elias had his full confidence to the end.

There were charming little incidents during these last days at the Portiuncula. To one of the Brothers who said to him, "Ask God to deal more gently with you, for it seems to me that His hand is laid heavily on you," Francis returned, "Did I not know that you spoke in simple purity I would henceforth shun your company, for you have dared to consider the divine counsels concerning me fit for blame." Struggling out of bed, he kissed the ground, exclaiming, "I thank Thee, O Lord God, for all my pains, and I beseech thee, that if it please thee, thou wilt add unto them a hundredfold."

It was in this spirit that a little while before, when staying at Greccio, he took a feather pillow that they had given him—hitherto he had used only a block of wood or a stone—and threw it at the Brother who went to him in the morning. "Take it away!" he cried. "I could not sleep. I believe the devil is in it!"

Yet he at last acknowledged that he had been too hard on "Brother Ass, the body," and now he humored his sick fancies occasionally. He had done this while in the bishop's palace at Assisi by saying, "I have no appetite, but I believe that if I had some of the fish called squail, perhaps I could eat it." Now at the Portiuncula he had a wish one night for some parsley. When Brother Cook was brought to him he said, "I have already picked all the parsley and I do not think I could find any more even if it were daylight. How could I distinguish it from the other herbs now that it is dark?" To this Francis said merely, "Never mind, Brother; bring me the first herbs you touch." He did so and there in the basket of herbs he had gathered was a bunch of parsley!

Now Francis wrote a letter to the Countess Settesoli, the tertiary he had always addressed by the private nickname of Brother Jacoba. He told her that he was dying: "Wherefore if you wish to see me alive, come at once to St. Mary of the Angels, and bring with you a shroud to wrap my body in and the wax that is needed for my burial. I pray you also to bring me some of the food that you used to give me when I was sick at Rome." It was a sweatmeat called *mostaccioli* made of sugar and almonds.

But even before the bearer of the letter could leave, Brother Jacoba arrived. "What shall we do, Father?" they asked him. "No women are allowed to enter here."

And Francis answered, "The rule does not apply to that lady, seeing that her great faith and devotion have brought her here from a distance." With her she had all the things Francis had asked for in his letter. Perhaps this was as miraculous as the Brothers supposed; perhaps it was rather an instance of her womanly understanding. She had added one thing Francis had not asked for: it was a quantity of incense. The shroud had been woven by her from the wool of the lamb he had given her three years before.

Francis wished that he could see Clare again, but he was too ill to go to her, and she was too ill to come to him. So he sent her a copy of his "Canticle of the Creatures" and a song he had composed for the Poor Ladies. This was his farewell. But he also sent her a last admonition which she incorporated in her Rule when it was approved twenty-seven years after his death. It was very brief: "I little Brother Francis, wish to follow the life and poverty of Jesus Christ Our Most High Lord and of His most holy Mother, and to persevere therein to the end. And I beseech you all, my ladies, and counsel you, to live always in this most holy life and poverty. And watch yourselves well that you in no wise depart from it through the teaching or advice of any one."

That admonition was the tenderest gift he could give.

As his end drew near he summoned the Brothers again. He wished to have a love-feast with them before he went. He asked that bread be brought, and, having blessed it, he gave to each one a morsel to eat, calling to mind the Last Supper. But he was too weak to break this bread himself.

He told the doctor to inform him when he saw death at hand. "It will be," he said, "the gate of life to me." Again he exclaimed, "Welcome, Sister Death!" Then he instructed the Brothers, "When you see my end approaching, lay me naked on the ground, and let me lie there for as long a time as one might take to walk a mile without haste." He ordered, too, that he should be buried in sackcloth, "in token and in example of humility and Lady Poverty." He asked that the Passion according to the Gospel of St. John be read. His attendant was already preparing to do that very thing, and the book opened at the desired place.

They stripped him as he asked and laid him on ashes. Lying there, with his face uplifted toward heaven and wholly absorbed in God's glory, he still did not forget to keep his left hand over the wound in his right side, so that it could not be seen. He said to them, "I have done what was mine to do; may Christ teach you what is yours."

The Brother who was acting as his personal warden at this time— for he always had someone to whom he rendered obedience— brought him a habit with the cord saying, "These I lend you, as unto a beggar; receive them at the bidding of holy obedience." At that conjuration he consented to be clothed, for what he was wearing was not his own.

Several times he had asked during the preceding days that his canticle be sung to him. But at the very end it was the hundred and forty-first psalm, the one that in the Vulgate begins, *Voce mea ad Dominum clamavi*. He joined in faintly, and before the brief psalm was finished he received death, still singing. It was October 3, 1226.

The evening had already begun to fall, but, though the lark is a bird that does not love twilight, great multitudes of larks gathered round the hut where he lay, perching on the roof or wheeling in flight singing. Their songs were even more joyous than was their wont as the saint passed to his glory.